The Danish Economy
An International Perspective

The Danish Economy
An International Perspective

Second edition

Torben M. Andersen
Bent Dalum
Hans Linderoth
Valdemar Smith
Niels Westergård-Nielsen

DJØF Publishing Copenhagen
2006

The Danish Economy
An International Perspective
Second edition 2006

© 2006 by DJØF Publishing Copenhagen
DJØF Publishing is a company of the
Association of Danish Lawyers and Economists

Print: Narayana Press, Gylling
Binding: Damm's Forlagsbogbinderi, Randers

Printed in Denmark 2006
ISBN 87-574-1540-4

DJØF Publishing Copenhagen
E-mail: forlag@djoef.dk
www.djoef-forlag.dk

Preface

An increasing need for a basic description of the Danish economy in English has developed because more and more courses are taught in English and more and more foreign students are studying in Denmark. At the same time, closer international cooperation has led to an increasing interest in Danish conditions from scholars and businesses in other countries.

We have attempted to give the book a broad non-technical content. Therefore *The Danish Economy* is designed for students in the first part of their education and for professionals and foreigners who want a comprehensive overview of the Danish economy, its institutions and its relations to the international economy. Furthermore, the chapters have been designed with reference to the use of the book both as a textbook and as a handbook for those who want to focus on special topics.

Selection of topics is a matter of personal judgement and preferences. However, we have attempted to include what is normally considered essential issues in order to give an adequate introduction to the Danish economy.

The writing of a textbook like this requires editorial and secretarial assistance. We thank the secretaries at the Department of Economics at the Aarhus School of Business and the University of Aarhus: Susan Stilling, Ann-Marie Gabel, Bodil Rasmussen and Gerda Christophersen, who had the patience and diligence to edit our manuscripts for the first edition and Ann-Marie Gabel who has taken care of the layout and finish of this second edition.

Aarhus, June 2006

Torben M. Andersen	Bent Dalum
Professor, Ph.D.	Associate professor, MA
Hans Linderoth	Valdemar Smith
Reader, Ph.D.	Associate professor, MA

Niels Westergård-Nielsen
Professor, Ph.D.

CONTENTS

CHAPTER 4:   FINANCIAL MARKETS AND MONETARY POLICY

CHAPTER 5:   THE DANISH LABOUR MARKET

Chapter 1

Growth and business cycles in the Danish economy

1.1. Growth and standards of living

The twentieth century brought an outstanding improvement in material living standards. At the turn of the century, most developed countries had an income level six times larger than at the beginning of the century when measuring the total income or production level by the gross domestic product (GDP)[1] per capita. On most other scores related to welfare, there have also been substantial improvements. While a newborn at the beginning of the century could expect to live some 40 years, the life expectancy of a newborn has now been doubled. Educational standards have improved substantially, and illiteracy is no longer a problem in the developed countries.

Denmark has followed this trend, as can be seen from Figure 1.1 showing the development in production and production per capita over the last 50 years. Average production per capita is now about 3.5 times as large as it was about 50 years ago. It is worth pointing out that this has been achieved despite the fact that average annual working hours towards the end of the 1990s were only about 2/3 of what they were in 1950.

---

1.   See Appendix A for an introduction to National Accounts.

Figure 1.1. Production and production per capita, Denmark 1948-2005.

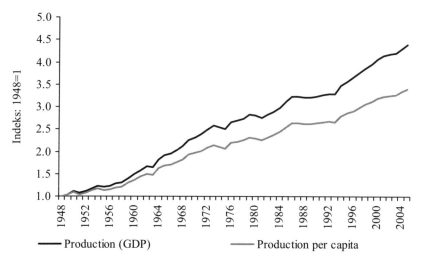

Note: Production measured by gross domestic product (GDP), index 1948 = 1.
Source: Adam databank and Ministry of Finance.

Comparing countries by their income (GDP) per capita (measured in Purchasing Power Parities, see Appendix A) puts Denmark on rank no 7 in 2004, and therefore among the richest countries in the world. The distribution of income is also in international comparison fairly equal, cf. below.

A more broad perspective in comparing countries can be taken by using the Human Development Index (HDI) (UNDP, 2005) according to which Denmark ranks 14th. The HDI is an attempt to construct a measure for international comparison of living standards which not only takes into account income per capita, but also health measured by life expectancy at birth and knowledge measured by a weighted average of literacy and school enrolment.[2] The HDI is a simple average of these three indicators. While there are a number of problems with the construction and interpretation of such measures of well-being across countries, they do yield useful summary information. The reason why Denmark's rank drops when going from income per capita to the broader HDI index is that the

---

2.   Denmark belongs to the group "High Human Development". For technical details see the annual report "The Human Development Report" published by UNDP.

life expectancy in Denmark (77 years) is below the average among highly developed countries (80 years). This reflects a general tendency that Denmark performs less well in comparisons involving health issues. In an evaluation made by WHO in 2005, Denmark is ranked 20th for a summary indicator including a number of health variables.[3]

In summary, even though neither production per capita nor the HDI can be interpreted directly as welfare indicators, they do both reflect that the material living standards have improved substantially over the past century and that Denmark is one of the most affluent countries in the world.

1.2. Sources of growth

The high level of material living standards and its continuing growth raise fundamental questions concerning the underlying causes. A first simple decomposition of production per capita can be made by noting that this depends on the fraction of the population in employment, how many hours they work and how much they on average produce per hour (productivity). Table 1.1 uses this reasoning for a decomposition of production per capita for 10 high income countries. The decomposition shows, however, that the high level of income per capita in Denmark is not explained by a high level of productivity, but rather from the fact that a large proportion of the population is contributing to the production results, i.e. a relatively high fraction of the population is active in the labour market. Working hours for the single workers are not particularly high in an international comparison. In short, the relatively high material living standard in Denmark is to a large extent driven by the fact that Denmark is a hard working nation, rather than by having a highly efficient and productive labour force. All of this, of course, should be seen relative to the fact that the comparison is made with other very affluent countries.

---

3.   See WHO World Health Report, 2005 at http://www.who.int/whr

Table 1.1.   Decomposition of production per capita for 10 high income countries 2004.

	Production per capita[1]	Employment/ population ratio[2]	Annual working hours[3]	Productivity per hour worked[4]
Norway	38,765	49.5	1,363	57.4
Ireland	35,767	45.4	1,642	48.0
Switzerland	33,678	56.6	1,556	38.2
Iceland	32,590	53.4	1,810	33.7
Austria	31,944	45.8	1,550	45.0
Denmark	31,932	50.4	1,540	41.2
United Kingdom	31,436	46.9	1,669	40.2
Canada	31,395	50.1	1,751	35.8
Australia	31,231	47.9	1,816	35.9
Netherlands	31,191	49.1	1,357	46.8
Belgium	30,851	40.2	1,522	50.4

1) GDP in PPP adjusted USD per capita.
2) Total employment relative to total population.
3) Average annual working hours. For Austria and Switzerland data refers to 2003.
4) GDP in PPP adjusted USD divided by total working hours.
Note: The countries in the table are not identical to the top 10 of countries ranked after GDP per capita due to lack of comparable data. The decomposition is based on $Y/P=(E/P)*H*(Y/HE)$, where Y=output, P=population, E=employment and H working hours.
Source: Calculations based on data from OECD, *Employment Outlook*, June 2005.

As all industrialized countries, Denmark has experienced substantial changes in the labour force participation and working hours over the years. The average labour force participation among those in the working age group (all persons between 16 and 66 years of age) has been reduced sharply. For males the downward trend has been undergoing for long, while for females it is a more recent phenomenon. The male labour force participation rate was about 95% in the 1960s (among age group 15-64), and is now close to 85%. For females it was around 35% until the mid 1960s, and then it increased to about 79% in the early 1990s. Since then it has also been decreasing and is now 76%. In recent years, there has been a small increase for both males and females. The rising labour force participation for women is one sign of the emancipation of women in society. It is also related to the expansion of the public sector (see below and Chapter 6) making this possible by offering both possibilities for childcare and job opportunities to women. The trend decline in the labour force participation rate is due to both earlier retirement and later entrance into the workforce partly caused by prolonged education. In an international comparison, the labour force participation is high in Denmark. In particular, the high labour force participation for females in Denmark stands out in comparison with the rest of EU (with the exception of Sweden). However, lower labour force participation for immigrants tends to lower the aggregate participation rate. See Chapter 5 for more information on the Danish labour market.

Working hours have also – as already stated – been on a trend decline. Average annual working hours (bargained normal working hours) were 2,400 in 1920, while they had fallen to about 1,650 hours in 2004. The fall is due to longer vacations and shorter working hours during the working week. It is to be expected that potential improvements in material well-being is split between increased consumption and increased leisure.

Since both labour force participation and working hours have been falling over the years, and production per capita has still increased substantially (Figure 1.1), it follows that productivity must have increased. This is indeed the case since average productivity per working hour in 2004 is more than three times higher than it was in 1960. This points out that the fundamental cause of improvement in material standard of living is improvement in productivity. Accordingly, the discussion about growth and policies to foster growth is focussing on factors influencing productivity (see Chapter 8).

The average productivity per working hour can be improved through several channels, where one obvious channel is investment in real capital. By expanding the stock of real capital available for production, the average productivity of labour can be increased. Moreover, investments often imply not only a change in the quantity of real capital, but also in its quality (new and better equipment etc.). Figure 1.2 shows the investment ratio, i.e. gross investments relative to GDP for Denmark and the average for EU-15 countries. There has been a general trend decline in the investment rate which is also the case for Denmark. However, the investment rate in Denmark displays a tendency to be below that of other European countries, and, moreover, there have been two significant dips in the investment ratio in association with recessions in Denmark. The investment share is also known to be relatively volatile since investments are very sensitive to the business cycle situation (see below). This is to be expected since investments in real capital are forward-looking decisions which therefore critically depend on expectations concerning future market opportunities. Note that the figure shows gross investments, and they do not directly translate into changes in the capital stock, since one also has to take into account depreciations of the existing capital stock. However, gross investments remain a key variable, also because it is mainly through investments that new technologies enter the production process.

Figure 1.2. Investment relative to GDP, Denmark and OECD-Europe 1960-2000.

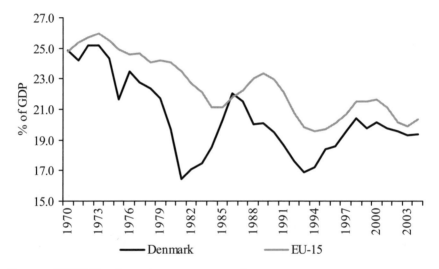

Source: OECD Database at www.sourceoecd.org

The quantity and quality of real capital are obviously of importance for growth, but equally important is the quality of labour input – the human capital. The latter includes the education and skills of the labour force, which in turn can be affected both by formal education and on-the-job training of various forms. Educational standards have been improved over the years. Thus, average years of education have been increased substantially, and a larger fraction of the population gets a higher education (see Chapter 5). However, it is difficult to assess human capital developments precisely since it is not only a question of formal education levels, but also the actual content and quality of these educations as well as on the job training, experience etc. Although the educational level is high in Denmark, it is still the case that about 1/5 of an age cohort does not get any education beyond compulsory schooling (Folkeskolen). This is high seen in relation to the high ambitions in the Danish welfare society where most people are expected to be able to find a reasonable, well-paying job and the fact that substantial public funds are invested in education.

Education and expansion of human capital are both driving forces for growth, but increased material well-being also increases the demand for education in a broad sense. That is, education has both a consumption value and an investment value in terms of improving the quality of the labour force, see Chapters 5 and 8.

There is one final and crucial aspect related to growth which is worth stressing. Growth is usually associated with new possibilities and structural changes. The growth process does not proceed by uniform productivity increases in all sectors and for all forms of economic activity, but is usually associated with substantial reallocations across sectors. Some sectors are declining and others expanding. Sectors may decline because demand turns in other directions, or in a relative sense when productivity increases imply that less labour is needed to maintain the production level. The latter makes resources available for other and new activities and thereby paves the way for further growth and improvements in material living standards. The agricultural sector in Denmark is a case in point. In 1950, about 30% of the employed worked in the agricultural sector. At the turn of the century the fraction is close to 3%. Still, agricultural production is much higher than in 1950. Productivity has increased by a factor close to 25. Therefore, less labour is needed, and still agricultural production is higher. Chapter 2 takes a closer look at the industry structure of the Danish economy and the changes which have taken place, and Chapter 8 provides an insight into the growth process and the possibilities of affecting it.

1.3. The Danish welfare model

Denmark ranks as one of the most affluent countries in the world, and is, at the same time, one of the most egalitarian[1] countries, i.e. economic possibilities are more equally distributed in Denmark than in most other countries. Table 1.2 shows for a number of countries various measures of inequality. The countries are ranked in terms of the Gini coefficient which is a metric often used to characterize the income distribution. The Gini

1: based on the belief that everybody is equal.

7

coefficient measures how far the distribution of income is from being completely equal, and a low value is thus tantamount to an equal distribution of income. By this measure Denmark has one of the most equal distributions of income in international comparison. The table also includes the ratio of income for the 10% richest to the 10% poorest, and for the 20% richest to the 20% poorest. This shows that the 20% richest earn more than 4 times the income of the 20% poorest. Using these metrics Denmark does not have the most equal distribution of income.

Table 1.2.   Measures of income inequality.

	Survey year	Richest 10% to poorest 10%	Richest 20% to poorest 20%	Gini coefficient
Denmark	1997	8.1	4.3	24.7
Japan	1993	4.5	3.4	24.9
Sweden	2000	6.2	4.0	25.0
Belgium	1996	7.8	4.5	25.0
Norway	2000	6.1	3.9	25.8
Finland	2000	5.6	3.8	26.9
Austria	1997	7.6	4.7	30.0
Netherlands	1999	9.2	5.1	30.9
France	1995	9.1	5.6	32.7
Canada	1998	10.1	5.8	33.1

1) Note data are not from the same year, and these data are not available for all countries.
2) Richest and poorest groups are defined from the income deciles, i.e. the 10% poorest is the first income decile, and the 0% richest is the t10 income decile
3) The Gini coefficient measures the difference between the actual distribution of income and the hypothetical situation where income is equally distributed across the population. The Gini coefficient is zero if the income distribution is equal, and 1 if all income is concentrated on one person. It can be interpreted as the fraction of total income in the economy which needs to be redistributed to attain an equal income distribution.
Source: Human Development Report 2005 (www.undp.org).

The issue of equality is intimately related to the welfare state, for which a primary aim is to equalize the opportunities and the consumption possibilities of individuals. The achievement of these objectives involves many aspects in relation to the organisation of society and the policies pursued including labour market policy, education policy, social policy and taxation policy. Societies differ in the role played by the civil society (family, friends etc.), markets and the public sector in the distribution of economic resources and thus for the organisation of the welfare society. In the Danish or Scandinavian welfare model, the public sector plays a central role. A basic principle for this model is universalism, i.e. all citizens have a right to the services and transfers offered by the public sector, and all are obliged to contribute to the financing via general taxation. In short, the model builds on a principle of individual rights and collective financing. Since, the model has been extended in terms of a higher level of standards for the services offered, as well as a tighter safety net via various forms of transfer income. Therefore, this model naturally implies a relatively large public sector. Figure 1.3 shows the size of the public sector relative to GDP for OECD countries in 2004. It can be seen that Denmark has one of the largest public sectors. The flip side of this is, of course, that Denmark also has one of the highest tax burdens (see Chapter 6).

Figure 1.3. Allocation of resources via the public sector, % of GDP 2004.

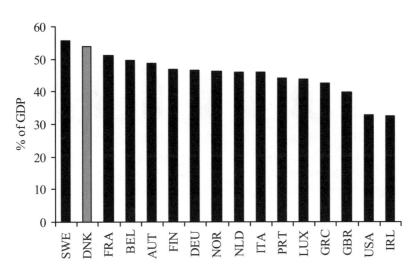

Source: OECD Database at www.sourceoecd.org.

The public sector has been growing since the 1960s, cf. Figure 1.4. Considering the development in more detail reveals that it can be split into two phases. In the first phase until the mid 1970s, growth was driven by public consumption, i.e. services like health care, education etc. provided to the population. In the second phase from the mid 1970s public consumption has been fairly constant (relative to GDP), but transfer expenses (unemployment benefits, social assistance, pensions and the like) have been driving the growth in the overall size of the public sector. The latter development is both a reflection of the increase in unemployment and the fact that some of the transfer schemes have been expanded. Capital expenses (interest rate payments) also rose from the 1970s and into the 1990s, because the government was running a budget deficit in the periods 1975 to 1985 and 1990 to 1996, and because the rate of interest was high in this period. During the second half of the 1990s, public finances turned into surplus and interest rates have been following, and therefore interest rate payment has been lowered (see below and Chapter 4).

Figure 1.4. Public expenditure decomposition, Denmark 1950-2004. % of GDP.

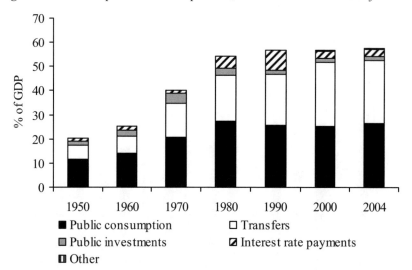

Source: Danmarks Statistik, STO and Økonomiministeriet, *Økonomisk Oversigt* Dec. 2000.

1.4. International relations

Denmark is a small country both measured in area (43,000 square km, which is 1.3% of the EU area) and population (5.3 million or 1.4% of the EU population). Due to the geographical characteristics and the natural resource base, international trade has played an important role for the Danish economy. Figure 1.5 shows measures of openness for EU countries. The figure shows the surprising fact that Denmark is not among the most open European countries when measured by the importance of trade. One reason for the low openness measure for Denmark is that this measure is downward biased by a relatively large public sector.

Figure 1.5.   Openness – EU countries, 2004.

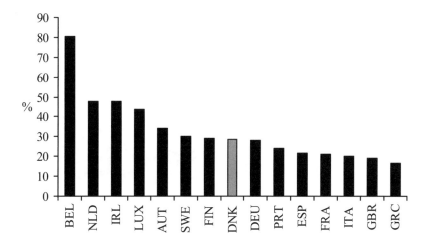

Note: Defined as ½ (X+M)/Y where X = exports, M = imports and Y = GDP.

Source: Danmarks Statistik: STO.

Capital markets are also tightly integrated internationally. This effectively means that there is no legal or tax barriers to the free movements of capital across countries and currencies. Such free mobility may be considered obvious today in light of the possibilities for electronic trade at extremely small costs and an infinite speed. However, it is worth pointing out that historically, capital flows have been tightly regulated. For many years, only capital movements tied to international trade in goods and services were allowed, but these restrictions have gradually been removed, and during the 1980s, the last restrictions were removed within EU (see Chapter 4). An indication of the role of international capital market integration is given by Figure 1.6 showing the interest rate in Denmark and the Euro area. It is seen that there has been a drastic reduction in the spread between the Danish and the Euro area interest rate, and that the former now follows the latter very closely. A necessary condition for this development has been the liberalisation of capital flows. This is not, however, in itself sufficient to eliminate the interest rate spread since this

11

requires a fixed exchange rate (see Chapter 4). In the Danish case, the convergence in interest rates has been made possible due to a convergence of Danish inflation to the Euro area level and the establishment of a credible exchange rate policy (see Chapter 4).

Figure 1.6. Interest rates: Denmark and Euro area, 1975-2005.

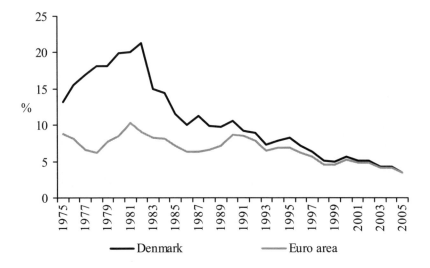

Note: Interest rate on 10-year state bond in Denmark and Germany. Before 1999 the German bond is in D-mark.
Source: Danmarks Nationalbank: Monthly Review.

Denmark is an active participant in many international institutions and organisations. Membership of EU was obtained in 1973. EU was initiated as a free trade area which gradually has been extended culminating with the approval of the "internal market" in 1986. The internal market means that, in principle, there is free mobility of goods, capital, services and labour within EU. Most EU countries have decided to adopt a common currency (euro) by forming the European Monetary Union (EMU)(see Chapter 4). The EMU is perceived to strengthen the integration process further. In a referendum in 2000, Denmark decided not to join the European Monetary Union, but it is still following a fixed exchange policy pegging the exchange rate to the core European currencies (earlier effectively to the D-mark, and now to the Euro). EU is continuously evolving, and it has developed into something much wider than a free-trade arrangement. Denmark has, however, decided[4] not to participate fully in all new areas of cooperation. The Danish policy debate on these issues has been very sensitive and reflects the concern of maintaining sovereignty for a small country.

1.5. The Danish business cycle

Although substantial increases in material well-being have been experienced, the growth process has not been smooth, as can be seen from Figure 1.1 and even more clearly from Figure 1.7 showing annual growth rates in real GDP for Denmark and Euro area countries. Such variations between periods with higher (upswings) and lower growth rates (downswings) or perhaps even negative growth rates (recessions) are systematically observed for market economies and are known as business cycle fluctuations.

The 1960s was a particularly good period in terms of growth, cf. Figure 1.7. Although there was some volatility in the growth rate, it was around a high level (on average 5% per year). In 1973/74, the development turned less favourable with the onset of the so-called oil crisis. Since then, there have been substantial variations in the business cycle. Summarizing the development since the early 1970s, there are three severe recessionary periods of which two were driven by international events, namely the so-called first and second oil crises in 1973-74 and 1980-81 (see Chapter 8), and a downswing in 1987-1993 driven by domestic factors. There have also been three expansionary periods, namely, in 1983-1986 driven by a strong increase in domestic demand, in 1993-2000 driven by both domestic demand and structural reforms, and after a brief interlude again an upturn starting in 2005.

---

4. The Maastricht treaty was not approved by a referendum in 1992. In 1993, a referendum approved the so-called Edinburgh agreement allowing Denmark to opt out of not only the economic and monetary union, but also the parts dealing with cooperation in areas such as military, police and judicial system as well as union citizenship. The Danish decision to stay outside the EMU was confirmed in a referendum in 2000.

Figure 1.7. Growth rates for GDP, Denmark and Euro area, 1961-2004.

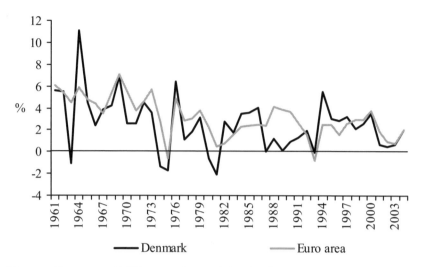

Note: Euro area: 12 EU countries participating in the EMU.
Source: OECD: *National Accounts*.

When considering the development in economic activity, it is useful to make a distinction between the trend (growth) component and the cyclical component. In the preceding discussion of long-run growth, outset was taken from the supply side, i.e. what has been the development in the supply of production factors and their productivity? Turning to short-run variations in economic activity or the cyclical components, it is more useful to approach the problem from the demand side, i.e. what are the main aggregate demand factors and how do they change over time? This is motivated by the fact that variations in aggregate demand play an essential role for changes in economic activity in the short run.[5] Figure 1.8 makes a decomposition of GDP growth into the effect of changes in domestic demand and net foreign demand. Two notable periods are the upswings in the 1980s and 1990s where domestic demand increased substantially and

---

5.   In Keynesian macro models aggregate demand is assumed to determine activity
      in the short run. In modern versions of this model, the interaction between
      supply and demand factors is stressed, but variation in aggregate demand is
      considered a main driving force behind business cycle fluctuations. In so-called
      real business cycle models, changes on the supply side are highlighted as the
      main driving force for both business cycles and growth.

thereby contributed to the upswing. In the recessionary interim period it is seen that domestic demand contributed to reduce growth rates, while net foreign demand prevented that the recession became too deep.

Figure 1.8.   Growth: Domestic and net foreign demand, Denmark 1960-2004.

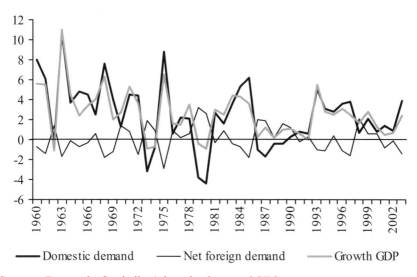

Source: Danmarks Statistik, Adam database and STO.

To further characterize business cycle fluctuations there are some regularities (stylized facts) on how the main aggregate demand components (private consumption, investments, public consumption, exports and imports) interact (see Appendix A). Table 1.3 shows some characteristics of the demand components. The largest component is private consumption and the smallest investments. The most volatile or erratic demand components are imports and investments, while private and public consumption display a variability of the same order of magnitude as GDP. Finally, one sees that private consumption, investments and imports are highly correlated with output, while public consumption and investments are not. These stylized facts suggest that a typical upturn is associated with increases in private consumption, investments and imports, while the pattern for exports and public consumption is less clear. The opposite obviously holds in a downturn. Note that since imports are highly pro-cyclical and exports essentially a-cyclical, it follows that the trade balance (exports minus imports) tends to be counter-cyclical, i.e. the trade balance tends to deteriorate in an upturn and vice versa. The qualitative properties revealed for the aggregate demand components over the business cycle for Denmark are so-called stylized facts found for all industrialized countries.

Table 1.3.   Stylized business cycle facts – Denmark, 1960-2003.

	Share of GDP[1] %	Volatility relative to GDP[2]	Correlation with GDP[3]
Private consumption	52	1.12	0.74
Investments	21	3.88	0.85
Public consumption	25	1.07	0.42
Exports	30	1.65	0.26
Imports	28	2.80	0.75

1) Calculated as the average value over the sample.
2) Calculated as the standard deviation of the growth rate in the demand component, relative to the standard deviation of the growth rate of GDP.
3) Calculated as the correlation between the growth of the demand component and the growth rate of GDP.
Source: Calculations based on data from OECD *National Accounts* ANA1-database.

Economies are interdependent through many channels, including trade via exports and imports. It is thus to be expected that there is a high degree of similarity in the business cycle between countries with much trade, i.e. if activity goes up in other European countries, one would expect this to improve activity in Denmark via more exports, and vice versa. Figure 1.9 shows how closely business cycles in EU-15 countries move measured by the correlation of the growth rate in the country to the average growth rate for EU-15.

Figure 1.9.   Correlation in business cycles with EU business cycles.

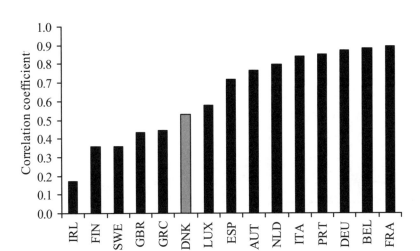

Note: Correlation coefficient between the growth rate of the country and the average growth rate for Euro area countries over the period 1971-2004.

Source: Calculations based on data from OECD Database at www.sourceoecd.org.

The figure shows two striking facts. First, there is a group of countries – core countries – which has a business cycle following the European business cycle rather closely; this includes countries like Germany, France, Italy, Portugal, Austria, Belgium and The Netherlands. Second, for some small and open countries – periphery countries – the business cycle does not follow the European business cycle very closely; this includes countries like Ireland, Denmark, United Kingdom, Finland and Sweden. The latter fact also shows that domestic factors can play a crucial role for business cycle developments even for small countries like Denmark tightly integrated in the European economy. One reason for this finding is that variations in domestic demand often play a crucial role for short-run variations in domestic activity, cf. above.

Figure 1.10. Unemployment rate: Euro area and Denmark, 1970-2005.

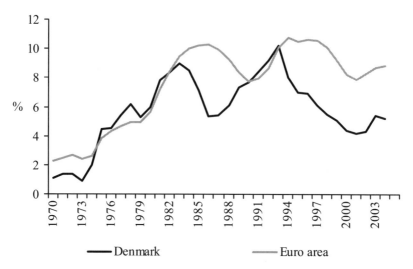

Source: OECD Database at www.sourceoecd.org

The reason why business cycle fluctuations attract much attention is both the direct implications they may have for the activity in various sectors, but also because they tend to induce changes in unemployment. While unemployment was very low in a period in the 1960s, it increased to a high level in the mid 1970s, and the registered unemployment rate remained at a high level until the mid 1990s, cf. Figure 1.10. During the years with high unemployment, there were naturally many policy attempts to cope with the unemployment problem (see Chapter 5). Most of these initiatives have been passive in nature aiming at reducing the registered unemployment rate by lowering labour supply through e.g. early retirement and a paid leave scheme, but there have also been more specific active measures aiming at bringing unemployed back to regular jobs (see next section). As can be seen from Figure 1.10, the unemployment curve for Denmark shows a break around 1993-1994, and the unemployment problem has been significantly reduced compared to the mid 1970s and 1980s. This change can partly be attributed to an improvement in the business cycle, but also to a shift in labour market policies with much more focus on active measures (see next section and Chapter 5). It is worth noticing that the entire reduction in unemployment over this period 1993-99 cannot be attributed to an increase in employment. Unemployment peaked with about 350,000 unemployed in 1993, in 1999 the registered unemployment was 158,000. In the same period, employment increased by about 132,000 people, hence close to 60,000 left the labour force or were taking part in active or passive labour market policies, and this contributed to the fall in the registered unemployment rate (see Chapter 5). In 2005-06, a further decrease in unemployment has materialized, and the unemployment rate is now back to the level at the onset of the oil crisis in the early 1970s. Note, however, that the number of people in working ages relying on public transfers has increased over this period (see Chapters 5 and 6).

Figure 1.11   Inflation, Denmark and Germany, 1961-2005.

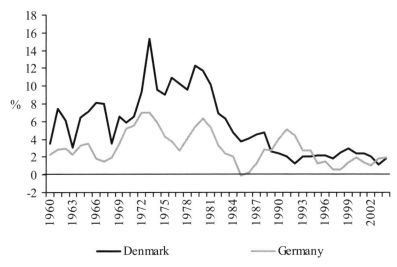

Note: Consumer price inflation.
Source: OECD Database at www.sourceoecd.org

Another macroeconomic concern is inflation. While growth proceeded with moderate inflation in the 1960s, high inflation was encountered in the 1970s despite the business cycle downturn and increasing unemployment. The reasons include increasing raw material prices (oil) and increasing wage demands to compensate for price increases and therefore inducing a wage-price spiral. This was reinforced by several devaluations made in an attempt to improve competitiveness, but at the same time fuelling inflation by increasing prices of imported goods. A disinflationary policy anchored in a fixed exchange rate policy (followed since 1982, cf. Chapter 4) initiated in the early 1980s brought inflation under control. Since the mid

1980s, Denmark has had a low and fairly stable rate of inflation close to the European average.

Alongside unemployment the current account of the balance of payments (see Chapter 3) has been a central variable for economic policy since the late 1960s. A systematic tendency for current account deficits seemed to arise, cf. Figure 1.12, and foreign debt started growing. This raised concerns that the situation was not sustainable. Accordingly, the current account has often been considered as a constraint on economic policy (see below). In recent years, the current account has shown a surplus, cf. Figure 1.12, not least due to increased revenue from oil and shipping. The deficits caused an increasing foreign debt which peaked at almost 50% in the late 1980s. The systematic current account surpluses have implied a reduction in foreign debt, and according to the most recent projections debt will be eliminated in 2007, and Denmark will start accumulating "foreign wealth".

Figure 1.12. Current account relative to GDP, Denmark 1970-2005.

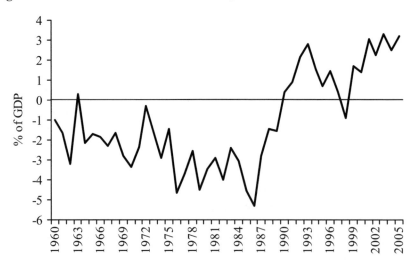

Note: Current account of the balance of payments relative to GDP.
Source: www.statistikbanken.dk.

Finally, public finances have displayed substantial variations over the years. In the 1970s, public finances deteriorated significantly due to the business cycle downturn and increasing unemployment. This is to be expected for a welfare state like the Danish, since its primary objective is to moderate the effects of economic downturns (see Chapter 6). There has thus been a rapid increase in public expenditure to transfers, while the traditional public-sector activities have not increased relative to GDP since the early 1970s, see Figure 1.4. Although the tax burden was increased over this period, there was a systematic tendency to run budget deficits, and this obviously resulted in an increasing level of public debt, cf. Figure 1.13. Since 1997, the public balance has been in surplus and the debt level has been reduced (see Chapter 6). This change is partly a result of the automatic improvements in the public budget which follows when activity is increasing and unemployment falling, and partly a result of a policy aiming at consolidating public finances (see Chapter 6).

Figure 1.13. Public sector primary balance,% of GDP 1971-2005.

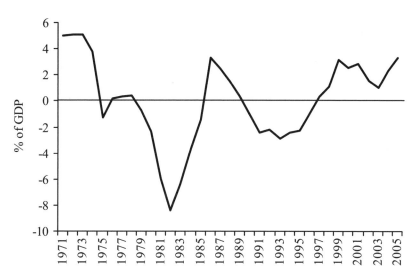

Note: The primary balance gives the differences between revenues and expenditures for the public sector.
Source: Danmarks Statistik. Adam database and STO.

1.6. Danish economic policy

The growth period in the 1960s led to an optimistic view on economic prospects. It was also a period with an optimistic view on the ability of policy makers to fine-tune the macroeconomic development. It was perceived that by management of macroeconomic policy instruments (in particular fiscal policy), it should be possible to avoid major swings in economic activity and unemployment. The subsequent development in the 1970s showed that macroeconomic management was very difficult, and a variety of different policy strategies have been pursued in an attempt to improve upon the macroeconomic performance.

The initial response to the international recession and the rise in unemployment in the mid 1970s was a so-called bridging policy. This policy was based on the perception that the recession was temporary and therefore could be mitigated by an expansionary demand management policy.

The perception that the recession was temporary soon proved wrong, and the overall policy strategy from the mid 1970s up to 1982 was guided by a so-called switching strategy according to which the twin problems of unemployment and current account deficits could be solved by switching private demand with a high import ratio into public demand with a lower import ratio. As a consequence, numerous policy packages included tax increases to curtail private demand and expansions of public demand and, in particular, public employment programmes. These changes did not necessarily take place simultaneously as the policy had a stop-go character with tax increases in times where the current account was considered out of control and public expansion in periods with focus on the unemployment problem.[6] This was the prime time of policy packages appearing frequently in an atmosphere of acute need for intervention. A loose exchange rate policy (crawling peg) was part of this strategy since discrete devaluations were believed to redo the harm of excessive domestic wage increases. Underlying this policy view was an accommodative attitude towards the labour market in the sense that the government accepted a responsibility for the employment level. Accordingly, the labour market policy was fairly passive concentrating on reducing labour supply and mitigating the economic consequences for the unemployed. This policy strategy was not very successful in terms of solving the overall macro problems. The problems of current account deficits and unemployment remained unsolved, while inflation and public debt were growing.

---

6. This period also saw several policy interventions to reduce the dependency of the Danish economy on import of energy. Gradually, the domestic production of oil and in particular gas was increased, and in the late 1990s, Denmark became a net-exporter of energy. See Chapter 8 for a more detailed explanation of the Danish energy sector and policy.

In the autumn 1982, there was a shift in government from a social democratic minority government to a liberal-conservative minority government. The new government launched an economic policy based on the idea that the problems underlying the Danish economy could only be solved in a medium-term perspective by an expansion of private sectors capable of facing international competition. The policy consisted of a disinflationary policy based on a fixed exchange rate policy and a tight fiscal policy. The policy shift signalled that the government attempted to leave more responsibility for the employment level to the labour market.

This disinflationary policy was initially very successful, and a change in the economic mood was observed accompanied by increases in private demand, higher GDP growth and a fall in unemployment from 1983 to 1986 (see Figures 1.8 and 1.10). This policy was to some extent killed by its own success, in the sense that the boom was larger than the economy could absorb. The upturn in the mid 1980s was associated with a substantial increase in domestic demand as both private consumption and investment soared, but it turned out that supply capacity could not match this increase. The capacity problems applied both to the production capacity of firms and the availability of labour with the needed qualifications. As a consequence, it led to a further deterioration of the current account and wage increases (in 1987) much in excess of the norms of the disinflationary policy. Since domestic demand was booming during this period, shortage of aggregate demand could be ruled out as the primary reason for the persistent unemployment problem. The fact that substantial wage increases were released in 1987 despite an unemployment rate around 8% can be taken as a strong indication that there were substantial adjustment problems in the labour market.

A fairly pessimistic view on the unemployment problem developed during the late 1980s and early 1990s, and the views that "one has to live with unemployment" and "there is no need for so much labour" became fairly widespread. A minority coalition government led by the Social Democratic party took over in 1992 and launched a paid leave scheme aiming at distributing the burden of unemployment more equally as well as a fiscal expansion (partly financing the transition period of a tax reform lowering marginal taxes and broadening the tax base) to create more jobs. Although a shift in the business cycle was to be expected after a prolonged recession, there is little doubt that the expansionary fiscal policy had a role in triggering the boom in economic activity and the fall in unemployment. The accompanying "break" in the unemployment figures changed the passive attitude which had characterized economic policy for more than a decade. The increase in employment showed that it was possible to do something about the problem, and a much more active attitude developed. This implied that the labour market and social policies were changed in the direction of strengthening requirements for active participation (see Chapter 5). An example of this is the so-called youth package, which implied that young people below the age of 25 could only remain on unemployment benefits for 6 months, subsequent to which they would have to start an education, accept a job offer or get lower benefits. Judging from the subsequent development in wage formation and unemployment, there is no doubt that the overall shift in policy had structural effects on the labour market, although it should be noted that the unemployment figures were also affected by policies moving people off the labour force (e.g. early retirement) and the business cycle situation. See Chapter 5 for details.

At the turn of the century, the business cycle turned less favourable although it was more a slow-down than a genuine recession. This was partly induced by international events like the stock market crash in 2000-2001 (see Chapter 4), the terror attack on the World Trade Center etc. It was also a period with very few policy initiatives.

The downturn was brief, and in 2005-2006 the business cycle situation has improved and brought unemployment to new record low levels. This has caused concerns for problems arising due to "lack of labour". Relative to the discussion in the later 1980s and 1990s on "excess supply of labour", the debate has thus taken a complete turn.

Currently (2006), macroeconomic conditions (low inflation and unemployment, surplus on public finances) are favourable, but there are some major challenges which have been attracting attention in policy debates. This includes the future of the welfare state in particular due to forthcoming changes in the demographic composition of the population (ageing), and the effects of globalization. The latter includes both the effects for the public sector and the labour market, and therefore issues like education, qualifications, research etc. are much debated. In short, the question is what is required in a forward looking perspective to maintain an extended welfare state and a position as one of the most affluent countries in the world (see also Chapter 6). For a discussion of these challenges and proposals, see Velfærdskommissionen (2006), Globali-seringsrådet (2005), Tænketanken fremtidens vækst (2005) and Trepartsudvalget (2006).

References

Andersen, T.M., S.E. Hougaard Jensen and O. Risager, 2000: Macroeconomic Perspectives on the Danish Economy: Problems, Policies and Prospects, in Andersen, T.M., S.E. Hougaard Jensen and O. Risager, *Macroeconomic Perspectives on the Danish Economy*, MacMillan.

Crafts, N., 2000: *Globalization and Growth in the Twentieth Century*, IMF Working Paper 2000-44.

Danmarks Nationalbank (The central bank of Denmark): *Årsberetning* (various issues).

Danmarks Statistik (Statistics Denmark): STO, various issues.

Danmarks Statistik (Statistics Denmark): 2005, *Statistical Yearbook.*

Det Økonomiske Råd (Danish Economic Council): *Dansk Økonomi* (various issues).

Erhvervsministeriet (Ministry of Business and Industry), 1998: *Erhvervs-redegørelsen.*

EU: *European Economy*, 1998, Brussels.

European Commission, 2000: *European Economy.*

Eurostat: Key Indicators, *Poverty rates after social transfers* (10/02/2001).

Eurostat: Statistics in focus, *Population and living conditions*, 9/2000.

Finansministeriet (Ministry of Finance): *Finansredegørelsen* (various issues).

Finansministeriet (Ministry of Finance): Økonomisk redegørelse (various issues)

Finansrådet (Danish Bankers Association), 1998: *Opsparing og fremtidig velfærd.*

Globaliseringsrådet, 2005, Danmark og globaliseringen – debatpjece om globaliseringens udfordringer for Danmark, Statsministeriet

Hansen, E.D., S.E. Hougaard Jensen og J. Rosted, 1994: *Dansk økonomisk politik – teorier og erfaringer.*

Hoffmeier, E., 1993: *Pengepolitiske problemstillinger 1965-1990*, Danmarks Nationalbank.

OECD 2001: *Main Economic Indicators.*

OECD 2005: *Employment Outlook*, June 2005.

OECD 2005: *OECD in Figures.*

OECD: *Economic Outlook*, various issues.

OECD: *National Accounts.*

Pedersen, P.J., C. Sørensen og C. Vastrup, 1987: *Træk af udviklingen i dansk økonomi efter 1960, i Råd og realiteter 1962-1987*, Det Økonomiske Råd.

Pedersen, P.J., 1996: Postwar Growth of the Danish Economy, in N. Crafts and G. Tonilo (eds.): *Economic Growth in Europe since 1954*, Cambridge University Press.

Trepartsudvalget, 2006: Livslang opkvalificering og uddannelse for alle på arbejdsmarkedet, rapport fra trepartsudvalget, Finansministeriet.

Tænketanken fremtidens vækst, 2005, Det nytænkende og fleksible samfunds, Økonomi og Erhvervsministeriet.

UNDP, 2005: *Human Development Report*.

Velfærdskommissionen, 2006, Fremtidens velfærd – vores valg (www.velfaerd.dk)

WHO, 2005: *World Health Report*.

Økonomiministeriet (Danish Ministry of Economic Affairs): *Økonomisk Oversigt* (diverse udgaver).

Web addresses

www.ae-dk.dk (Economic Council of the Labour Movement)
www.di.dk (Danish Industry)
www.dors.dk (Economic Council)
www.dst.dk (Official hompage for Statistics Denmark)
www.ecb.org (European Central Bank)
www.europa.eu.int (Eurostat)
www.fm.dk (Ministry of Finance)
www.imf.org (IMF)
www.nationalbanken.dk (The central bank of Denmark)
www.oecd.org (OECD)
www.oem.dk (Ministry of Economy)
www.statistikbanken.dk (Statistics Denmark – online data)
www.undp.org (UNDP)
www.who.int (WHO)

Chapter 2

Industry structure

2.1. Introduction

The growth process has brought an outstanding improvement in material living standards. This applies both in a quantitative and qualitative dimension since the process has not only implied expanded quantities but also new options (e.g. electronic communication and more time for leisure). Hence, underlying the growth process is both increasing productivity as well as reallocations. Some activities would need less labour, some are not in demand anymore and new activities are expanding. This process implies structural changes, and one important dimension of these changes is a change in the sectional structure of the economy.

This chapter takes a closer look at the industrial structure in Denmark considering both how it has developed into the current structure but also some of the future challenges. If Denmark is to maintain a position as one of the richest countries in the world it is important to consider whether the existing industry structure is solid and optimal for further growth. Thus, the industry structure of today is the result of the economics of the past and it is not necessarily the best point of departure for securing future prosperity.

This chapter is structured as follows. Section 2.2 provides a general introduction to the main forces linking growth to structural change. Section 2.3 outlines some of the basic features of the historical development and the present day structure of production in Denmark. The next sections deal with primary (Section 2.4), secondary (Section 2.5) and tertiary (Section 2.6) private sectors. Government provision of various services is extended in Denmark and therefore the public sector is in itself an important sector, which is discussed in Section 2.7. Section 2.8 focuses on some major challenges for the structural characteristics of the Danish production sector in an international context.

Chapter 2

2.2. Basic factors behind structural change

What are the main factors behind structural change? Economic growth and structural change can be considered as two sides of the same coin. Growth can in broad terms be caused either by an expansion in input (land, labour or capital) or an increase in productivity allowing an expanded output for given inputs (see Chapter 8). The latter can be interpreted as being driven by expanded knowledge in a broad sense ranking from new technologies over improved education to changes in the organisational structure. Increased productivity allows more to be produced for the same inputs. However, technological advances and new knowledge usually also open new opportunities. Growth is in general not only characterized by more of the same. The qualitative dimension is important. The process creates new opportunities some of which are important for the production process itself and some of which are important also for consumers and thus generates new demands. Two important examples are the electric engine and the computer. These two inventions have turned out to be very important not only in the production process but also expanding the opportunity set for consumers. From this it follows that the growth process creates new options and thus a change in the production and employment structure in society.

This process is reinforced by the fact that the growth process via increases in income may affect the demand structure. When basic needs as food and housing are satisfied consumers turn to other items when they can afford it. Some activities would thus be in relatively less demand (income elasticity less than 1) when income grows, and others would be in relatively increased demand (income elasticity above 1). As an example consumers used about 50% of their income on food and the like in 1950 and today it is less than 20%. Increase in income thus implies change in consumption patterns, which is reflected in the composition of demand. Consumers can afford new types of products or services, such as cars, television, computers, mobile phones and Internet access.

Considering the linkage between growth and structural process it follows that it runs both ways. Structural changes are a prerequisite[1] for growth, but growth does also cause structural changes. In broad terms the growth process has been associated with first structural changes from primary sectors into secondary sectors. A change which was strong in Denmark in the 1950s and 1960s and it was associated with a shifting of labour from agriculture into manufacturing sectors. Productivity in agriculture increased dramatically. Jobs and higher wages in manufacturing were the attractions that caused a major transfer of people

1: something that is necessary before something else can happen or be done.

28

from rural regions to the cities. The second wave has been expanding tertiary sectors (services) both private and publicly. Actually, employment in secondary sectors started decreasing already in the late 1960s. In recent years the expansion of service sectors has been rather strong, and international trade in services is also increasing partly due to liberalization and technological changes (electronic communication).

In considering the fundamental interaction between growth and structural change one can highlight the following key factors:

Endowments of natural resources: Taking a historic perspective it is rather evident that the resource endowment for Denmark has been conducive for agriculture, fisheries, sea transport etc. Other countries like e.g. Sweden and Finland have had a resource base providing options for industries related to forestry, such as wood, paper and pulp and even paper machinery and wooden furniture. Natural resources have thus historically been an important determinant for the production structure and therefore also for the direction of trade. In high income countries the resource base has played a decreasing role during the 20th century. Present day industries are not closely rooted in the natural resource base. A fact also reflected in trade statistics showing that the large part of growth in international trade is not driven by cross-country differences in natural resource endowments (se Chapter 3).

Technological change can be singled out as the most important driving force for increases in productivity (as discussed in Chapters 1 and 8). Technological advancements has meant improved scope for specialization and allowed substitution of labour for capital increasing the productivity of labour. Some of this has made it possible to improve productivity in existing forms of production, but also opened for new product methods and products. Moreover, technological changes have fostered closer international integration via lower trade and communication costs. This has further improved the scope for specialization and exchange of technology via both trade and foreign direct investments (see Chapter 3).

Human capital is a broad term capturing the education and qualification of the work force including both formal training, on the job training, experience etc. Technological change is knowledge driven and therefore human capital plays an important direct role for the growth process. In addition technological change tends to have a skill-bias decreasing the number of unskilled (low qualification jobs) and increasing the number of skilled (high qualification jobs). Accordingly human capital and its expansion is a critical factor for the growth process, and also for change in the structure and composition of labour demand.

1: a natural quality or ability that someone has.
2: provides conditions that make it easy, in this case, to fish etc.

Political, cultural and institutional factors are equally important to the technological factors in determining growth. This ranges from the specific organisational aspects related to firms and work-places to more broad aspects related to thrust, political stability etc. Recently these factors have been summarized by the term social capital as a factor of production equally important to natural capital, real capital and human capital. Alike the traditional capital concepts social capital can be accumulated but it may also depreciate, and it can therefore not be taken for granted.

Exposure to international trade is also important in shaping the structural development. The gains from trade are associated with specialization and division of labour, and therefore also with structural changes (see Chapter 3). This, in turn, leads to the most efficient allocation of productive resources globally, according to standard economic theory. As noted above international trade may interact with technological factors in inducing growth and therefore structural changes.

In Chapter 8 growth and growth policies are further discussed while the following sections turn to the structural composition and its changes.

2.3. The structural composition of Danish production

At the aggregate[1] level it is useful to split the economy into three main sectors: *primary*, *secondary* and *tertiary* sectors or industries.

The *primary* industries are characterised by exploiting natural resource endowments directly, such as agriculture, fishery and extraction of minerals, oil and gas. The *secondary* industries include manufacturing, construction and utilities (energy and water). While these two sectors deliver physical goods, the third sector consists of the *tertiary* or service industries.

Table 2.1.   Main sectors in Danish production 1820-2004, measured at GDP, %.

	1820	1900	1950	1966	2004
Primary	55	30	21	9	5
Secondary	19	26	36	35	22
Tertiary	26	44	43	56	73
Total	100	100	100	100	100

Source: 1820-1950:. Hansen S. Aa.: *Økonomisk vækst i Danmark*, Bind I, Akademisk Forlag 1974, www.statistikbanken.dk.

1: The total after a lot of diff. figures or points have been added together

The relative role of these three sectors has changed dramatically over the years, cf. Table 2.1. In a long term perspective, primary sectors have been on a declining trend. In 1820 it was the main sector constituting 55% of GDP while it was diminished to only 5% in 2004. Secondary sectors have followed an inverted U-path, first increasing and then decreasing in importance. The peak level was in the 1950s and 1960s with a level slightly above 1/3 of GDP. The tertiary sectors have also been important (26% already in 1820) but have been on an upward trend and it is currently accounting for about ¾ of GDP.

In broad terms we have thus seen a shift from primary over secondary to tertiary sectors in the underlying growth process. This pattern is quite common for the growth process experienced by most high income countries. However, there is some variation in the absolute importance of the various sectors across countries. The point is that the growth process has induced significant structural changes, and therefore also a change in the areas in which one might expect to find the scope for further growth.

Leaving the historical trends to take a more detailed perspective on the role of various industries Table 2.2 provides measures in terms of share of employment and value added for the importance of various sub-sectors from the mid 1960 and up to the present. By considering both employment and value added it is possible to put some perspective on the role of productivity (more output for less labour input) as well as on the question on where is people employed, and which sectors are most important for value added.

Among the *primary* industries, the long-term decline of the relative size of agriculture has continued after 1966, see Section 2.4.[1] This is more pronounced for employment than for value added, which indicates substantial productivity increases. However, raw materials has increased its share of value added since the mid-1980s, which reflects oil and gas extraction from the North Sea. See Chapter 7.

1. The industry categories are based on the DB93 system used for classification of approximately 0.5 million firms. DB93 is the Danish version of the EU NACE nomenclature (Rev. 1), which is based upon the UN ISIC, Rev. 3. The first four digits in NACE are identical with DB93. At the six-digit level DB93 contains approximately 800 industries.

Table 2.2. *Structure of Danish industries 1966-2004. Employment and value added (%).*

INDUSTRY	Employment		Gross value added	
	1966	2004	1966	2004
PRIMARY INDUSTRIES	***14.7***	***3.8***	***9.0***	***5.2***
Food, beverages and tobacco	5.1	2.7	4.8	2.6
Textile and clothing	3.8	0.4	2.2	0.3
Wood and furniture[1]	2.5	1.0	1.7	0.9
Paper and printing	2.5	2.1	2.4	1.9
Chemicals	1.7	1.8	1.9	2.5
Non-metallic mineral products	1.4	0.7	1.4	0.6
Basic metals, fabricated metals and machinery	8.8	6.2	7.6	5.4
Manufacturing	*25.9*	*14.8*	*22.1*	*14.2*
Utilities	0.6	0.5	1.8	2.1
Construction	8.8	6.0	11.4	5.3
SECONDARY INDUSTRIES	***35.3***	***21.3***	***35.2***	***21.6***
Wholesale and retail trade	14.3	14.0	16.6	10.8
Hotels and restaurants	2.0	3.1	1.3	1.7
Transport, post and tele	7.0	6.6	9.3	8.8
Finance and insurance	2.0	2.6	3.0	5.4
Real estate and renting services	0.3	1.6	3.9	12.7
Business service	2.3	8.8	2.7	7.7
Domestic services and car repair	4.1	2.2	2.9	1.6
Government services	13.2	31.1	12.9	23.0
Other services	4.9	4.9	3.4	1.5
TERTIARY INDUSTRIES	***50.1***	***74.9***	***55.8***	***73.2***
Total	100	100	100	100
Employment (1000)	2,237	2,679		
Value added (billion DKK)			69	1,035

1. Including jewellery and toys.
Source: www.statistikbanken.dk and STO 2005.

Secondary industries have experience a substantial decline both in terms of relative importance for employment and value added since the mid-1960s. Food, beverages and tobacco as well as textiles and clothing have experienced a decreasing trend in their shares of total value added. Chemicals have shown an increasing share of value added and a (smaller) increase of its employment share. The biggest manufacturing industry is fabricated metals and machinery ('engineering'). However, the most pronounced structural change among the secondary industries is the fall of the share of construction from 11.4% to 5.3% of value added in the period 1966-2004, while the employment share only decreased from 8.8% to 6.0%. A pattern indicating serious long-term productivity problems in the industry.[2]

The decrease in the share of the two main commodity-producing sectors is reflected in the increase of the *tertiary* industries. Basically, this has been caused by the substantial increase in government services, which nearly doubled its share of total Danish employment from the mid-1960s to the mid-1970s (see also Chapters 1 and 6). This increase continued, although at a slower speed, until the mid-1980s, after which the share has stagnated. In 2004, government services amounted to about one third of employment and one quarter of gross value added. Among market services, business services and real estate services have had a relatively striking growth. The growth in business services is partly due to the fact that firms in this industry are increasingly taking over areas of activity from firms in primary and secondary industries.

2.4. Primary industries

As noted above the changes for primary industries and in particular agriculture have been dramatic. Just before the second world war, agriculture constituted 20% of GDP and 25% of employment.[3] Today, agriculture etc. only makes up about 2% of gross value added (GVA, for a definition see Appendix A) and less than 4% of employment, cf. Table 2.3. This pattern is common for all European countries. In 2003, the agricultural share of total GVA (including horticulture and forestry), was 2.0% in Denmark and 1.9% in EU(15), varying from 0.5% in Luxembourg to 6.0% in Greece.[4] The situation is slightly different from the ten new

---

2. See also the discussion of this issue in Chapter 8.
3. Mogensen, G. Viby (1972), p. 8.
4. www.europa.eu.int/comm/eurostat.

member states of EU (NMS). In these countries agriculture accounts for a larger share of GDP than the EU(15) average and the proportion of the working population engaged in agriculture in NMS is more than three times as high as the EU(15) average.[5] This is consistent with the fact that the countries have a lower income level and have progressed less in the growth process than the "old" EU countries.

Table 2.3.   Danish primary industries as a percentage of total industries, 1966 and 2004.

	Gross value added		Employment	
	1966	2004	1966	2004
	------------------------ % ------------------------			
Agriculture etc.[1]	8.8	2.2	14.6	3.6
Extraction industries	0.2	3.0	0.1	0.2
Total primary industries	9.0	5.2	14.7	3.8

1) Agricultural services, horticulture, forestry and fishing.
Source: www.statistikbanken.dk and STO 2005.

Agriculture and extraction of crude petroleum and natural gas are by far the most important primary industries measured by GVA and therefore those sectors are dealt with more thoroughly in the next two sections. Employment in the extraction industry, however, is of no significance, because this industry is very capital intensive.

Even though Denmark is surrounded by the sea and has a relatively big fishing fleet, GVA and employment in the fishing industry only make up about 0.2% of total industries GVA and employment. The fishing industry is a declining industry. The Common Fisheries Policy (CFP) of the EU forms the framework for the Danish fishing industry. Especially important are the quotas fixing a maximum catch of the different species within specified areas. The quotas are necessary to prevent over-fishing and to keep a sustainable fish stock.

2.4.1. Extraction of oil and gas

A striking structural change for Denmark is a transformation from being an importer to becoming an exporter of energy.

---

5 .   Agricultural Policies in OECD Countries: Monitoring and Evaluation 2005, p. 68.

While a concession to explore and produce oil and natural gas was given to A.P. Møller in 1962 (and later to other companies) oil production did not start until 1972. Production began to grow steadily from 1980, and in 2004 total oil production was 828 PJ (10^{15} Joule). Ranked after the UK and Norway, Denmark is now the 3rd largest oil producer in Western Europe. The result is that oil production in 2004 was 139% above oil consumption. Danish natural gas has been extracted since 1984 and in 2004, production was 356 PJ of which 43% was exported.[6]

Oil and gas production has, especially in recent years, been important in the Danish economy due to increasing production and escalating oil prices. In 2004, the value of Danish oil and gas production was about 3% of total GVA, oil and natural gas made up 8% of total exports[7] and 2-3% of taxes were founded on oil and gas production.[8] The Danish Energy Agency has estimated that oil and gas activities will contribute DKK 29 billion to the current account in 2005 (oil price 40$/barrel) corresponding to about 2/3 of the total surplus.[9]

At the end of 2004, the R/P ratio (reserves/production) is estimated to be 12. Oil production peaked in 2002 and according to a production forecast prepared by the Danish Energy Agency, oil production will fall after 2005. Based upon long-term sales contracts, the natural gas production is expected to be approximately unchanged between 2005 and 2009. Based upon production forecasts, one must therefore conclude that the extraction industry is a declining sector.

2.4.2. Agriculture

The agricultural sector is most influenced by the EU's Common Agricultural Policy (CAP). The details of this policy framework are outlined in Chapter 7.3.

Considering the agricultural sector and in particular the pricing of farms is an interesting case example of the implications of regulations. The EU agricultural policy implies subsidization through various mechanisms of farmers aiming at improving the income levels of farmers. When Denmark joined EU in 1973, the higher prices within the EU were

6 .   Energistyrelsen: *Energistatistik* 2004.
7 .   www.statistikbanken.dk.
8 .   Energistyrelsen: *Danmarks olie- og gasproduktion* 2004.
9 .   Energistyrelsen: *Danmarks olie- og gasproduktion* 2004 and SE: *National-regnskab og betalingsbalance* 2005:12

1 : something you allow somebody :
2 : The guverment pays part of its cost.

capitalized into higher farm prices. Hence, existing farmers benefited from the price increase while new farmers did not benefit.

Figure 2.1. *Fixed gross capital formation in agriculture in constant prices, and the price of farms in DKK/ha, deflated by the consumer price index. 1970-2004, 1970=100.*

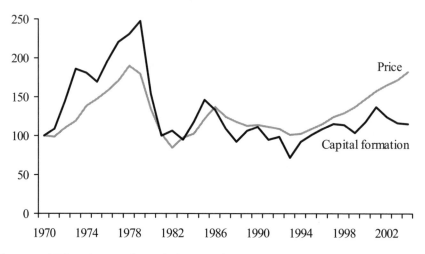

Source: STO, *Nationalregnskabsstatistik* 1987 and 1993 as well as www.statistikbanken.dk.

Similarly, CAP was also part of the reason for the huge increase in capital formation (investments) in the 1970s. Around 1980, therefore, the agricultural sector was heavily in debt and since much of this debt was borrowed at fixed interests rates, farmers were hit hard by the adjustment of the Danish economy to a lower level of inflation and thus, lower nominal interest rates after 1982 (See Chapter 1). Since 1993, prices on all kinds of real property have escalated, especially due to low interest rates, see also the development of house prices in Section 7.5.

A number of farmers are still having a very high interest burden, measured as net interest payments/net farm income in spite of low interest rates, cf. Table 2.4. On average, in the period 1998-2004 the interest burden was 83% of net farm income. The other EU countries have no similar interest burden.

Table 2.4 also reveals that farm income fluctuates substantially. The fluctuations of farm income are caused by variations in crop yields and producer prices. Moreover off-farm salary and profit from other business make up a substantial part of current income, even on full-time holdings.

Table 2.4.   Current income on full-time holdings[1], thousand DKK per holding.

	1998	1999	2000	2001	2002	2003	2004
1. Net farm income	368	396	583	654	465	449	532
2. Profit from other business	41	46	49	51	63	62	63
3. Off-farm salary	34	29	28	29	33	42	43
4. Total salary and net income (1+2+3)	443	471	660	734	561	553	638
5. Net interest payments[2]	330	359	389	417	433	460	472
6. Current income (4-5)	157	112	271	317	128	93	166

1) Farms requiring a labour input of at least one man-year.
2) Including rent.
Source: www.foi.dk. Fødevareøkonomisk Institut: *Landbrugsregnskabsstatistik.*

The agricultural sector has seen a continuous of new technologies in the form of better machines and more rational buildings contributing to an increasing productivity. New kinds of fertilizers, pesticides, high-yield plants and livestock have also increased productivity. In addition, holdings have become bigger and more specialized. The number of holdings with both cattle and pigs has declined rapidly, while the number of holdings with either cattle or pigs, or without both, has increased.

Table 2.5.   Holdings by size of area in EU countries, 2003, %.

	- 4.9 ha	5.0-19.9 ha	20.0-49.9 ha	50 ha -	Total
Denmark	4	38	31	9	100
EU(15)[1]	56	24	11	3	100

1) Excluding Portugal.
Source: Danmarks Statistik, *Landbrug* 2004.

For many years, the number of holdings has decreased about 2-3% a year[10] and today, the average farm size in Denmark is considerably above the EU(15) average, cf. Table 2.5. Average size in the ten new member states is about 50% below the EU(15) average.[11]

---

10.   Danmarks Statistik: STO.
11.   Agricultural Policies in OECD Countries: monitoring and Evaluation 2005, p. 87.

The adjustment in farm size has been accompanied by a corresponding adjustment in the use of labour. There has been a continuous decline in the number of self-employed and assisting spouses, while the number of permanent workers has increased in recent years. In 2003, the number of non-family permanent workers corresponds to 40% of the number of farms.[12]

Table 2.6 shows that the value of livestock products is just under 2/3 of total sales. Ten years ago, the value of livestock products was just above 2/3 of total sales.

Table 2.6. Value of agricultural sales, 2004.

	---- % ----
Crop products	35
Livestock products	65
Natural milk	19
Cattle	4
Pigs	32
Other products	9
Total sales	100

Source: Danmarks Statistik, *Landbrug* 2004.

Pigmeat is a very important agricultural product in Denmark making up about 10% of total pigmeat production in EU(15), while the production of beef (including veal) and milk in Denmark only makes up 2% and 4%, respectively, of the production in EU(15).[13]

The exports of food and livestock, including export subsidies from EU, were 10% of total Danish exports in 2004.[14]

2.5. The secondary industries

The main sub-sectors of the secondary industry are utilities, construction and manufacturing, cf. Table 2.2.

---

12. Danmarks Statistik: *Landbrug* 2003.
13. Danmarks Statistik: *Landbrug* 2004.
14. Danmarks Statistik: *Landbrug* 2004 and SE: *Udenrigshandel* 2005:2.

2.5.1. Utilities

Utilities consist of producers of water and energy – in terms of heating and electricity - for households and firms. Until recently, these producers were mainly publicly owned and/or heavily regulated. From 1998 the Danish electricity market has gradually been liberalised and from around 2003 a series of mergers and acquisitions, also with international partners, have been envisaged. Most of the companies are in a process of deregulation and privatisation, as has been the case in many other countries. The utilities area has been liberalised some years later than tele-communications, but in the most recent period the speed of transformation has been increased significantly in Denmark.

The share of value added in 2004 was four times larger than the employment share, cf. Table 2.2, reflecting capital intensive production methods. Total employments amounted to 13-14.000 persons. Utilities have traditionally been considered as 'natural' monopolies, but technological change and the new approaches to deregulation have entered the scene.

DONG, originally a publicly owned gas extraction company, has emerged as the largest group in the sector.[15] From 2005 DONG (owned by the Danish government) has taken over the majority of the Jutland-Funen utility Elsam. The Swedish Vattenfall (owned by the Swedish government) has, however, also acquired influence in the Danish sector through e.g. ownership of one third of Elsam. The Copenhagen-Sealand region is dominated by Energi E2, where DONG has acquired 2/3 of the shares. At the bottom line of this rather complicated recent restructuring of the sector it appears that energy production and distribution is dominated by DONG, Vattenfall and a group of smaller regional actors, still with a the municipal sector involved in ownership relations. The government has, though, merged a group of distribution companies (Eltra, Elkraft and Gastra) in Energinet.dk as a government owned company with responsibilities for overall planning of the electricity and gas transmission network in Denmark.

---

15. 2004 data from the November 2005 issue of *Berlingske Nyhedsmagasin*, "Guldnummer" (The Golden Issue). This account is made annually and is an useful source of information on large companies in Denmark. Also the Danish Association of Engineers publishes surveys based on this source as special reports in the weekly magazine "Ingeniøren" (The Engineer). The latter publishes annual surveys on construction, ICT and manufacturing, but not specifically on utilities.

2.5.2. Construction

The construction industry produces buildings for industry and private households and the physical infrastructure in terms of roads, bridges, airports, harbours etc. Among the EU countries the relative size of construction varies somehow. In 2004, the share of gross value added in Denmark was 5.1% compared to an EU-25 average of 5.7%.[16] The absolute size of employment was approximately 160,000, cf. Table 2.2. In a cross country perspective the general pattern appears to be an inverse relationship between the relative size of this industry and income per capita. The construction sector is generally considered to be operating in local or national markets with respect to building materials and building style and does not experience intense international competition such as in manufacturing. Public regulation is playing a substantial role at all levels, ranging from the level of construction activity seen from a macroeconomic point of view to detailed specifications and control of building standards in private homes, although the EU internal market in principle has opened up for international competition on building materials. The regulations of the rental market are described and discussed in Section 7.5.

The Danish construction sector has shown a stagnant productivity growth for more than three decades and there have been recurrent complaints of bad quality of new houses from consumers. These features have been analysed extensively in a series of government initiated studies, especially because the industry has experienced substantial growth in production and earnings during the 1990s and again in the 2000s. As shown in Table 8.2 total factor productivity growth has stagnated since the mid-1960s. It has been shown that labour productivity during 1970-95 grew approximately 100% in Sweden, 60% in Germany and 25% in the Netherlands while it stagnated in Denmark.[17] The poor Danish productivity performance has been attributed to a lack of 'innovation culture' in the construction industry combined with a 'lock-in' effect in a more traditional division of labour between a rather large amount of not sufficiently co-ordinated partners. The latter include architects, independent engineering consultants, building companies ('construction entrepreneurs' in the Danish vocabulary) and a long series of

---

16.   Danmarks Statistik: STO 2005, p. 173. The internationally comparable data in STO deviates slightly from Table 2.2.
17.   The same applies for growth of labour productivity, cf. By- og Boligministeriet & Erhvervsministeriet (2000).

subcontractors.[18] Lack of R&D departments and of a co-operative culture between the firms possessing complementary knowledge within the industry is apparently among the decisive features.

The low productivity is one of the important factors behind a major consolidation process, which has been envisaged by the industry in recent years, whether through mergers of foreign take-overs. The biggest construction company is MT Højgaard with approximately 5,000 employees in 2004.[19] The second largest, measured by employment, is NCC (i.e. NCC Construction Denmark and NCC Roads), which is part of a large Swedish multinational construction company. NCC has been formed through take-over and mergers of four Danish construction companies during 1996-99. Among the five largest is also the Swedish owned Skanska Denmark. These two Swedish companies are among the large multinational firms in the international construction industry. They appear to be in a position to be better able to solve the problems of internalising coordination problems in the construction process together with R&D activities. They appear to be better geared to create a persistent knowledge accumulation, which has been the more standard way of organising innovative activities in manufacturing during almost a century.

2.5.3. Manufacturing

In 2004 the relative size of Danish manufacturing was 14.2% of gross value added and 14.8% of employment equal to nearly 400,000 jobs, cf. Table 2.2. The relative share of manufacturing is lower than the OECD average around 17% of gross value added.[20] Although the Danish share was no. 22 out of 30 OECD countries shown for 2002 it is on the other hand slightly larger than the shares of the US, the Netherlands and the UK. In general, there does appear to be a simple causal relation between the more general macroeconomic performance of developed countries and the relative size of their manufacturing sectors.

---

18. These issues have been analyzed by Erhvervsfremmestyrelsen [2001].

19. The source of the company information is the annual "Guldnummer" from Berlingske Nyhedsmagasin. The most recent is from November 2005. MT Højgaard is the result of a merger between Monberg & Thorsen and Højgaard & Schultz in 2001.

20. According to *OECD Science, Technology and Industry Scoreboard 2005*, Figure F.6, p. 168-69.

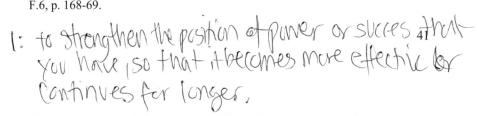

1: to strengthen the position of power or success that you have, so that it becomes more effective or continues for longer.

41

A predominant view in the public debate has been that the manufacturing sector plays a particular important role for the wealth of a nation, and many policy debates seem to take it for granted that "the more you have of it the better". This view was often advanced in the period 1964-89 with systematic deficits on the current balances, but also more recently in relation to the globalization debate and the question of "what should support us in the future". However, this view is not supported by economic theory which does neither provide a particular important role to specific sectors nor on the 'optimal' size of major sectors, such as manufacturing. In a market economy the important test of value added is made in the market in the form of a willingness to pay.

The internal structure of manufacturing is shown in Table 2.2. In 1966 the three largest manufacturing industries measured by employment were 1) the broad engineering sector ('basic metals, fabricated metals and machinery'), which also includes electrical and electronic equipment; 2) food, beverages & tobacco and 3) textile & clothing. The latter was surpassed as the third largest by paper and print, when measured by value added. In the mid-1960s around one third of Danish manufacturing was, thus, concentrated on low income elasticity products[21] with a rather low growth potential.

The most visible structural change over the period has been the substantial decrease of the textile and clothing industry in line with the general pattern for the OECD countries. Although the food, drink and tobacco industry has experienced a declining share it is still rather big in international context.

Among the large companies in the *food processing* industry is Danish Crown, the largest pork and meat manufacturer in Europe and the second largest pork manufacturer in the world. Danish Crown is the sixth largest Danish company with 24,000 employees in 2004, of which the majority was employed in Denmark.[22] Arla Foods, the dairy company, is the third largest company in Denmark with 21,000 employees (globally). Arla is a Danish dominated merger of the previous MD Foods and Swedish Arla. It is the second largest dairy company in Europe. Both companies are the modern outcomes - through a long series of mergers - of the co-operative production movement, which emerged from the late 19th century. They are by their very nature not listed at the stock exchange but owned by the

21. Low income elasticity means that demand increases with less than one percent, when incomes increase with one percent.
22. The ranking is based on turnover data from Berlingske Nyhedsmagasin's "Guldnummer", November 2005.

farmers. Although they are large within their fields, these companies are not broad conglomerates in the sense of the huge European food companies, like Nestlé of Switzerland and the Anglo-Dutch Unilever. The similar Danish companies have a size of less than 10% of their big European food counterparts. The Danish brewery Carlsberg is an incorporated company and publicly traded company with a total of around 32,000 employees (globally). The size of Carlsberg, the 9th largest Danish company, is more in line with some of the biggest multinational breweries in Europe.

Wood and furniture is dominated by small and medium sized firms, of which especially the manufactures of 'Scandinavian design' furniture are well known internationally. *Paper and print* as well as the *chemicals* industry have increased their relative share of manufacturing gross value added. The growth of the latter has been dominated by pharmaceuticals, where, Novo-Nordisk (21,000 employees globally) is among the world leaders in diabetes care products, while Novozymes is a world leader in enzymes (4,000 employees). However, similarly to the food industry Novo-Nordisk, the eleventh largest Danish company, is a big player in two markets but small compared to the multinational pharmaceutical companies, which have turned into conglomerates[1] with a much wider product portfolio.

Basic metals, fabricated metals and machinery, the broad collection of industries ranging from shipyards via mechanical and electrical engineering to electronics with the common label of *engineering*, has increased its share of manufacturing employment from 34% in 1966 to 42% in 2004 (measured by value added from 34% to 38%). Denmark is not the home for any multinational giants in these industries either. The biggest company is Danfoss (global employment of 17,000 persons), a world leader in heating regulating equipment for households and compressors for cooling equipment. Grundfos is the second largest in the engineering field (global employment of 13,000), a world leader in pumping systems. The Danish electronics industry is small and concentrated on development of wireless communications systems, hearing aids and instruments & electro-medical equipment.

In the *non-metallic mineral products* industry, which has experienced a decreasing share of manufacturing, there is a group of internationally oriented building materials companies, such as Rockwool International (mineral and stone wool) and Aalborg Portland (cement), as well as a broad portfolio within other categories of building materials, such as Velux (windows), Vest-Wood (doors).

1: A large business organization consisting of several diff. companies that have joined together.

43

Danish manufacturing consists in general of mainly of small and medium sized enterprises, so-called SMEs. The most competitive companies may be among the leaders within their specific field of specialization, such as e.g. Novo-Nordisk, Novozymes, Danfoss and Grundfos, but they are very seldom large multinational companies with a broad product portfolio.

2.6. The private service sector

The private service sector includes industries such as wholesale and retail trade; hotels and restaurants; transport, storage and communication; financial intermediation and other business service. Together with public and personnel services they make up the entire service sector.

The private service industries have become a relatively larger part of the Danish economy over the last decades. In accordance with the broad experience of the OECD area, more than 40% of the Danish GDP was produced by the service industries[23] in 2003. Besides the importance of the service sector due to its relative size, most economists believe that services are even more important as a driver of economic growth and productivity development. Thus, according to OECD (2000,2001) service has become an increasingly *dynamic* part of the economies. Becoming more exposed to competition because of globalization, deregulation and use of information and communication technology (ICT), improvements in productivity and general performance have been the result in most countries. Besides its own business opportunities because of the new technology, the service sector has an important role for investments in ICT made by other industries because of the need for consultancy services, upgrading of knowledge and the increased role for co-operation in the innovation process. As a consequence, knowledge-intensive sectors such as R&D and innovation-producing industries, consulting, computing and engineering services have grown in importance over the last 5-10 years.[24]

Despite the importance of business services in connection with the knowledge-based economy, it is still a rather diverse sector ranging from the high-tech industries just mentioned to low-skill and low-technology

---

23. Private consumption of dwellings not included in service industries.
24. The importance of knowledge-intensive services industries may be underestimated when using value-added figures as an indicator of importance, because of difficulties in measuring and assigning quality changes correctly.

sub-industries such as personnel services, cleaning etc. Consequently, the dynamics of service sub-industries are rather mixed.[25]

Box 2.1.   Definition of the private service sector.

> OECD (2000)[26] discusses the concept of services and declares that *"services deliver help, utility or care, and experience, information or other intellectual content – and the majority of the value in intangible rather than residing in any physical product"*. Alternatively stated, services industries are characterized by typically not producing material goods. Consequently, the output of the production process cannot be stored, e.g. a hair cut at a hair dresser, transportation of goods from producer to retail store or a consultancy service.

2.6.1. The private service sector

The gross value added of the Danish private service sector was DKK 413 billion or nearly 40% of the total Danish GDP in 2004. The total employment in the service sector was 982,000 persons, which amounted to 36% of the total employment in Denmark. Consequently, both indicators stress the dominance of the service sector in the Danish economy. The service sector includes a number of dissimilar sub-sectors. Table 2.7 illustrates their relative importance and growth performance over the last decade.

The far most dominating sub-sector is trade. The trade industries (wholesale and retail sales incl. motor vehicles) represent over one fourth of services GVA and more than 40% of the total employment in services. Trade is characterized by its services, i.e. buying and selling goods thereby facilitating the flows of goods between agents within the economy. The domestic product of wholesale, defined as trade between producers, wholesale companies and retail sales agents, is larger than retail sales, DKK 85.0 vs. 47.8 billion. The difference is caused by the fact that part of wholesale activities relates to imports and exports (20%) and trade of intermediates between production and other wholesale firms, whereas retail trade is defined as sales to the final consumer. Thus, increased

---

25. The difference between the manufacturing sector and the service sector is not always that clear. Thus, bundling services with commodities, e.g. hotline support, installation of software in new hardware in connection with the buying of a new PC etc., make the distinction irrelevant in some cases.

26. OECD: Science, Technology and Industry Outlook (2000) p. 131.

specialization in production tends to increase the sales volume and consequently value added of the wholesale sector for a given level of turnover at the retail desk.

Table 2.7.   Employment and gross value added (GVA) in the private service sector, 2004, and annual real growth, 1994-2004.

	Total employment		Gross value added		Annual growth rate 1994-2004	
	Persons (1000)	%	Billion DKK	%	Total employ- ment	GVA (const. price)
					------ % p.a. -----	
Sale and repair of motor vehicles etc.	60.3	5.6	19.9	3.3	0.7	0.1
Wholesale, exc. motor vehicles	180.6	16.8	85	14.1	1.5	4.7
Retail trade and repair, exc. motor vehicles	207.7	19.4	47.8	8.0	1.6	1.7
Hotels and restaurants	85.8	8.0	20.9	3.5	1.9	-0.6
Transport	129	12.0	79.9	13.3	0.1	5.2
Post and telecommunications	51.9	4.8	29	4.8	0.2	7.1
Financial intermediation and insurance, etc.	72.9	6.8	66.8	11.1	0.0	2.1
Dwellings, Real estate and renting activities	43.2	4.0	156.7	26.1	1.6	1.6
Business activities	241.7	22.5	94.9	15.8	4.1	3.9
Private service industries, total	1073.1	100	600.9	100	1.7	3.1
All industries	2,758.4 0		1,236.20			

Source: Danmarks Statistik: STO 2005. p. 130,131 and 136.

The two last columns of Table 2.7 reflect the long-run development in trade with considerably higher growth in value added as compared to employment growth, caused by significant productivity gains. Furthermore, the significant growth of retail trade reflects the upturn of the middle of the 1990s in the Danish economy.

Another large sector within services is transportation which contributes with nearly DKK 80 billion. Note that transportation has a larger share of total GVA than the corresponding share of total employment and furthermore, the growth in employment has only been slightly positive parallel to considerable growth (5.2%) in value added, suggesting significant productivity improvements in the second half of the 1990s and in the beginning of the new Millennium. The development of the transportation sector is mainly explained by increased demand for transportation services due to specialization in the Danish economy. In fact, the business cycle of the transport sector is closely related to the development in the trade sector.

Business activities account for 16% of the gross value added of the whole service sector. This sector is quite heterogenous and includes a number of different sub-industries, i.e. computer and related activities, R&D activities, legal activities, accounting and book-keeping etc., consulting engineers, advertising, cleaning activities and other business activities. Since the late 1980s, this sector has experienced a huge growth, mainly due to specialization and the increased tendency for outsourcing from other sectors. Of course, the massive growth in the use of information and communication technology (ICT) has in itself provided a breeding ground for economic expansion of industries such as software consultancy and supply and consultancy in general.

The post and telecommunication sector has experienced a massive growth in value added over the last decades, which of course is due to the increased demand for fax facilities, internet access, mobile telephones and other communication services. In total, the real annual growth rate has been 7.1% since 1994. The fast development in ICT, however, has been labour saving and as a consequence, there has been nearly no growth in the employment of the sector.

Finally, financial intermediation and insurance etc. cover the activities of banks, life and non-life insurance companies, pension funds institutions and auxiliary activities to financial institutions (see also Chapter 4). This sector has experienced stagnating growth in value added as well as zero growth in employment. The latter is mainly due to mergers between banks and insurance companies with fewer branches as a consequence. Furthermore, especially financial intermediation has been able to exploit the productivity potentials in ICT.

2.6.2. Firm size and market structure

Figure 2.2 illustrates the size distribution of firms within the services sector. The figure is based on the total number of firms within services, 142,000, and the turnover of the whole sector, DKK 1,520 billion. It is easily seen that the distribution of firms is completely different from the distribution of turnover. Thus, the small firms (i.e. firms with less than 1 full-time equivalent employee, (FTE), account for more than 50% of the number of firms but their share of the total turnover is less than 10%. On the other hand, the large firms (firms employing more than 100 FTEs) account for no more than 0.5% of all firms within service but they have nearly 40% of the total turnover.

Figure 2.2. The total number of firms and the total turnover in the private service sector by the size of the firm, measured by number of full-time employees (FTE), 2003.

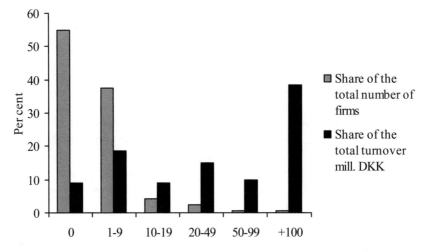

Source: Danmarks Statistik: SE: Generel Erhvervsstatistik og Handel 2005:16 Table 3.

Focusing on the large firms, Table 2.8 shows that usually their share of the total number of firms is low – around 0.5%. However, except for real estate & renting and to some extent hotels & restaurants, their share of total turnover in the domestic market is much larger.[27] Large firms are dominating especially within post and telecommunication (88% of industry turnover), transportation (62% of industry turnover) and also retail trade and repair excl. motor vehicles (turnover share equal to 46%). The largest firms in the first mentioned industry are Post-Denmark, owned

27. Note that the large firms normally have become multinationals. Therefore turnover from foreign companies is not included in Table 2.2 that relates to the domestic markets.

by the Danish State, and TDC, which was totally privatized in 1997. Liberalization of the Danish telecommunication sector has created more competitive conditions in some market segments, especially the market for mobile telephone services and internet connections. The large companies within retail trade are to be found in the market for everyday necessities. Thus, the combined market share of Dansk Supermarked (partly owned by A.P. Møller group, see below) and the cooperative chain COOP-Denmark was nearly 70%.[28]

Table 2.8. Number of firms and turnover in firms within the service sector with more than 100 employees (FTE), 2003.

	Number of firms, FTE >100	Total turnover, FTE > 100 (mill)	Number of firms in % of all firms	Turnover in % of industry turnover	Average turnover (mill) in firms with FTE > 100.
Sale and repair of motor vehicles etc.	42	27,823	0.5	21.3	662.5
Wholesale, exc. motor vehicles	175	178,536	1.1	29.7	1020.2
Retail trade and repair, exc. motor vehicles	78	105,741	0.3	46.4	1355.7
Hotels and restaurants	26	5,220	0.2	16.0	200.8
Transport	111	144,727	0.8	61.6	1303.8
Post and telecommunications	24	51,719	2.1	88.2	2155.0
	84	..	1.8	..	..
Real estate and renting activities	31	3,801	0.1	6.4	122.6
Business activities	208	66,488	0.5	38.2	319.7
Private service industries, total	779	584,055	0.5	38.4	749.7

Source: Danmarks Statistik: SE: *Generel Erhvervsstatistik og Handel* 2005:16 Table 3.

As noted above the transportation sector also has a myriad of small firms with a few large and dominating firms having a large share of industry turnover (62%). Large companies in this sector are the AP-Møller Group, (Maersk shipping and air transport), Torm (shipping), Scandinavian

---

28. See the Council of Economic Advisors (2005) for at discussion of the competitive conditions in Danish industries.

Airlines System Denmark, Sterling Airways (air transport), DSB (train transport) and DSV (logistics and road transport).

Finally, it should be mentioned that nearly all large Danish transportation firms are international conglomerates and partly operate from companies owned abroad. Therefore, it is difficult precisely to estimate their share of the domestic turnover within specific industries.[29]

2.6.3. Prospects for services industries

The structural changes of the last decade in the Danish economy (see above) imply an increasing role for service industries. This trend change can be given various explanations. One is that basic needs have been fulfilled (food, housing etc.) and therefore households turn their attention to other needs. In economic terms this can be phrased that many service activities have an income elasticity above one, and therefore growth and increasing incomes tend to increase the demand for services. Another explanation is that it for certain service activities (especially human services like care) are difficult to increase productivity. Therefore these activities will tend to have an increasing relative price (sometimes termed the Baumol effect) and therefore constitute a large fraction of spending when productivity in general goes up.

Irrespective of the precise driving mechanism it is a fact that the service industries have been growing rapidly, and that this process is expected to continue. There is a widespread consensus among economists that the services industries have become much more crucial for the persistence of this process and consequently for the sustained economic growth, see OECD (2001). According to Danmarks Statistik (2005)[30] they account for more than 70% of the growth in the GVA in Denmark over the period 1994-2004.

The expansion of the service industries is related to the discussion about the role of knowledge for value added in the growth process. Many service sectors are basically knowledge driven, and therefore knowledge as a factor of production has attracted much attention. As a consequence investments in intangibles, i.e. expenditure for education and research and development have come into focus. Moreover the sector supplies a number of services that have become more and more important. Thus, upgrading

---

29. See Berlingske Nyhedsmagasin "Guldnummer" which is published in November each year. It includes account information on the top 500 large Danish firms.

30. Danmarks Statistik (2005): STO2005, p 131.

of knowledge and the increased role of co-operation and networking in the innovation process have created a number of services industries. Outsourcing and specialization of knowledge-intensive problems have drawn the economic structure in the same direction. As a consequence, knowledge-intensive sectors such as R&D and innovation-producing industries, consulting, computing and engineering services are sectors of increasing importance as intermediators of new technology. Furthermore, R&D and innovation coming from the service sector may stimulate new production of advanced final consumer or investment goods or technological processes. Inventions, productivity gains and development of new technology in e.g. engineering firms support the building of e.g. advanced airliners, other goods or even infrastructure. Thus, the knowledge-based economy tends to accelerate specialization and the relative importance of knowledge-intensive services industries supporting the rest of the economy.

The development in R&D and innovation within the Danish service sector stresses these arguments. Over the last 10 to 15 years, services have performed a larger share of business R&D. In 2003, its share of business R&D was 42% against 24% in 1988 (the right axis), see Figure 2.3.

Figure 2.3. *The share of services in business R&D (BERD) left axis) and the R&D intensity of the service sector (right axis), 1988-2003.*

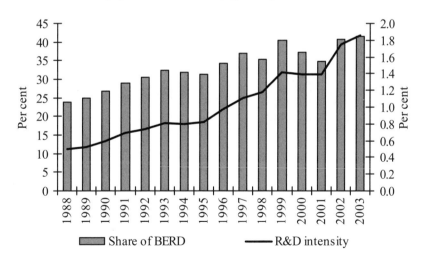

Source: Danish Business Sector R&D Statistics, various issues and the Danish National Accounts, various issues.

R&D performed in Danish services constitutes an increasing share of business R&D, see OECD (2006). In 2001 the service sector accounted for one third of business R&D, but in 2003 this share had increased to more than 40%. Comparing with the Nordic countries the service sector R&D in Denmark is on line with Sweden and Sweden, but in Finland the private service accounts for only 20%.Among the OECD countries the service industry in Iceland and New Zealand perform more than 60% of the business sector R&D, but for OECD as a whole the service sector R&D seems les important than in Denmark. Accordingly, the R&D structure of the Danish economy seems relatively favorable in order to gain from the future evolution of the knowledge-based economy.

Thus, R&D performed in the service sector has become relatively larger in general terms. Looking at the R&D intensity (the left axis in the figure), which has been defined as the R&D expenditure in per cent of value added, there has been a quite persistent increase, i.e. from less than 0.5% in 1988 to 1.9% in 2003, giving support to the general arguments in the beginning of this section.

2.6.4. The Danish services sector in an international perspective

The rising significance of services (private and public) is not a unique Danish phenomenon. Between 1994 and 2004 approximately 4/5 of the GDP growth within EU-25 countries came from growth in the (private and public) service sector.[31] Figure 2.4 accentuates for the most recent period the importance of private services for various countries.

Except for Norway and Sweden the services sector grows relatively to other industries for all countries represented. The GDP share of the private Danish service sector rises to 47% in 2004, which corresponds to an increase of 1.5 percentage points since 1994. In the UK, Belgium, Italy and Finland, however, services have grown relatively faster, i.e. between 3 and nearly 7 percentage points in the same period. The relatively modest development in the service sector's share of GDP for Denmark is mainly due to the growth in public services and the business upturn of the second half 1990s in Denmark.

---

31. Own computations based on STO 2005.

Figure 2.4.   Private services' share in GDP in various countries, 1994 and 2004, %.

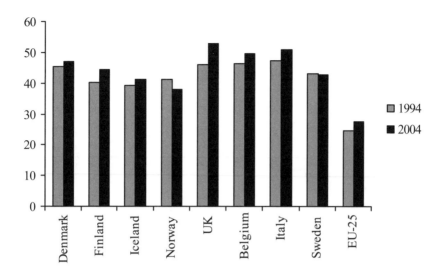

Note: Private service includes industries in NACE 5000-7900. Iceland: 1994-
        2002, UK: 1991-2003, Belgium: 1994-2003, EU-25: 1995-2004.
Source: Danmarks Statistik: STO 2005, p. 173.

2.7. The public sector

In Denmark the public sector plays a large role by providing various
services like education, health care, police, administration etc. Since the
public sector mainly is a producer of these services it follows that it in
terms of both value added an employment is an important production
section. We shall consider these aspects in some detail in this section
while Chapter 6 looks at these activities from the perspective of the Danish
welfare model

The public sector includes general government and public
corporations, see Table 2.9. The general government sector consists of the
institutional units which, in addition to fulfilling their political objectives
and their role of economic regulation, produce principally non-market
services and redistribute income and wealth. Public corporations are
corporations subject to control by government units, with control being
defined as the ability to determine general corporate policy by choosing

appropriate directors, if necessary. Public corporations produce goods and services to the market.

Table 2.9.   The public sector employment and gross value added as percentage of total employment and gross value added, 2003.

	Employment [1]	Value added [2]
	------------------- % -------------------	
General government	34.7	23.3
Public corporations	3.8	6.0
Total public sector	38.5	29.3

1) Full-time equivalents (FTE).
2) At factor prices.
Source: Danmarks Statistik: SE *Offentlige finanser* 2005:5, and SÅ 2005 Table 276 and 390.

Table 2.9 shows that public corporations make up a larger share of value added than of employment and that the opposite is the case for general government. Public corporations are capital intensive which entails a high labour productivity meaning that each individual worker produces a relatively large quantity of goods and services. The relatively low share of gross value added in the general government sector compared to the share of employment can partly be explained by relatively low wages in this sector compared to the private sector.

In the national accounts statistics, public corporations are grouped together with private firms in the industries to which they belong. Electricity, gas and water supply make up 36% of value added in public corporations, while transportation, post and telecommunications account for 37% and financial intermediation, business activities and personal services for another 22%. Unlike many other countries, the Danish State is not involved in manufacturing. In recent years, employment in public corporations has been declining due to privatisation.

With rising incomes the demand for relatively more services increases in the health sector (more and better treatment), social sector (increasing standards), childcare sector (because of increasing participation rate for women at the labour market), and education (a higher proportion of the population going on to higher education). This has been the pattern in the Western industrial countries, including Denmark, see Tables 2.10. and 2.11.

Table 2.10. Share of total employment and gross value added in sectors mainly belonging to general government services.

	Employment			Gross value added		
	1966	1982	2004	1966	1982	2004
	---------------------- % ----------------------					
Public administration etc.	3.7	8.1	6.3	4.9	8.3	6.5
Education	3.9	7.1	7.4	3.9	6.0	5.8
Health care activities	3.0	5.9	5.5	3.6	5.2	4.5
Social institutions	2.6	8.4	11.6	2.4	5.8	6.4
Total	13.3	29.5	30.8	14.8	25.2	23.1

Source: www.statistikbanken.dk.

The substantial growth after 1966 is not only due to an increase in the demand for these services but also to the fact, that public sector services are characterised by relatively low productivity growth. Rising labour productivity means that each individual worker produces a larger quantity of goods and services. This implies that sectors with low productivity growth have, ceteris paribus, a rising share of employment.

The fact that the share of employment has increased considerably more than the share of gross value added can be explained by a rising number of part-time employees in the public sector and by the fact that there has been a relatively large increase in the number of low-wage employees, e.g. in childcare centres and old people's homes, cf. the especially high growth rate in the share of employment in social institutions. Another important reason is that wages in the public sector have fallen relatively since the mid-1970s.

The level (quantity and quality) of non-market services is to a wide extent determined by political decisions. A tight fiscal policy in the early 1980s thus put a brake on the growth in public expenditure and consequently, on the growth in general government services as a share of value added. In fact, a considerable decline in the share of gross value added has taken place in other sectors than social institutions since 1982, see Table 2.10.

Table 2.11 shows that Denmark is not unique with respect to the resources used by the public sector.

Denmark has higher shares than the other countries with respect to employment, though not much different from Belgium and Finland, while Italy's shares are much lower.

Table 2.11. Public administration, education, health and social work etc. as a percentage of total employment and gross value added, 2003.

	Employment	Gross value added
	--------------- % ---------------	
Denmark	33	24
Germany	24	17
Belgium	33	23
Netherlands	28	24
Finland	31	19
Italy	22	17
United States	28	21

Source: www.sourceOECD: *National Accounts of OECD Countries.* Volume II.

In recent years there has been some debate about whether the public sector should be in the producer role or whether it to a larger extent should delegate and out-source the actual production to private enterprises. The argument being that it thereby would be possible to expose the supply to a market test via competition which in turn could create room for cost savings or improved qualities. If the public sector remains responsible for deciding on the supply and the financing of these activities this would not violate basic principles of the welfare state (see Chapter 6). Whether such gains can be reaped is much debated, and proposal on outsourcing is in general considered rather controversial.

2.8. Perspectives

Growth is closely associated with structural changes. This chapter has considered the historical changes but also some of the perspectives and challenges in a forward looking perspective. It has been pointed out that the growth potential is likely to be in service industries in general and knowledge intensive activities in particular. However, Danish manufacturing contains a rather large element of industries with a fairly low growth potential in food processing, building materials and various mechanical engineering industries.

In order to give a condensed view of some salient features of the entire industrial structure the so-called 'Resource Area Statistics' presents data on e.g. employment and exports aggregated across industrial classifications to broad areas including related industries.[32] In 2002, 23% of private sector employment and 22% of exports of goods and services were related to the Danish food sector, such as agriculture, food processing manufacture, agricultural machinery, fertilizers, wholesale and retail as well as various knowledge dissemination activities. On average, it can be expected that the growth potential of a substantial part of these activities is below the average of business activities in general. The same may apply to the construction 'resource area', consisting of construction, building materials, wholesale and retail, housing, engineering consultants, etc. which amounted to 25% of private sector employment and 9% of total exports in 2002.

A third major 'resource area' is transports which covered 21% of exports and 16% of employment. The large share of exports reflects Denmark as a big shipping nation and the home nation for one large multinational conglomerates, A.P. Møller-Mærsk (62,000 employees in shipping, ship building, oil and gas extraction, retail sale and manufacturing), which is the largest container shipping company in the world. The transport 'resource area' does not count as a high-technology industry per se, but the previous growth record has been visible and that may also apply for the future growth potential.

The large share of the 'resource areas' in food and construction may, *potentially, represent a kind of structural handicap for future growth* of the business sector. Such a view may, however, be too narrow or even misleading. In fact, there have been several sub-industries with no evident high-tech characteristics, such as furniture and windmills, which have experienced substantial domestic and international growth. The constant renewal of the older, more 'mundane', industries may also be an important source of growth.

---

32. See Danmarks Statistik *SE: Generel erhvervsstatistik*, 2004:17.

References

Andersen, T.M., Dalum, B., Linderoth, H., Smith, V. & Westergård-Nielsen, N. (1999): Beskrivende Økonomi, 6. udgave, Jurist og Økonomforbundets Forlag, Copenhagen 1999.

Berlingske Nyhedsmagasin (2005): *"Guldnummer"*, November 2005.

By- og Boligministeriet (Danish Ministry of Housing and Urban Affairs) & Erhvervsministeriet (Danish Ministry of Business and Industry) (*2000): Byggeriets fremtid - fra tradition til innovation.*

Center for Forskningsanalyse, University of Aarhus (The Danish Centre for Studies in Research and Research Policy): *The Danish Business Sector R&D Statistics*, various issues.

Cornwall (1977): Modern Capitalism: Its Growth and Transformation. London: Martin Robertson.

Council of Economic Advisors (2005): *The Danish Economy, Fall 2005.* Copenhagen.

Danish Energy Agency (Energistyrelsen) (1999): Oil and Gas Production in Denmark.

Danmarks Statistik (Statistics Denmark): Danish National Accounts. Various issues.

Danmarks Statistik (Statistics Denmark): DSTB/WEFADATA.

Danmarks Statistik (Statistics Denmark): Landbrug.

Danmarks Statistik (Statistics Denmark): Nationalregnskabsstatistik.

Danmarks Statistik (Statistics Denmark): SE: *General erhvervsstatistik*, 2004:17.

Danmarks Statistik (Statistics Denmark): SE: *Generel Erhvervsstatistik og Handel.*

Danmarks statistic (Statistics Denmark): SE: Nationalregnskab og betalingsbalance 2005:12.

Danmarks Statistik (Statistics Denmark): SE: Offentlige Finanser 2005:5.

Danmarks Statistik (Statistics Denmark): SE: Udenrigshandel 2005:2.

Danmarks Statistik (Statistics Denmark): Statistisk Årbog (SÅ) 2005.

Danmarks Statistik (Statistics Denmark): *Statistisk Tiårsoversigt* (STO) 2005.

De danske Landboforeninger (Danish Farmers' Union) (2000): Land økonomisk Oversigt 2000.

Edquist, C. (1997): Systems of Innovation: Technologies, Institutions and Organizations. London: Pinter Publ.

Energistyrelsen (Danish Energy Agency) (1999): Energistatistik, 1999.

Energistyrelsen: Danmarks olie- og gasproduktion 2004.

Energistyrelsen: Energistatistik 2004.

Erhvervsfremmestyrelsen (Danish Agency for Trade and Industry) (2001): *Proces- og Produktudvikling i Byggeriet – Analyserapporten.*

Erhvervsfremmestyrelsen (Danish Agency for Trade and Industry) (2001a): Proces- og Produktudvikling i Byggeriet – Perspektivrapporten.

Fiskeridirektoratet (Danish Directorate for Fisheries) (1999): Fiskeristatistisk Årbog. 1999.

Fødevareøkonomisk Institut: Landbrugsregnskabsstatistik.

Freeman (1987): Technology Policy and Economic Performance: Lessons from Japan. London: Pinter Publ.

Hansen S. Aa.: Økonomisk vækst i Danmark, Bind I, Akademisk Forlag 1974.

Hansen, S. Aa. (1974): Økonomisk vækst i Danmark, Bind 2. København: Akademisk Forlag, 1074.

Kutznets, S. (1971): Economic Growth of Nations. Cambridge Mass.: Harvard University Press.

Lundvall (1992): National Systems of Innovation: Towards a Theory of Innovation and Interactive Learning. London: Pinter Publ.

Maddison, A. (1982): Phases of Capitalist Development. Oxford: Oxford University Press, 1982.

Mogensen, G. Viby (1972): Landbrug og øvrige primære erhverv, Copenhagen.

Nelson (1993): National Systems of Innovation: A Comparative Study. Oxford: Oxford University Press.

OECD (1999): Historical Statistics 1960-1997.

OECD (2000): *Science, Technology and Industry Outlook 2000.*

OECD (2000): System of National Accounts, Glossary.

OECD (2001) *Innovation and Productivity in Services, Industry services and trade,* OECD Proceedings 2001

OECD (2005): *OECD Science, Technology and Industry Scoreboard 2005.*

OECD (2006): *Research and Development Statistics Volume 2006.1,* SourceOECD Science and technology Statistics, www.sourceoecd.org April 2006.

OECD 2006, Going for Growth, Paris, www.sourceoecd.org

OECD: Agricultural Policies in OECD Countries: Monitoring and Evaluation 2005. (www.sourceoecd.org).

OECD: National Accounts of OECD Countries.

OECD: National Accounts of OECD Countries. Volume II. (www.sourceoecd.org).

OECD: The Anberd Database.

Statens Jordbrugs- og Fiskeriøkonomiske Institut (Danish Institute of Agricultural and Fisheries Economics): Landbrugets økonomi.

Web addresses

www.cfa.au.dk (Center for Forskningsanalyse, University of Aarhus (The Danish Centre for Studies in Research and Research Policy).

www.em.dk (Danish Ministry of Business and Industry)

www.europa.eu.int/comm/eurostat

www.fao.org (FAO)

www.fm.dk (Danish Ministry of Finance)

www.foi.dk

www.fvm.dk (Danish Ministry of Food, Agriculture and Fisheries)

www.imf.org (International Monetary Fund)

www.landbrug.dk (links to Danish agricultural institutions etc.)

www.men.dk (Danish Ministry of the Environment and Energy)

www.oecd.org

www.sourceoecd.org (through university libraries)

www.statistikbanken.dk (databank at Statistics Denmark)

www.worldbank.org (World Development Indicators)

www.wto.org (World Trade Organization)

Chapter 3

International trade

3.1. Introduction

International integration is attracting widespread attention under the heading globalization. It is a process which is widely perceived to affect the interdependence[1] between countries fundamentally and therefore have radical consequences for economic performance.

The process of international integration is driven both by technological changes (e.g. lower transport and information costs) and political decisions (e.g. WTO agreements; EU decisions like the single market and EMU). This process is extending the market, not only in size but also in scope allowing for more division of production and therefore exploitation of gains from specialisation. It is also changing preferences as well as the production possibility set. Changing travel patterns and the instantaneous flow of information at a global level is enhancing knowledge concerning norms and habits in foreign countries, which in turn shapes new demands. Equally, a speedy transfer of information also affects production possibilities by allowing for more rapid and less costly flows of knowledge about new production possibilities and market opportunities. The most visible effects of the process of international integration are found in the areas where transactions across countries can be observed like in financial markets and in international trade, but it affects society through a variety of more or less visible channels.

In popular debates one often finds arguments suggesting that international integration is a new process. This reflects a general misunderstanding. International integration is an old phenomenon, which has increased faster in some periods than in others. It has been an integral part of the productivity increases underlying improvements in material well-being, cf. Chapters 1 and 8. It is therefore useful to see recent developments in a historical perspective. Consider information flows. Global information networks have existed for many years and have

1: A situation in which people or things depend on each other.

steadily been improved by inventions including the telegraph (1832), telephone (1876), and communication satellites (1964). Clearly, information and communication flows have been facilitated considerably by the World Wide Web.

Box 3.1.   International organisations.

World Trade Organisation (WTO) was formed in 1995 with the purpose of achieving further trade liberalisation through negotiation and setting up an impartial means of settling disputes. In 2005 WTO had 145 countries including China. Today WTO members account for more than 90% of global trade.

WTO grew out of the *General Agreement on Tariffs and Trade (GATT)*, which came into force in 1948. Tariffs and other barriers to trade were gradually lowered through a number of so-called trade rounds, which were long lasting negotiations. More and more topics were included over the years. Intellectual property, dispute settlement, textiles, agriculture and the final creation of WTO were among the topics negotiated at the last round, the Uruguay Round, which lasted from 1986 to 1994.

International Monetary Fund IMF), founded in 1944, provides the machinery for consultation and collaboration on international monetary problems for its 184 member countries. The purposes of IMF are to promote exchange stability, to avoid competitive devaluations, to assist in the establishment of a multilateral system of payments etc. The traditional task of IMF has been to advise about economic policy to avoid balance of payments crises and to help countries undergoing a crisis by granting a loan.

The World Bank (184 member countries, founded in 1944) is the world's largest source of development assistance. The bank provides loans to poor countries on a long-term basis.

Organisation for Economic Co-operation and Development (OECD) was created in 1961, but its origins date back to 1947 when the Organisation for European Co-operation (OEEC) oversaw the launch of the Marshall Plan for reconstruction of Europe. Today OECD includes 30 member countries. OECD is known for its regular reports on the economic situation of its member countries and as a source of comparable statistical data.

North American free Trade Area (NAFTA), founded 1992. Member states are the United States, Canada and Mexico. The purpose of NAFTA is to phase out all tariffs and virtually all other trade barriers between the three countries.

The key effect of this is not to create global information networks, since they have existed for decades, but to make them more flexible and widely accessible to firms and households. In addition the information technology also allows for more flexible and less costly trade in e.g. financial markets (see Chapter 4 on globalization of financial markets) and allows for easier trade in commodities and services which can be delivered in electronic form.   Product

Physical transport cost is an important determinant for international trade. In recent years there have been notable reductions in transport costs. This obviously applies to services etc. which can be delivered electronically, but also for physical transport costs have been lowered. Notable recent advances include container transport allowing for more flexible and divisible forms of transport, which aided by information technologies also serve to reduce transport costs by exploiting the transport capacity more efficiently. However, physical transport costs remain an important factor for international trade of goods.

This chapter takes a closer look at international trade. Section 3.2 starts by considering trends in international trade, while Section 3.3 considers the European Integration process. The trade patterns for Denmark are considered in Section 3.4, and issues relating to competitiveness and the balance of payments are addressed in Section 3.5 and 3.6, respectively.

3.2. International trade

Turning to trade we currently experience a fast increase in trade flows. However, it is important to keep in mind that some of this increase is actually an adaptation to barriers to trade inflicted during the crisis years between the two world wars. Since WWII the process of trade negotiations has dismantled these barriers. Figure 3.1 gives measures of global trade in terms of the value of exports relative to gross domestic product. This is a measure of openness often used since it measures the amount of trade relative to production or income. While such numbers, especially for the early years, should be interpreted with care, they do show that global trade has been on a roller coaster. Trade was at a high level in the initial period of the twentieth century, but then dropped due to protectionist policies pursued in the inter-war years. Subsequently, trade has increased again as a consequence of free trade negotiations in GATT and WTO, as well as regional trade arrangements (like EU and NAFTA). Much of the increase in trade experienced in the second half of the twentieth century can thus be seen as a return to previous trade levels, and it is not until the 1970s that trade was at a level comparable with that prevailing at the start of the century. Since then trade has continuously increased to record levels.

Figure 3.1.   Global trade – the long-run trend.

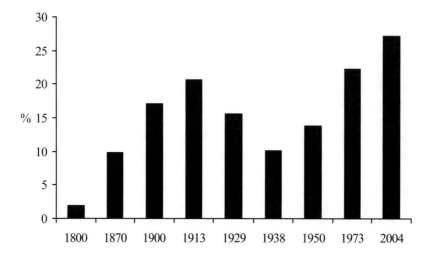

Note: Trade share defined as ½(import+export) divided by GDP.
Source: Taylor (2002) and www.wto.org.

The fact that trade matters significantly more for economic activity than in the past is captured by Figure 3.2 showing the development in trade and economic activity for the period 1950 to 2004. Over this period economic activity has grown dramatically (see Chapters 1 and 8), and global GDP in 2004 is more than 7 times larger than in 1950. However, even these high growth rates are nothing compared to the growth in international trade which in 2004 was about 25 times larger than in 1950. In short international trade matters much more for value added than in the past.

Figure 3.2.   Global trade and economic activity: 1950-2004, 1950 = 100.

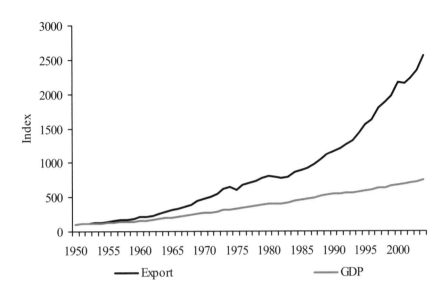

Source: www.wto.org

In this process of increasing international trade, there has also been a change in the nature of trade. While most trade at the start of the twentieth century was driven by differences in natural resource endowments, it has more recently been more dominated by so-called intra-industry trade. The latter is trade in basically similar or related products, which are, however, differentiated along one or more dimensions, and the producers are located in a single or few countries supplying several markets with their specific product. In 1913 about 64% of total world merchandise trade was in primary products, and the remaining in manufactured goods. Currently primaries constituted only 25% of world trade, while manufactures made up the remaining 75%. (Crafts 2000). This path is documented in Figure 3.3. showing that international trade in agricultural product is a factor 6 larger than in 1950, for fuel and mining a factor 9 larger, and for manufactures a factor 50 larger. In recent years trade in services have become increasingly important.

Figure 3.3.   The character of global trade, 1950-2004, 1950=100.

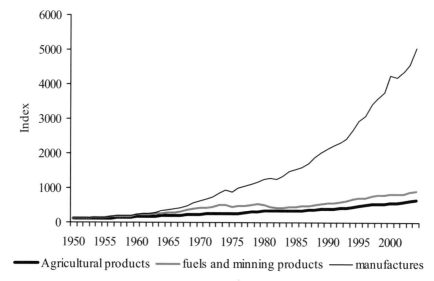

Note: The Figure shows the development in trade volumes.
Source: www.wto.org

The shift in the nature of trade reducing the importance of natural resources is mirrored in a significant increase in intra-industrial trade. Intra-industrial trade is trade between the same industries in various countries. Intra-industrial trade may arise from three sources: horizontal differentiation (e.g. different brands), vertical differentiation (e.g. different qualities) or vertical specialization of the production process (outsourcing of parts of the production process). The important thing about intra-industrial trade as compared to inter-industrial trade is that it tends to imply that production is less dependent on close proximity to natural resources or final consumers. It follows that these activities can more easily be relocated across countries and thus potentially different labour markets.

While international trade has been liberalised considerably over recent decades, it would be misleading to conclude that there is free trade at the global level. First, tariff barriers to trade remain. As an example so-called free trade areas like the EU maintain tariffs on imports from outside the union on e.g. agricultural products. In fact the agricultural sector remains the most protected sector (see Section 7.4). Second, even though tariffs have been reduced it is possible to impair international trade through non-tariff barriers. These may include bureaucratic rules concerning approval of products, specialised national product standards etc. Hence, even within free trade areas like the EU there remain substantial barriers to trade, and there is some indication that many countries have resorted to such measures to protect domestic producers, as a substitute for tariff protection. As an indication the number of notifications of non-tariff or technical barriers to trade reported to the WTO has been increasing in recent years.

Another increasingly important factor is the enhanced mobility of firms, that is, the incentive of firms to set up foreign production units, to acquire foreign firms or to merge with foreign firms. This is reflected in an increasing number of multinational firms and increasing levels of foreign direct investments. The increase in foreign direct investments is a more recent phenomenon with a significant increase during the 1990s, cf. Figure 3.4. Since then it has level off, although it is still at a much higher level than earlier. A very important fact is that direct investments flows tend to be balanced in the sense that many countries experience an increase in inflows (foreign firms establishing themselves in the domestic economy) but with an equal increase in outflows (domestic firms establish themselves abroad).

Figure 3.4.   Foreign direct investments, inflows and outflows: 1970-2004.

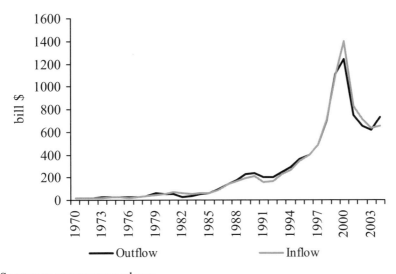

Source: www.sourceoecd.org.

An important aspect of the globalization process is the fact that new countries enter the global economic scene. This is the case for a number of Eastern European countries where some have become members of the EU (see below), but also a number of Asian countries. In particular, India and China are becoming important for the global economy. Since these countries account for about 1/3 of the world population this is a change with a large potential impact. In policy debates one often finds exaggerated claims on the importance of these countries for Western countries. It is true that the increase in international trade for these countries is high, but it has started at a very low level. More important is the fact that the increase tends to be balanced, that is, Western countries import more from these countries but we also export more to them. This reflects that increased globalization is a vehicle through which these countries can attain higher growth and improved living standards. Dividing countries into global regions Figure 3.5 shows the share of the various regions in global trade. It is seen that both Europe and Asia have experienced an increasing share, whereas American regions have experienced a relative decline.

Figure 3.5.   Global regions – share of global trade – selected years 1948-2004.

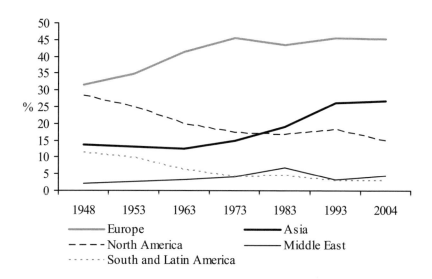

Source: www.wto.org.

Finally note that large immigration flows have also been part of the globalization process also historically. As an example USA experienced immigration in the second half of the 19th century to the turn of the century of about 7% per year of the resident population. From 1890 to 1991 about 20% of the population emigrated from some of the Nordic countries. Currently, most industrialised countries are experiencing increasing immigration flows, and in policy debates this is often associated with one of the major visible signs of globalisation.

3.3. European integration

In Europe the integration process is reinforced by political decisions aiming at further integration within the European Union. This started in 1957 as a "Coal and Steel Union" with the aim of ensuring free trade in these products. Subsequently, the scope of the co-operation has been extended, and the membership has been increased to 25 countries in 2004, and this number may expand, see Box 3.2.

Since its start the scope of the EU has gradually been widened. Integration with respect to trade culminated with the establishment of the single market in 1986, formally to be fully implemented at the end of 1992. The basic aim of the single market has been to ensure free trade.

EU is continuously evolving, and an important step has been the establishment of the European Monetary Union, which was formally initiated in 1999 and became fully operative from 2002 (see Chapter 4 for further details).

Box 3.2.   European Union (EU).

In 1957 the foundation of what today is known as the European Union was laid by the establishment of the European Economic Community (EEC) between six countries (Belgium, France, Germany, Italy, Luxembourg, The Netherlands). The original idea was to create a free trade area. The EEC was enlarged by Denmark, Ireland and Great Britain in 1973, and has over the years been in a process where the cooperation has developed beyond the narrow idea of free trade, and the areas of cooperation have gradually been expanded. A major step in this process has been the approval of the so-called "Internal (single) Market" in 1986 – to be fully implemented by 1992 – aiming at ensuring free trade and mobility of factors of production within member states. A further step was taken by the treaty on the European Union – known as the Maastricht treaty – introducing the idea of a European citizenship, extending the areas of cooperation to legal and policy matters, and launching the common currency (the Euro – see also Chapter 4).

Over the years the European Union has been enlarged with Austria (1995), Finland (1995), Greece (1981), Portugal (1986), Sweden (1995), and Spain (1986) to the s-called EU-15 or "old member states". In 2004 ten new member states entered EU (EU-10): Lithuania, Estonia, Latvia, Poland, Hungary, Czech republic, Slovenia, Slovakia, Cyprus, and Malta. Rumania and Bulgaria have applied for membership and Macedonia, Croatia and Turkey are so-called candidate countries for membership.

The common budget is about 1.25% of total GNP in the EU. Since the European Union is a customs union vis-à-vis non-EU countries, tariffs (e.g. agricultural levies) have contributed to the revenue of the union. More important is a fee (about 90% of EU's revenues) which is calculated based on the value added tax base and the GNP in the member countries.

Important items on the expenditure side of the union – besides administration – include the common agricultural policy (see Chapter 7), and the structural policies aiming at correcting for unequal areas within the union.

The important institutions of the European Union are:

The Council of the European Union is the main decision making institution. It is made up of representatives of the member states governments at the ministerial level.

The European Commission is the executive institution responsible for implementing European legislation, but it also has the right to propose initiatives. The president of the commission is appointed by the council, and member states propose commissioners to be responsible for specific areas of responsibility.

The European Parliament has 626 representatives and is elected every five years (first time in 1979). Originally, the parliament was a purely consultancy assembly, but over the years some of its power has been strengthened. Law bills now have to be formally agreed on by both the European Parliament and the Council of the European Union. The parliament also approves the European union budget and supervises the executives of the union.

The effects of European integration are very visible in a number of aspects ranging from policy decision to trade statistics. European integration is also clearly visible in financial markets for the obvious reason that a number of countries share the same currency (=Euro) and thus monetary policy (see Chapter 4). All European countries have experienced a strong increase in trade, and Europe accounts for an increasing share of global trade, cf. figure 3.5. However, the bulk of this increase is with other European countries and thus a reflection of the tighter European integration. This can be seen from Figure 3.6 considering the EU-15 countries as one unit (disregarding trade between these countries) and measuring the trade this area has with outside countries. It is seen that the trade share for the consolidated EU-15 has not had a trend increase. That is, Europe is roughly as open at the start of the 21st century as it was thirty years ago, despite the process of international integration. Since trade has been growing it follows that most of the trade I concentrated within Europe. This suggests that we are not experiencing a globalisation, but rather a Europeanization. Interestingly figure 3.6 shows that the US has become more open over this period.

Figure 3.6.   Trade shares.[1] EU(15)[2] and USA.

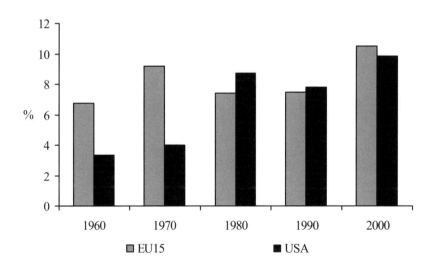

1)   ½ (import + export) divided by GDP.
2)   Extra trade.
Source: Velfærdskommissionen (2005).

It is an implication of European integration that market entry and penetration and thus competition across European countries have been reinforced. Since the geographical proximity to natural resources and final customers matter less than in the past, it follows that production and thus employment can more easily relocate across countries. The implication of this is quite clear for all European countries and can be summarized by considering the increasing role of intra-industrial trade. The growth in intra-industrial trade has been dramatic, and its share of total trade has increased from about 1/3 in 1970 to currently about 60% of the total trade. Figure 3.7 shows a measure[1] of the role of intra-industrial trade for the "old" EU countries.

The fact that European integration is driven by intra-industry trade is of great importance for the interdependencies between European countries. Since it implies that more and more trade is in commodities which in principle could be produced anywhere in Europe, it follows that competitiveness and comparative advantages come to play an increasingly larger role for where production and thus employment is located.

The EU implies free mobility of labour. Labour mobility across the old member states has been low and does not seem to change much. However, the enlargement of EU has raised concerns about migration flows from the new Eastern European Member countries. In particular there has been a concern about the immediate implications for labour markets (inflows of cheap labour) as well as the medium term consequences for welfare systems. Therefore some countries have opted for a transition period in which free mobility of labour from the new member stats is not allowed. Moreover all EU countries face an immigration pressure from low income countries, and it is widely debated how to avoid massive immigration. At

---

1. *Intra-industry trade* is calculated by the so-called Grubel-Lloyd index given as

$$GL_i = \left[1 - \frac{|X_i - M_i|}{X_i + M_i}\right]100$$

where the index is calculated for a given industry, and X and M are exports and imports from this industry, respectively. If X and M are of an equal size in a given industry the index is 1. If a country has exports X and no imports (M = 0) the index is 0. |X-M| is the so-called absolute value, which by definition is positive. For textbook treatments of intra- versus inter-industry trade, see Begg, Fisher and Dornbusch (2000, chap. 33) and Krugman and Obstfeld (2000, chap. 6).

the same time most countries are trying to attract educated and qualified immigrants.

Figure 3.7. Index for intra-industrial trade, EU14 countries. 1970-2002.

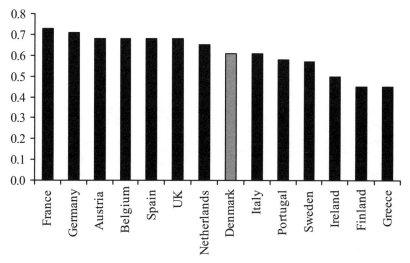

Note: When countries exchange products mainly from identical industries (intra-industry trade) the Grubel-Lloyd index is close to 1. When countries exchange products mainly from different industries (inter-industry trade) it is close to 0. The figure includes all EU-15 countries except Luxembourg.

Source: Fridas and Carballas (2004)

To sum up we can conclude that the European situation today is characterised by strong globalisation of financial markets, strong Europeanisation of product markets, and national labour markets.

3.4. The Danish trade pattern

Although transport and information costs as well as legal barriers for trade have been reduced it remains a fact that geography matters for trade patterns. In general countries tend to trade more with their "neighbours" this reflect not only lower transport costs but also similarities in income levels, preferences etc. This also applies for Denmark which has most of its trade with other EU countries, cf. Table 3.1.

Table 3.1. Structure of Danish foreign trade 1973-2004

	Exports			Imports		
	1973	1994	2004	1973	1994	2004
EU (15)	66	64	66	68	70	68
Euro-area (12)	32	45	44	41	52	50
Germany	13	24	18	20	23	22
UK	20	9	9	11	7	6
Sweden	14	10	13	16	11	14
Non-EU (15)	34	36	34	32	30	32
US	7	5	6	7	5	3
Norway	7	6	5	5	5	4
Japan	1	4	3	3	3	1
China	-	0	3	-	2	4
Total	100	100	100	100	100	100
Bill. DKR	37	273	455	35	232	400

Source: STO 2005 and 1976.
Note: The Euro-area is defined as the 12 present member countries in1994 and 2004. Greece is not included in 1973. 'Germany' was only West Germany 1973. Data for trade with China were not available in STO 1976 for 1973.

Actually trade with the present Euro-area has been strengthened. Over the period 1973-2004 the export share has increased from 32% to 44% and the import share from 41% to 50%. Since Denmark is pegging its exchange rate to the Euro it follows that the fixed exchange rate applies to slightly less than 50% of foreign trade.

The most outstanding change 1973-94 has been the switch from trade with the UK to Germany. Export of food to the UK has been a driving force of Danish economic growth during the 19th and 20th century. But the dependency on (mainly) food exports to the UK has decreased from one fifth to one tenth of total exports. This has basically been reflected in an increase in the share of exports to Germany from 13% in 1973 to 24% in 1994. This structural shift has mainly been an export phenomenon. In the same period imports from Germany have only increased from 20% to 23% and the UK share has decreased from 11% to 7%. However, in the most recent 10-year period of 1994-2004 the share of exports to Germany has decreased from 24% to 18% reflecting a persistent recession in Germany. During 1994-2004 there has been some change of the country pattern of imports. Within EU-15 the Swedish share has increased and the

German decreased. Within the non-EU countries the Japanese share has decreased and the Chinese increased significantly.

As noted above there has been a strong increase in trade among European countries in particular an increase in intra-industrial trade. There is, however, a striking difference in the country pattern of intra-industry EU trade as shown in Figure 3.7. The small, but rich, countries appear to have a substantially smaller share of intra-industry trade than the large countries. The latter group is able to sustain exports of products from a larger portfolio of industries, while the small countries need to specialise their exports to a higher degree.

Inter-industry trade has traditionally been explained by national differences in endowments of production factors. These are typically supply of labour, capital and 'land' (agriculture, mining, forestry, etc.). This explanation may be valid for the emergence of the early 20th century trade patterns for many present day industrialised countries. Among the group of small high-income OECD countries this pattern has been prevalent for such countries as Sweden (e.g. paper & pulp, wood products, iron ore & metal products), the Netherlands (food), Finland (paper & pulp, wood products), Norway (fish, shipping, shipyards, oil) and Denmark (food, fish, shipping, shipyards).

For these countries increasing export of manufactured goods has typically been through a gradual process of adding value to their endowments of resources, initially given by nature. This has typically happened through upgrading the products (e.g. better food) or through developing machinery and equipment for the production processes. The latter process has often been used in connection with e.g. agricultural and food-processing machinery, machinery for paper and pulp production, ships, mining equipment, maritime communications and navigation equipment, etc.[2]

During recent years the debate has generally focused on the increasing amount of intra-industry trade, caused by product differentiation and economics of scale.[3] The 'old' trade pattern was based on the endowment of natural resources. However, this old pattern is still highly visible in the trade patterns from the group of small high-income OECD countries that Denmark usually is compared with. Not to say that the export structures can be explained by the 'old' theories in any simple way either. But this upgrading of their original (natural resource based) endowments is still a stylised feature of their export pattern, and represents a major challenge

---

2.   See Andersen, Dalum and Villumsen (1981) and Fagerberg (1995)
3.   One of the most prominent proponents for the so-called 'New Trade Theory' has been Paul Krugman. See e.g. Krugman and Obstfeld (2006) Chapter 6.

(or potential threat?) to their future standard of living. According to this view the 'old' industries are not considered to represent the high growth industries of the future.

This view that the sectoral composition matters[4] has, however, been challenged. It has been argued that it does not matter in what kind of industries a country is specialised. What matters are gains from being specialised as such (in whatever industries).[5] This is related to the debate about innovation efforts, as discussed in Chapter 8.

The export structures of four small high-income OECD countries are compared in Table 3.2. It is a general feature of such patterns that they are (i) distinctly different from country to country and (ii) they change rather slowly.[6]

Among the OECD countries only US, Japan, UK and Ireland were specialised in high-tech industries in 1990.[7] During the 1990s this pattern changed somehow, when also the Netherlands joined this group, with Finland, Sweden and Denmark at or close to the OECD average. In the Swedish and Finnish case two ICT companies, Ericsson and Nokia, were the major force behind the increased high-tech specialisation (especially due to very rapid increase in mobile communications), although pharmaceuticals also was of importance for Sweden. The Dutch case has been a combination of pharmaceuticals and the computer industry.

It is a striking feature that all of the small countries have the common characteristic of being specialised in exports from the low-tech industries. Among the countries shown, Denmark is the one with the most marked specialisation pattern in these industries.[8] Denmark and the Netherlands are highly specialised in food exports, Denmark in furniture and Sweden and Finland in wood products. Sweden and Finland are also clearly specialised in exports of paper and printed materials. These are some of the features behind the rather low share of intra-industry trade shown in Table 3.2.

---

4. In economic theory this view has been promoted through the framework of New Growth Theory by Grossman and Helpman (1991).
5. This view is vigorously expressed in Krugman and Obstfeld (2006) Chapter 11.
6. See Dalum, Laursen and Villumsen (1998). The long-term results point towards de-specialisation. The speed of the process is however quite slow.
7. For a definition of the categories of technology intensity, see *OECD Science, Technology and Industry Scoreboard 2005*, Annex A. The case of Ireland is a true outlier, as being the most high-tech intensive export economy in the OECD. Ireland has the role of an assembly and production hub for large US and UK multinationals in electronics and pharmaceuticals.
8. The low-tech industries are shown as the upper five rows of Table 3.2.

Table 3.2.   Export[1] specialisation[2] in manufacturing - 4 OECD countries.

	OECD[3]		Denmark		Sweden		Netherlands		Finland	
	1990	2003	1990	2003	1990	2003	1990	2003	1990	2003
Food, bev. and tobacco	7.2	5.9	**3.8**	**3.5**	0.3	0.5	**2.7**	**2.4**	0.3	0.3
Textiles and clothing	6.2	5.1	1.0	1.4	0.4	0.4	0.8	0.7	0.5	0.3
Wood products	1.2	1.0	1.4	1.4	**3.8**	**3.7**	0.4	0.3	**5.9**	**5.4**
Paper and printing	4.4	3.4	0.8	0.7	**3.8**	**3.4**	0.9	1.0	**7.2**	**6.1**
Other manufacturing	2.7	2.7	**2.0**	**1.9**	0.8	0.8	0.6	0.5	0.4	0.4
Chemicals, petr. & rubber	16.9	19.5	-	-	-	-	-	-	-	-
Chemicals.	9.9	9.9	0.5	0.5	0.5	0.5	**1.6**	1.5	0.5	0.5
Rubber & plastics	2.8	2.9	1.4	1.3	09	0.9	1.1	0.9	0.7	0.7
Petrol. refineries	2.4	2.3	0.8	0.8	1.3	1.4	**3.5**	**2.8**	0.6	1.5
Pharmaceuticals	1.8	4.4	**2.1**	**2.1**	1.4	**1.6**	0.8	0.9	0.5	0.3
Non-met. mineral prod.	1.8	1.5	1.0	0.9	0.6	0.6	0.8	0.5	0.6	0.9
Basic metals	9.3	7.4	0.6	0.7	1.3	1.4	0.9	0.8	1.2	1.2
Machinery & electronics	49.9	53.3	-	-	-	-	-	-	-	-
Non-electrical mach.	13.4	11.3	1.21	1.2	1.1	1.2	0.6	0.6	1.1	1.0
Computers	4.7	4.6	0.4	0.5	0.6	0.3	1.4	**2.9**	0.3	0.2
TV, telecom & semicond.	5.4	8.2	0.6	0.6	1.0	1.1	0.6	0.9	0.9	**2.3**
Shipbuilding	0.7	1.0	**3.0**	0.9	1.0	0.5	0.7	0.6	**4.4**	**3.5**
Motor vehicles	13.9	15.3	0.2	0.2	1.0	1.0	0.3	0.3	0.3	0.2
Aerospace	3.7	3.4	0.5	0.0	0.4	0.4	0.6	0.2	0.0	0.1
Electrical Machinery	3.9	4.6	0.6	1.3	0.9	0.9	0.6	0.6	0,.8	1.0
Instruments	3.7	4.3	1.1	1.0	0.9	0.8	0.7	1.3	0.5	0.7
Other transport equip.	0.5	0.6	0.4	1.2	0.6	0.7	0.6	0.7	1.4	0.2
Total manufacturing	100	100	1.0	1.0	1.0	1.0	1.0	1.0	1.0	1.0
High-tech industries	19.4	24.9	0.8	0.9	0.8	0.9	0.8	1.2	0.5	1.0
Medium-high technology	41.5	41.7	0.6	0.7	0.9	0.9	0.8	0.7	0.7	0.6
Medium-low technology	17.1	15.1	0.9	0.9	1.1	1.1	1.3	1.1	1.1	1.4
Low technology	21.7	18.2	**2.0**	**2.0**	1.3	1.2	1.4	1.3	**2.1**	**1.7**
Total manufacturing	100	100	1.0	1.0	1.0	1.0	1.0	1.0	1.0	1.0

1) Export data only contain manufactured goods (in current USD).
2) 'Specialisation' is the relative share of national exports from a given industry compared with the OECD average. If the indicator is above 1.0 the country has an above-average export share - i.e. is 'specialised'. Values above 1.5 are shown in bold.
3) Distribution of OECD manufacturing exports.
Source: OECD (2001) Annex Table D. 7.2.1 and D.7.2.2
            OECD (2005) Annex Table F.7 and F.8.

In this latter context the lack of Danish specialisation in ICT hardware is striking. Denmark has not had companies which have developed into 'domestic' multinationals of the Ericsson-Nokia-Philips type in Sweden and Finland. Among the high-tech industries Denmark is only specialised in pharmaceuticals. One important caveat here is how to classify industries according to technologies. The approach used associates given sectors with a different technological level based on their output, and not the production process. This can give quite a misleading picture since production technologies can be rather sophisticated even in traditional sectors, such as the agricultural and food processing sector.

The discussion here is related to the question of which industries will be the "growth engines" of the future and whether the historical industrial structure in Denmark would be an impediment for growth and competitiveness (see also the discussion in Section 2.8). However, it should be stressed that trying to identifying the 'good' and 'not so good' industries/sectors is problematic, and after all the test in a market economy is a market test in the sense of whether some is produced for which there is a demand and a willingness to pay.

3.5. Terms of trade and international competitiveness

The prices at which goods and services are traded are as important as the quantities. An important concept is the terms of trade which is defined as the unit value index for exports divided by the corresponding index for imports, both measured in DKK, see Figure 3.8 (see also Appendix B). In short it gives the relative price of what we export/sell to what we import/buy, and an improvement in the terms of trade is thus the same as saying that export prices have increased more than import prices. Is an increase in the terms of trade good or bad news? It depends on the reason for the increase. If the increase is caused by e.g. an increase in foreign demand for products produced in Denmark, this is good news, demand is going up and the price for our products increases. If the increase is due to increasing costs of production domestically, it may be bad news, since the relative price increase tends to reduce demand for our products. However, whether the real income generated from trade goes up or down depends on the elasticity of demand – if demand is very elastic, real income decreases and oppositely if demand is not very elastic.[9]

Figure 3.8. Price development for export and imports, and the terms of trade, 1991-2004.

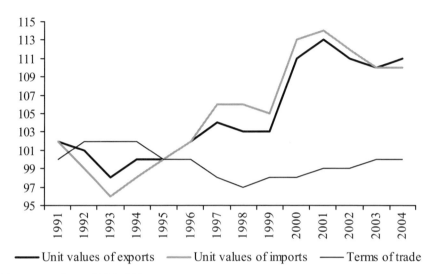

Note: Indexes 1995=100
Source: Danmarks Statistik, STO

The development in the terms of trade for Denmark is shown in Figure 3.8. It is seen that there has been no major changes on the last years since export and import prices have shown similar developments.

The development in the terms of trade is closely related to the issue of competitiveness. This is a concept intended to capture the ability of domestic firms to compete with foreign firms, but it is hard to define precisely. The factors influencing international competitiveness are obviously many, and among the most important are: i) cost factors like wages, interest rates, taxes, ii) productivity and effectiveness in production, distribution and marketing, iii) product characteristics and developments, iv) product market structures including barriers to trade, v) institutional setting: the political system, the function of labour markets, etc.

---

9.   The Marshall-Lerner condition captures this, see Krugman and Obstfeld (2000) pp. 481-484.

One often used measure focussing on the cost aspect is wage competitiveness. This is motivated by the fact that the wage costs of production are an important determinant of the competitive position, and that some of the other factors are either fairly similar across countries or – at least in the very short run – fixed. Comparing wage costs across countries requires three ingredients – domestic wages, foreign wages and the exchange rate. An example is given in Table 3.3 with wage competitiveness as calculated by the Council of Economic Advisors. The table shows changes in competitiveness, i.e. whether wage competitiveness is improving or deteriorating. It is more meaningful to talk about changes in competitiveness than its level. Changes in wages may be an indicator for the direction of change in competitiveness in the short run.

The table gives foreign wage increases as a weighted average of wage increases for trading partners weighted by their importance for Danish foreign trade. Since foreign and domestic wages development cannot be readily compared since the exchange rate may change the table includes change in the effective exchange rate, which is a weighted average of exchange rates with weights depending on trade shares (see also Chapter 4). If DKK depreciates relative to foreign currencies, Danish wage increases measured in foreign currency are lower, and oppositely if DKK appreciates. In the table a positive number for the effective exchange rate corresponds to a depreciation of DKK and therefore an improvement in competitiveness and vice versa.

Table 3.3.   Wage competitiveness.

	1995	1997	1999	2001	2003	2005
Growth rate of wage costs per hour						
Foreign[1]	3.5	3.0	2.1	3.4	2.7	2.4
Domestic	3.8	3.9	4.0	3.4	4.0	3.1
Relative wage[2]	-0.4	-0.9	-1.9	3.4	-1.3	-0.8
Change in effective exchange rate[3]	4.1	-3.0	-1.9	-0.1	4.7	0.0
Change in wage competitiveness[4]	-4.4	2.1	-0.6	4.0	-6.0	0.7

1) Wage increase in foreign countries weighted by their importance for Danish foreign trade.
2) Difference between domestic and foreign wage increases. A positive number indicates an improvement in competitiveness.
3) Effective exchange rate given by trade-weighted average of foreign exchange rates. A positive number indicates an increase in the value of DKK, and thus a deterioration of competitiveness.
4) Change in relative wage minus the change in the effective exchange rate. A positive number indicates an improvement in wage competitiveness.
Source: Council of Economic Advisors (F2000, F2001, E2005).

Table 3.3 shows that wage competitiveness has both improved and deteriorated in recent years. Domestic wage increase has displayed a tendency to increase faster than foreign wages. During some periods changes in the effective exchange rate have improved competitiveness and in others deteriorated it. Since the effective exchange rate can change rapidly this also shows why changes in exchange rates often attract much attention. Another implication is that if wage increases are given in the short run, it follows that a change in the exchange rate (a devaluation) can be a quick way to improve wage competitiveness. As discussed in Chapter 1, this type of policy was pursued in the late 1970s and the early 1980s. A devaluation of the exchange rate tends, however, to increase the price of imported goods and thus inflation, which in turn exerts an upward pressure on wage demands. If this takes place, the end result may be an unchanged wage competitiveness, but increased inflation. To avoid this situation is an important rationale for the fixed exchange rate policy which has been pursued since 1982 (see Chapter 4). Although DKK is fixed against the euro this only fixes the exchange rate for approximately half of foreign trade (cf. above), hence the effective exchange rate can fluctuate despite the fact that a fixed exchange rate policy is pursued.

One question is whether the calculation of wage competitiveness displayed above is misleading since it does not correct for productivity increases. Obviously, wage increases should be seen relative to productivity. This can be done by calculating unit labour costs which measure the wage costs of producing one unit of output. This measure is not without problems since wage increases tend to increase observed productivity because less productive activities are no longer profitable. Hence, assessing wage competitiveness by using unit labour costs is also problematic.[10]

These problems lead to attempts to distinguish between *price* versus *non-price factors* (or 'structural competitiveness'). Such a distinction is not clear-cut, though. The various factors affecting competitiveness listed above are not independent. Many factors may thus determine competitiveness, such as technological development, labour market incentives and organisational culture at the firm level. Technological development may, however, improve not just production processes and productivity (and prices), but also the characteristics of the products and their quality. In the long term these developments may be the most

---

10. In the text book case with a Cobb-Douglas production function and competitive firms it follows that average unit labour costs are independent of the wage rate.

important determinants of competitiveness, but they are difficult to measure empirically. Among the indicators most often applied to measure technological development is R&D expenditure and patent counts, cf. Chapter 8.[11]

The difficulty of defining the concept of international competitiveness precisely has often caused controversies. Some international economists have even warned against the very use of the term. According to the influential international economist Krugman (1994) its analytical foundations are usually unspecified and weak. However, often in the debate measures of competitiveness are presented, where the performance for the entire economy (or a major part of it, such as manufacturing) is related to various explanatory factors. This is among other things caused by the fact that it is necessary to try to measure the concept to make empirical analysis.

To sum up, it is difficult both define and measure competitiveness. The discussion on international competitiveness may be narrowed down to be one of how to sustain and improve incomes per capita of a country. This question is taken up again in Chapter 8.

3.6. The balance of payments

Considering the overall development in export and import (prices and quantities) it is of interest to know the overall balance in trade. Is there a surplus or deficit, and which financial implications will such differences have?

To assess the overall implication of trade and financial flows it is useful to consider the balance of payment for the entire economy cf. Table 3.4. Essentially this gives an account of the in- and outflow of foreign currency generated by trade in goods and services, and financial transactions.

Considering the rows in Table 3.4 each entry gives a possible source of inflow and outflow, namely, trade in goods (row 1), trade in services (row 2), interest rate payments and transfer (row 3), trade in financial assets (row 4) and direct investments (row 5). The last row gives the change in the stock of foreign reserves of the Central Bank.

---

11. One of the most comprehensive surveys of the relation between technology, competitiveness and international trade is Dosi, Pavitt and Soete (1990). See also Wakelin (1997) and Laursen (2000).

Table 3.4 Balance of payments – basic principles

	Inflow of foreign currency	Outflow of foreign currency
1	Export of goods	Import of goods
2	Export of services	Import of services
3	Interest rate payments, transfers etc. from abroad	Interest rate payments etc. to abroad
4	Selling financial assets abroad	Acquisition of financial assets abroad
5	Direct investments in Denmark	Direct investments abroad
6	Increase in stock of foreign reserves	Decrease in stock of foreign reserves

The sum of row 1 and 2 – trade in goods and services – is given net-exports or the trade balance. Adding row 3 we get the current account of the balance of payments. If this is in surplus there is a savings surplus in the Danish economy vis a vis other countries, and vice versa in the case of a deficit. For this to be possible there must be a corresponding financial flow, i.e. a savings deficit must somehow be financed and a surplus allows us on a net basis to acquire foreign assets. The sum of row 4 and 5 is giving the so-called capital account. The sum of row 1-6 in net terms must always be zero, that is, to any international transaction there is a corresponding in- or outflow of foreign currency.

In table 3.5 the current account for Denmark for 2004 is displayed in a form correspond to the principles given in Table 3.4. In 2004 there was a surplus on the trade balance of almost 74 bill. DKK. In net terms interest payments and transfers (to the EU, less developed countries etc) amounted to 38 bill DKK. This partly reflects that Denmark for a number of years has been running a deficit on the current account and therefore has been accumulating a foreign debt, see Chapter 1. In 2004 the current account therefore displayed a surplus of 36 bill. DKK. The table shows that this savings surplus corresponds to a (net) acquisition of foreign assets of 42 bill. DKK, and a reduction of the stock of foreign reserves by 6 bill. DKK. Therefore overall we have accounted for the total in- and outflow of foreign currency to Denmark, and therefore the balance of payments is in balance. Hence the term the balance of payments.

The stock of foreign reserves play an important role in Denmark since we pursue a fixed exchange rate policy (see Chapter 4). The stock of foreign reserves held by the central bank acts as a buffer when the net demand of DKK is increasing or decreasing.[12] In a system with flexible exchange rate the exchange rate would have to adjust when the demand for the currency changes, and in principle there is no need for a stock of foreign reserve.

Table 3.5 Current Account, Denmark 2004, bill. DKK

		Inflow	Outflow	Net
1	Goods (fob.)	448.9	393.4	55.5
2	Services	225.6	207.2	18.4
	Trade balance			73.9
3	Interest rate payments, transfers etc.	107.1	145.1	- 38.9
	Current account			35.9
4+5	Capital account			- 42.2
6	Reduction of the stock of foreign reserves			6.4
	Sum of rows 1-6			0

Source: STO2005

The developments over time of the components of the balance of payments are shown in Figure 3.9. Denmark had a systematic deficit on the balance on goods from the 1960s until the mid 1980s, and on the current account balance from the 1960s to the early 1990s, see Figure 3.7.

In addition to the trend changes it is also rather evident that business cycle factors (domestic as well as foreign) exert a considerable influence on the trade balance. The trade balance tends to evolve counter-cyclical, that is, it improves in a downturn and deteriorates in an upturn, cf. Chapter 1.

The long period with deficits on the current account implied that the foreign debt level was increasing, cf. Figure 3.10. This raises the interest rate payment on the foreign debt, which in turn tends to deteriorate the current account, see Figure 3.9. The development in interest rates is therefore critical for the development in both the current account and the debt level. In particular during the 1980s the effective real interest on the foreign debt was very high and this contributed to accelerating the increase

---

12. The reserve assets are also referred to as accommodating items on the balance of payments.

in the debt level, while during the 1990s it has been falling and thus has contributed to reducing the growth of debt level.

Figure 3.9. The balance of payments sub-balances since 1960, net receipts (balance), % of GDP.

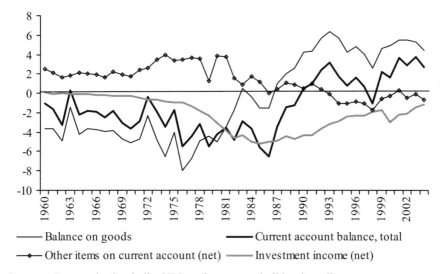

--- Balance on goods   Current account balance, total

--•-- Other items on current account (net)   Investment income (net)

Source: Danmarks Statistik: STO and www.statistikbanken.dk.

In relation to this it should be noted that the real value of the debt in DKK also depends on changes in exchange rates and asset prices. The fall in the debt in 2004 was only DKK 12 billion while the surplus on the current account was DKK 36 billion. This difference can thus primarily be attributed to rising stock and bond prices.[13]

Another important factor influencing the current account and thus debt developments is that during the last 10-15 years Denmark has been able to produce enough oil from the North Sea to become a net-exporter. In recent years the effect of this has been reinforced by increasing oil prices. High oil prices in recent years thus contributed significantly to improvements in the trade balance. According to OECD (2006, p. 16) about 40% of the surplus on the current account can be attributed to net oil export in 2005.

The current account balance has often played an important role for economic policy (see Chapter 1). The reason is that it has been taken as an indicator of either the competitive position of the Danish economy or the

---

13. Danmarks Nationalbank: Kvartalsoversigt 4. kvartal 2005.

sustainability of the economic situation. Systematic deficits were thus taken as a signal that the situation was unsustainable and policy measures were taken to change the situation. Usually the situation was perceived to be one of excessive domestic demand leading to fiscal contractions or one of competitiveness problems leading to a devaluation. This role of the current account has been criticised by pointing to the fact that the current account is the difference between investments and savings in the economy. A deficit corresponds to a net savings deficit and a surplus to a savings surplus. In a world with liberalised capital movements there is no need according to this viewpoint to be concerned with the current account. If there is a savings deficit currently, it is because agents use capital markets to make intertemporal reallocations, and those taking loans will be responsible for paying them back. Others have argued that this is correct only in a world with no imperfections. Hence, there is still a point in using the current account as an indicator which – alongside other indicators – should be used in planning economic policy. Related it has been argued that systematic current account deficits have effects on financial markets and make the economy more vulnerable to shocks. The swing from systematic deficits to a surplus on the current account has meant that this debate is less heated, and the development on the current account has played a less important role for economic policy in recent years than it did in the past.

Figure 3.10. The Danish foreign debt, % of GDP, 1960-2004.

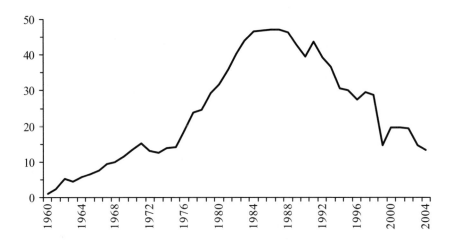

Source: Danmarks Statistik: STO and www.statistikbanken.dk.

References

Andersen, E.S., B. Dalum and G. Villumsen (1981): *International Specialization and the Home Market. Aalborg*: Aalborg University Press.

Andersen, T.M., N. Haldrup and J.R. Sørensen (2000): Economic Policy.

Andersen, T.M., N. Haldrup and J.R. Sørensen (2001): International integration and labour demand, Working paper, University of Aarhus.

Begg, D., S. Fischer and R. Dornbusch (2000): Economics. McGraw-Hill.

Coppel, J. and M. Durand (1999): Trends in Market Openness, OECD Working Paper.

Council of Economic Advisors: Dansk Økonomi, Forår 2000.

Council of Economic Advisors: Dansk Økonomi, Forår 2001.

Crafts, N. (2000): Globalization and Growth in the Twentieth Century, IMF Working Paper WP/00/44.

Dalum, B., K. Laursen and G. Villumsen (1998): "Structural Change in OECD Export Specialisation Patterns: Despecialisation and "Stickiness"", *International Review of Applied Economics,* Vol. 13, No. 3.

Danmarks Nationalbank (The central bank of Denmark): Monetary review – 4th Quarter 2000.

Danmarks Nationalbank: Kvartalsoversigt 4. kvartal 2005.

Danmarks Statistik (Statistics Denmark): SE Nationalregnskab og betalingsbalance, 2000:2.

Danmarks Statistik (Statistics Denmark): *Statistisk Tiårsoversigt* (STO) 1976.

Danmarks Statistik (Statistics Denmark): *Statistisk Tiårsoversigt* (STO) 2005.

Danmarks Statistik: SE Nationalregnskab og betalingsbalance. 2005:12.

Danmarks Statistik: Statistisk tiårsoversigt (STO).

Dornbusch, R., S. Fischer and Startz (2001): Macroeconomics. McGraw-Hill.

Dosi, G., K. Pavitt and L. Soete (1990): The Economics of Technical Change and International Trade. Hemel Hempstead: Harvester Wheatsheaf.

Fagerberg, J. (1988): "International Competitiveness", Economic Journal, Vol. 98, June.

Fagerberg, J. (1995): "User-producer Interaction, Learning and Comparative Advantage", *Cambridge Journal of Economic*, Vol. 19.

Fagerberg, J. (1996): "Technology and Competitiveness", Oxford Review of Economic Policy, Vol. 12, No. 3.

Grossman, G. and E. Helpman (1991): *Innovation and Growth in the Global Economy*. Cambridge Mass.: MIT Press.

Jensen, B. and J. Jessen (2000): Sammenhæng mellem geografisk branche-koncentration og eksportspecialisering. Unpublished cand.oecon. master thesis, Aalborg University.

Krugman, P. (1994): "Competitiveness: A Dangerous Obsession", Foreign Affairs, No. 73.

Krugman, P. and M. Obstfeld (2000): International Economics – Theory and Policy. 5th edition, Addison-Wesley.

Krugman, P. and M. Obstfeld (2006): *International Economics – Theory and Policy*. 7th edition, Addison-Wesley.

Lauritzen, F. and A. Hoffmann (1997): "Konkurrenceevnen som et mål for erhvervspolitisk succes?", Nationaløkonomisk Tidsskrift.

Laursen, K. (2000): *Trade Specialisation, Technology and Economic Growth*. London: Edward Elgar.

Ministry of Finance (1999): Finansredegørelse 98/99. Copenhagen.

OECD (1999a): "Open Markets matter: The Benefits of Trade and Investment Liberalizations", Policy Brief.

OECD (1999b): *Science, Technology and Industry Scoreboard, 1999*. Paris.

OECD (2001): *OECD Science, Technology and Industry Scoreboard 2001*. Paris.

OECD (2005): *OECD Science, Technology and Industry Scoreboard 2005*. Paris.

OECD (2006): Economic Surveys – Denmark, Paris.

Pedersen, L.H., 1999: Velfærdseffekter af betalingsbalanceunderskud i en lille, åben økonomi, i Lotte Langhoff-Ross (ed.): Socialøkonomisk debat gennem 25 år, Jurist- og Økonomforbundets forlag.

Sørensen, P.B. (1999): Betalingsbalancemålsætningen – en kommentar, Nationaløkonomisk Tidsskrift, 137, 360-387.

Taylor, A.M., 2002, Globalization, Trade and Development: Some Lessons from History, BNER working paper 9326.

Vastrup, C. (1999): Kan betalingsbalancen være et problem, in Lotte Langhoff-Ross (ed.): Socialøkonomisk debat gennem 25 år, Jurist- og Økonomforbundets forlag.

Velfærdskommissionen (2005): Fremtidens velfærd og Globaliseringen.

Verspagen, B. and K. Wakelin (1997): "Trade and Technology from a Schumpeterian Perspective", International Journal of Applied Economics,Vol. 11, No. 2.

Wakelin, K. (1997): Trade and Innovation – Theory and Evidence. London: Edward Elgar.
World Bank (1995) and (1998/99): World Development Report.

Web addresses

www.dors.dk (The Economic Council)
www.ecb.int (ECB)
www.em.dk (Ministry of Trade and Industry)
www.europa.eu.int (EU)
www.europa.eu.int/comm/eurostat
www.europa.int/comm/eurostat (Eurostat)
www.fm.dk (The Ministry of Finance)
www.imf.org (International Monetary Fund)
www.nationalbanken.dk (The central bank of Denmark)
www.oecd.org (OECD)
www.oem.dk (The Ministry of Economics)
www.sourceoecd.org (through university libraries).
www.statistikbanken.dk
www.un.org (UN)
www.worldbank.org (World Bank)
www.worldbank.org (World Development Indicators)
www.wto.org (World Trade Organization)

Chapter 4

Financial markets and monetary policy

4.1. Globalization of capital markets

Developments on financial markets often make it to the headlines. Huge changes in prices of bonds or stocks as well as exchange rates can arise suddenly causing substantial wealth re-allocations. This is so since financial markets are flexible price markets in which prices adjust instantaneously to changes in supply and demand. Since returns on investments in financial assets depend critically on future developments including the future price of the asset itself, it follows that price determination is influenced by expectations formation. This naturally implies that the market can be erratic since market sentiments concerning the future can change rapidly and that substantial changes in prices can occur when new information changing expectations concerning the future is brought to the market.

Financial markets are becoming increasingly global for two major interrelated reasons. One reason is political since most countries have lifted restrictions on the movement of financial capital across countries. As recent as in the early 1980s, many countries still had restrictions on capital movements (formally restrictions on capital mobility were not eliminated within the EU until 1990), which made it difficult for foreign investors to invest in domestic markets and for domestic investors to buy foreign financial assets.[1] The restrictions on capital mobility have their origin in an epoch where financial markets were less developed and in which restrictions on capital mobility made it easier for monetary authorities to manage exchange rates and/or domestic monetary conditions.

The other reason for the globalization of capital markets is that advances in information technologies have facilitated trade across the globe to an extent that instantaneous trade at virtually no cost is possible

---

1. Various forms of capital market restrictions are documented in "Exchange Arrangements and Exchange Restrictions" published by IMF.

from any computer linked to the internet. News and trade can thus flow instantaneously around the globe. The global interdependence is often brought to the forefront when there are major general changes, e.g. stock price changes in one part of the world which have an immediate effect on the rest of the world. Recent major examples include the turmoil during 2000 and early 2001 when stock prices of, in particular, information and communication companies plummeted. The global nature of markets is captured by the fact that the correlation in stock price movements between Europe and the US since 2000 has been almost 0.9.

Figure 4.1.   Share prices, USA, Japan and Euro area, 1994.1-2006.2.

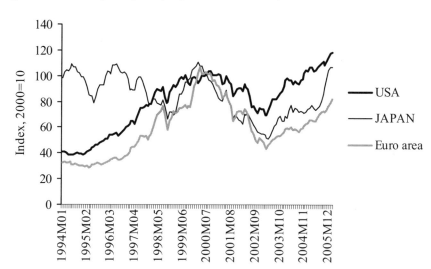

Note: General market index for the respective countries, index 2000=100
Source: www.sourceoecd.org

These institutional changes have not only made markets more global, but have also expanded the trade volumes in financial markets. This is due to the expansion in trading volumes following integration of markets, but also to the fact that financial markets become more sophisticated with product innovations in terms of so-called derivatives. A derivative is a financial asset which is derived from other financial assets (see Box 4.1.). Getting a precise idea of the size of financial markets is difficult due to the global nature of markets. According to IMF (2005), the global value of bonds, equities and bank assets was 152,327 billion USD or almost 370% of world GDP in 2004. Another indication of the expansion of the volume and nature of trade in financial markets is given in Table 4.1. It is based on transactions in foreign exchange markets for the countries most integrated in international capital markets. The table shows the average daily turnover measured in USD. For comparison note that total GDP for the whole year 2004 for USA and EU countries was 25,000 billion USD. It is quite obvious that volumes of trade have increased enormously, and that they are huge seen relative to incomes and trade flows.

Table 4.1.   Net turnover in global foreign exchange markets. Billion USD per trading day.

	1989	1992	1995	1998	2001	2004
Spot transactions	317	394	494	568	387	621
Forward	27	58	97	128	131	208
Foreign exchange swaps	190	324	546	734	656	944
Other(1)	56	44	53	60	26	107
Total	590	820	1,190	1,490	1,200	1880

Note: Numbers are based on average trading per trading day in April the respective years, (i) includes estimated gaps in reporting.

Source: Bank of International Settlements, Triennial Central Bank Survey, Foreign exchange and derivatives markets in 2004, 2005.

Another interesting aspect brought forward by the table is that trade in derivatives is driving the increase in trade volumes, whereas traditional spot trade increases only moderately. The purpose of these derivatives is basically to allow for better possibilities of risk diversification. As an example, consider a company selling goods with payment in foreign currency due in say 9 months. The firm has a currency risk, since the value of foreign currency in terms of domestic currency may change. If the firm does not want to carry this risk it has the possibility of selling the amount of foreign currency on a future contract, i.e. selling it today at a known price but with future delivery (9 months), a so-called forward contract. In this way the company will immediately know the value in domestic currency of the foreign money received after 9 months. More sophisticated trading is also possible. Trade in financial assets to diversify risk often releases a string of trades. Return to the example from before. The forward contract made by the firm with e.g. a bank will transfer the currency risk from the firm to the bank, but in case the bank does not want to carry the risk or only wants to carry part of it, it may engage in further trades to diversify the risk. This often takes place and therefore there is a strong multiplier in the sense that a given initial transaction causes a string of subsequent trades. Therefore, trading volumes in financial markets often amount to several times production activities. Another important implication of the various financial instruments or derivatives is that they make speculative trades possible. If you think that a given currency is going to increase in value in the future, you can buy the currency forward at a favourable price, that is, you buy at a low price today (if this belief is not shared with all other market participants) and then make a profit by selling it at a higher price in the future (if your belief turns out to be right).

Box 4.1. Instruments in financial markets.

There are a number of different ways in which to trade in financial markets. In the foreign exchange market there are the following possibilities:

Spot trade: Two currencies are traded against each other for settlement no later than two trading days after the transaction date.

Forward or outright forward trade: Two currencies are traded against each other for settlement later than two days after the transaction date.

Forward exchange swap (fx-swap): Contract involving a cash trade and a counterpart forward contract. By a fx-swap one attains a loan or placement in one currency against security in another currency.

Currency swap: Contract to swap current instalments, equivalent to loans in different currencies.

Currency option: Contract conferring the right to sell or buy a currency at a predetermined price at a predetermined time. By a call-option one achieves the right to buy, and by a put-option one achieves the right to sell.

Trade in forwards, swaps and options is also available for other financial assets, e.g. bonds and stocks (see below). These forms of trade are termed derivative instruments, since they derive from other underlying assets.

There are two important caveats to take into account when considering the globalization of capital markets. First, it is important to stress that perfect capital mobility is not tantamount to capital markets being perfect. The former refers to a situation with i) no restrictions in terms of legal barriers or taxes on the movement of capital between countries, and ii) low information- and transactions costs. A perfect capital market is a much more demanding concept requiring that capital markets offer a complete set of markets in which to diversify risk, i.e. to lend and borrow conditional on all possible future states of nature at actuarially fair prices.[2] Second, although the increase in global trade is indisputable, it remains a fact that many financial assets are effectively not traded internationally. One particularly important asset is human capital, where the possibilities

---

2.   By a fair or actuarially fair price is understood that the price reflects the probabilities of various future states of nature.

of trading based on future human capital have not improved despite the liberalization of capital markets. It is also well-established that there is a so-called home bias in portfolio allocation in the sense that portfolios have an over-representation of domestic securities relative to what seems to be the optimal trade-off between return and risk.

This chapter provides an introduction to monetary and exchange rate policy as well as financial markets. The first part deals with European exchange rate and monetary policy and outlines the room for an independent Danish monetary policy, given that we pursue a fixed exchange rate policy and have fully liberalized capital movements. The second part considers in detail financial institutions and markets.

4.2. European cooperation in exchange rate and monetary policy

4.2.1. Historical background

European countries have a long tradition of cooperation on exchange rate management. Up to 1971, there was an international exchange rate cooperation known as the Bretton Woods system, but turmoil in foreign exchange markets caused the system to break down. In 1972, a European arrangement for maintaining fixed exchange rates was launched. This system became known as the snake arrangement since it essentially implied a target zone. That is, the participating countries decided on a central parity for their currency vis-a-vis other currencies, but variations within a certain bound were allowed. The system was changed over the years as was the participating countries. From 1979 to 1992, the rules of the system were unchanged within the Exchange Rate Mechanism of the European Monetary System defining a band of +- 2.25% around a central parity. This parity was defined relative to a weighted average of the participating currencies.[3] The system was multilateral in the sense that the obligation to maintain the exchange rate within the band was mutual, that is, if e.g. DKK was depreciating towards the ceiling vis-a-vis the DEM, the DEM had to be appreciating relative to DKK and therefore both Denmark and Germany would have an obligation to maintain the exchange

---

3. Technically relative to the ECU, which was defined as a weighted average of the participating currencies.

rate within the band. This is a natural arrangement given that an exchange rate is a relative price between two currencies, but in practice, the largest burden tended to be on the depreciating (weak) currency. The reason is that the country subject to a depreciation pressure on its currency tends to lose foreign reserves.

Over the years, there have been many discrete devaluations (changes in the central parity in the system). However, during the latter half of the 1980s and in the early 1990s the system was operating well and there were few devaluations. Turmoil in European foreign rate markets starting in 1992 eventually made the system break down in 1993. Formally, the system was not discontinued because the bands were extended to +-15% to accommodate the tensions created in foreign exchange markets, but in reality, it ceased to be a fixed exchange rate cooperation because the band became so wide that it did not effectively restrain exchange rate movements. There was no interest in reestablishing the system because the plans for the Economic and Monetary Union (EMU) were already well under way at this time.

4.2.2. The Economic and Monetary Union

The idea of strengthening European cooperation by making it a common currency area with the same currency and monetary policy for all EU countries has existed since the early days of the cooperation. This idea gathered momentum by the Delors report released in 1989 proposing a three-stage process towards the Economic and Monetary Union (EMU) with a common currency (Euro), namely, preparation, convergence, and full implementation. Effectively, exchange rates for the participating countries were irrevocably fixed in 1999, and the Euro replaced national currency in 2002. The following countries participate: Austria, Belgium, Finland, France, Germany, Greece (member since 2001), Italy, Ireland, Luxemburg, Portugal, Spain and The Netherlands. Among the old EU-members, Denmark, Sweden and the United Kingdom decided to stay outside. The new EU members admitted into EU in 2004 are not participating in the EMU, but some of them would eventually like to join the EMU (Slovenia is likely to be the first of the new member states in EU to join the EMU).

Membership of the EMU implies that the countries share the same monetary policy laid down by the European Central Bank (ECB), cf. below. Associated with participation in the EMU is the so-called Growth and Stability Pact (GSP) including norms on fiscal policy, namely that the budget deficit is not allowed to exceed 3% of GDP and that the public debt must not exceed 60% of GDP. These conditions were also part of the entry conditions but they were interpreted loosely to ensure that some potential member country did not disqualify for membership by not meeting the fiscal norms.

Since the launch of the EMU the Growth and Stability Pact has attracted much attention. A number of countries (e.g. Germany, France and Italy) have formally violated the norms (too large budget deficits) and should be sanctioned according to the pact. However, political concerns have implied that no such sanctions have been implemented. There has been much debate about the norms. A crucial dilemma arises because countries tend to have larger budget deficits in recessions (due to automatic budget effects, cf. Chapter 6), and therefore the requirement may be that a country in a recession should pursue a more tight fiscal policy to fulfil the requirements of the pact. Proponents of the pact argue that the idea of the pact is to force policy makers to plan their fiscal policy properly in due time to avoid these problems. In 2005, the European Commission adopted a proposal to make the pact more flexible. This includes a less rigid interpretation of the norms and the implementation of the sanction.

The situation in the three old EU countries staying outside the EMU (Demark, UK and Sweden) is quite different. Denmark rejected the EMU in a referendum in 1993, and again in 2000. Still, the maintained policy is to pursue a fixed exchange rate policy to the euro area (see below). Denmark has adopted a narrow band for variations of DKK relative to the Euro of +- 2.25%. Sweden and the UK have both adopted a wait-and-see position and pursue a flexible exchange rate policy with inflation targeting.

4.2.3. ECB and monetary policy

The backbone of the European and Monetary Union is the European Central Bank (ECB). Since member countries have the same currency, the ECB is determining monetary policy for all the participating countries. The objective of the common monetary policy is quite clear, thus the statutes state that the primary objective is "...to maintain price stability. Without prejudice to the objective of price stability, it shall support the general economic policies in the Community with a view to contributing to the achievement of the objectives of the Community". The Euro has a floating exchange rate vis a vis other countries.

A crucial feature is that ECB shall operate independently as stated clearly in the statute: "... when exercising the powers and carrying out the tasks and duties conferred upon them by this Treaty and this Statute, neither the ECB, nor a national central bank, nor any member of their decision making bodies shall seek or take instructions from Community institutions or bodies, from any government of a Member State or from any other body. The Community institutions and bodies and the governments of the Member States undertake to respect this principle and not to seek to influence the members of the decision making bodies of the ECB or of the national central banks in the performance of their tasks."

As noted the primary objective of monetary policy within the euro area is price stability. This has been formulated in quantitative terms to mean that the increase in the Harmonized Index of Consumer Prices (HICP) should not increase by more than 2% annually. This is to be interpreted as a medium term strategy meaning that inflation in a single year slightly above 2% would not be violating the policy objective, provided the average over a few years is below 2%. Later it has also been made clear that price stability means that negative inflation should be prevented.

Various instruments are used in the actual implementation of monetary policy. For the management of extreme short-run (overnight) variations in liquidity in the financial sector, there is an overnight lending and deposit facility in the ECB. To steer interest rates and liquidity in the euro area, open market operations are used. They can take on many forms, but an important and regular part is so-called repurchase activities for maturities of two weeks and three months. A repurchase arrangement basically implies that the central bank provides liquidity based on other assets as collateral. A further instrument in the management of the financial system is a minimum reserve requirement on financial institutions within the Euro-system, where the reserve requirement for each institution depends on the risk profile of its balance sheet.

4.3. Danish exchange rate and monetary policy

A basic insight of monetary theory is that a situation with perfect inter-national capital mobility, a fixed exchange rate and an independent mone-tary policy is not tenable (Mundells incompatible trinity). Given perfect capital mobility, a choice must be made between either having a fixed ex-change rate leaving no room for an independent monetary policy or letting the exchange rate float in which case there is room for an independent monetary policy. For all single countries of the EMU, the situation is like the first option, although they as a group follow the second option. The United Kingdom and Sweden have decided to follow the second option.

The Danish position on this issue has always been to pursue a fixed exchange rate policy. The main argument for this choice has been that for a small and open economy, a floating exchange rate will lead to a very volatile exchange rate which in turn will harm foreign trade. A fixed exchange rate (vis-a-vis the most important trading partners) will contribute to a stabilization of relative prices (terms of trade) and therefore be beneficial for trade which is essential for a small economy.

4.3.1. Exchange rate policy

Denmark has participated in the European exchange rate cooperation from the start of the snake arrangements set up in 1972 via exchange rate mechanisms within the European Monetary System to the arrangement currently made with the EMU (cf. above). Although, the official position has always been that a fixed exchange rate policy was pursued, the interpretation of the meaning of "fixed" has changed over the years. In the late 1970s, a crawling peg policy was effectively followed as the Danish government e.g. undertook four discrete devaluations in the period 1979-82. This policy was abandoned in late 1982 when a new government declared a fixed exchange rate policy as an integral part of its disinflationary policy (see Chapter 1 for details). This policy remains in force and has broad political support. It is noteworthy that the fixed exchange rate policy has not been contested in the debate in relation to the Danish referenda on participation in the EMU. Hence, although Denmark has decided against participation in the EMU (latest at the referendum in 2000), the fixed exchange rate policy remains in place.

In practice, a fixed exchange rate does not imply that the exchange rate is fixed in the literal sense that the price in DKK of any foreign currency is fixed. This would be impossible because an exchange rate is a relative price. Hence, in practice a fixed exchange rate is defined relative to some benchmark currency or groups of currencies reflecting the importance of the currencies for foreign trade. In the Danish case, the anchor is the Euro, i.e. Denmark pursues a fixed exchange rate policy vis-à-vis the Euro. Figure 4.1 shows the development in the exchange rate between DKK and Euro as well as the effective exchange rate. The latter is a weighted average of all exchange rates, with weights equal to the importance of the currency for Danish foreign trade. It is seen that while there are some fluctuations in the effective exchange rate, the fixed exchange rate policy has been rather successfully evaluated due to its ability to stabilize the exchange rate DKK-DEM. The figure also underlines the point that this does not imply that the exchange rate is fixed in the literal sense since the exchange rate peg only fixes the exchange rate to some trading partners (approximately 50% of Danish foreign trade, cf. Chapter 3).

One issue is whether the official policy is a fixed exchange rate, another is whether it is credible to the market that the exchange rate will not be changed. Some indication of how the market evaluates the credibility of the exchange rate can be found from the interest rate spread between countries (on otherwise comparable securities). If the fixed exchange rate policy is fully credible, the spread should be zero, while a credibility problem tends to imply a spread different from zero reflecting how the market prices the expectations and the risks associated with possible changes in the exchange rate.

Figure 4.2.   Exchange rate DKK-DEM and effective exchange rate DKK 1999.1-
          2006.1.

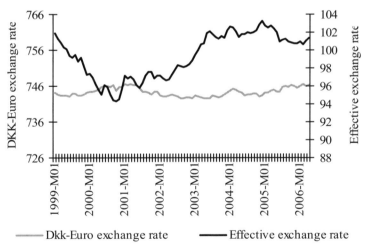

Note: Effective exchange rate is calculated as a weighted average (weights determined by trade in industrial products) of the exchange rates for Denmark's 25 most important trading partners. Note that the scaling is different, and therefore given changes in the figures do not correspond to the same relative change in the two exchange rates.

Source: Danmarks Nationalbank: Database, www.nationalbanken.dk

Figure 4.2 shows the interest rate spread between Denmark and Euroland.[4] It is seen that the spread was very high in the early 1980s before the fixed exchange rate policy was formulated more explicitly. The prevailing spread up to the early 1980s reflected not only a credibility problem but also the fact that all restrictions on capital mobility were removed in this period. Subsequently, we see a sharp fall in the interest spread and it has remained at a low level since 1998, indicating that the fixed exchange rate policy had attained much credibility in this period. The reduction in inflation (see Chapter 1) was a particularly important contributing factor to this development. However, credibility is not an absolute thing, and it can easily change depending on both internal and external factors which may affect the incentives to change the exchange rate. It is seen from the figure that although the interest rate spread has been reduced to a low level, there are fluctuations. In particular, periods of turmoil on international capital markets can quickly change the spread, as is seen by the increase in the autumn of 1998 caused by the so-called Asian crisis.

Figure 4.3.   Interest rate spread DK-Germany, 1987.01.-2006.4.

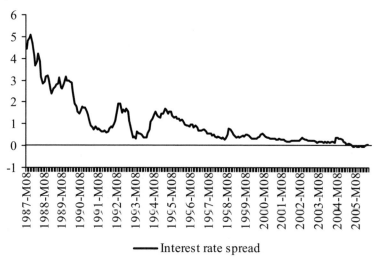

——— Interest rate spread

Note: Spread between 10-year state bonds Denmark and Germany, monthly averages.

Source: Danmarks Nationalbank: Database, www.nationalbanken.dk.

---

4.   Before 1999, the interest rate in Germany was used because the fixed exchange rate policy had the D-mark as the anchor.

Although nominal interest rates have fallen rapidly, this is not mirrored one-to-one in real interest rates. Real interest rates have been on an upward trend during the 1970s and 1980s, but the trend has recently been reversed and real rate of interest has for some years been rather low.

4.3.2. Monetary policy

As already noted, there is no room for an independent monetary policy in the Danish case given the fixed exchange rate policy and the perfect mobility of capital across borders. This means that the Danish monetary policy has to be passive in the sense of being devoted to the objective of supporting the fixed exchange rate. The fixed exchange rate policy means that the central bank is a price setter in the foreign exchange market always willing to buy Euro at a fixed price. Variations in supply and demand must therefore be accommodated by the central bank. In a situation where the net demand for DKK is positive, the central bank supplies DKK to the market and increases its stock of foreign reserves (i.e. its holdings of foreign currency), whereas in a situation with a negative net demand (positive net supply), it receives DKK and depletes its stock of foreign reserves. Clearly, there is an asymmetry since it is technically much easier for the central bank to cope with a positive rather than a negative net demand for DKK. The simple reason is that the central bank at its own discretion can increase the supply of DKK, but in the case of a negative net demand, it may face problems if its stock of foreign reserves is depleted. If so, the central bank is not able to honour its obligation of buying and selling DKK at a fixed price. In practice, the stock of foreign reserves is not an absolute constraint since the central bank has borrowing facilities with other central banks, and it may participate in a multilateral exchange rate cooperation where other countries share some of the burden of adjustment. Nonetheless, changes in the stock of foreign reserves are an indication of the viability of the fixed exchange rate policy. In a so-called exchange crisis where pressure on a given currency suddenly builds up, one usually sees a sharp depletion of the stock of foreign reserves. Figure 4.3 shows the stock of foreign reserves possessed by the central bank of Denmark. As an example of a currency crisis building up, consider the early autumn of 1998 where a crisis originating in Asia and Russia was causing turmoil in foreign exchange and financial markets. This development also implied that the DKK came under pressure, and the stock of foreign reserves fell rapidly. In such a situation, the central bank can try to increase short-term interest rates in an attempt to prevent capital from "floating" out of the country and therefore to support the fixed exchange rate policy. Figure 4.2 shows that the interest spread on DKK was increasing in this period. This brings us to the monetary policy instruments.

Figure 4.4.   Foreign reserves.1996.7-2005.12.

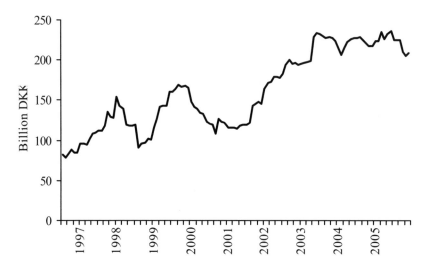

Note: Monthly average.
Source: Danmarks Nationalbank: Database, www.nationalbanken.dk.

Despite the absence of a possibility of pursuing an independent monetary policy, the Danish central bank has a unique position in the liquidity market in DKK for the obvious reason that it is the unique supplier of DKK. Management of liquidity is important since the need for liquidity can vary substantially over time (e.g. around dates for tax payments) and with the business cycle situation. Hence, for the financial system to function smoothly it is essential that the central bank manages the liquidity in DKK. Moreover, management of liquidity, and thereby short-term interest rates, can be used to temporarily support a fixed exchange rate. By reducing liquidity and raising short term interest rates the central bank makes it less attractive to "leave" DKK for another currency, and this reduces the pressure on the stock of foreign reserves.

Box 4.2. Monetary policy and the money market.

The central bank can affect prices in the short end of the money market. The money market is a market for liquidity, i.e. assets with very short maturities (from days or weeks up to one year) are traded between financial institutions. By affecting the market conditions in the very short-end of the market, the central bank can affect the money market and thereby the terms which financial institutions offer their customers. In the implementation of monetary policy, the central bank offers possibilities for either depositing or acquiring liquidity in the central bank. Deposits are known as folio-deposits with the associated interest rate (folio-renten) which corresponds to the discount rate (diskontoen). Today, the latter is not directly used in any transactions, but it serves to signal the monetary policy stance. Moreover, the central bank conducts weekly auctions where financial counterparts can either borrow with collateral in other financial assets or they can place excess liquidity in certificates of deposits. The associated rate of interest is the lending rate, which is equivalent to the rate of interest for certificates of deposit. The rate at which the central bank offers liquidity to the money market is known as the lending rate, and it is a short rate since these arrangements have a maturity of two weeks. By changing the liquidity offered to the market or the terms for depositing liquidity, the central bank can influence short term interest rates. Given the Danish exchange rate policy, it follows that changes in the monetary policy of the central bank of Denmark have to follow the changes undertaken by the European Central Bank rather closely.

The money market also includes transactions directly between financial institutions, but mostly in maturities longer than those applying for transactions with the central bank. The tomorrow/next interest rate is an uncollateralized day-to-day interest for money market lending. The CIBOR (Copenhagen Interbank offered rate) is a reference rate of liquidity offered in the inter-bank market on an uncollateralized basis. The CIBOR is an average of interest rate offered in the market. CIBOR is calculated for eight different maturities: 1, 2, 3, 4, 5, 6, 9 and 12 months.

4.4. Financial markets and institutions

Financial markets perform two essential tasks for a decentralized market economy to function effectively. The first arises from the fact that a market economy is a monetary economy in the sense that it is based on exchange of goods for money in contrast to a barter economy where goods are exchanged for goods. The existence of means of payments (money) clearly reduces transactions costs and facilitates trade. Equally important is trust - means of payments are accepted as final payment because it is expected that others will accept the means of payments as final payment. Financial institutions - primarily banks - have a crucial role in providing liquidity needed for the transactions taking place in the economy. While the existence of money (coins and notes) issued by the central bank is the basis on which financial institutions (particularly banks) operate, it is also clear that financial institutions play an essential role for the practical operation of the payments system. Increasingly, physical money (notes and coins) is replaced by electronic forms of payments supplied by financial institutions (credit cards, e-banks etc.).

The second major function is to intermediate between agents having a savings surplus and agents having a savings deficit. Financial institutions play two important roles. First, information is imperfect and scattered in a decentralized market economy and therefore there is a need to match agents with a savings surplus with agents with a savings deficit. Second, what agents with a savings deficit have to offer is not necessarily what agents with a surplus demand. Agents with a savings deficit want to borrow to finance current consumption or investments based on future income. The horizon for such decisions is usually long, implying that there can be both a substantial risk and a commitment in lending directly to a specific borrower. Agents with a savings surplus are looking for a way to place funds for a period of time, and they value an investment which has little risk and which is flexible or liquid, that is, it is possible, if necessary, to realize the funds. Financial institutions can offer financial assets which intermediate between these two different needs. The basic principle is pooling, i.e. a homogeneous type of asset - say a bond - is offered to a heterogeneous group of borrowers. The institutions, in addition, have experience in evaluating the credit-worthiness of borrowers. The asset is homogeneous, i.e. it does not depend on the fortune of a single borrower and can be traded at the stock exchange. In this way, financial institutions offer better terms for both agents with a savings deficit and surplus, and this justifies the existence of such institutions.

Given the important role of the financial system for a decentralized market economy, it cannot be left uncontrolled. Control takes place at two levels. First, the central bank, in its role as supplier of money, controls the quantity and terms at which liquidity is supplied in the economy through its monetary policy (see Section 4.3). Second, there are well-defined rules regulating the operations of various forms of financial institutions, the leverage they are allowed in their operations (see below), solvency etc. The Danish Financial Supervisory Authority has the task of monitoring the institutions and controlling that rules and regulations are followed. The overall framework for the financial sector is regulated by the law on financial enterprises (lov om finansiel virksomhed), while specific laws regulate the details for specific forms of financial institutions. Given the globalization of financial markets, cross-border activities of financial institutions become more important. To cope with this, EU rules have been introduced to regulate cross-border financial activities and the financial leverage of financial institutions.

4.5. Financial institutions

This section explains the major types of financial institutions, their operations and regulations. Table 4.2 lists the main types of financial institutions and their importance measured by their total balance. The table also shows that the financial sector has been growing rapidly measured by the total balance of the institutions.

Table 4.2.   Total balance, financial institutions, 1986-2004.

Billion, DKK	1986	1991	1996	2001	2004
Banks	720	1,013	1,172	1,987	2,532
Specialized credit institutions	19	27	36	53	60
Mortgage credit institutions	656	829	991	1,378	2,121
Stock broker	...	19	1	1	1
Investment funds	32	23	56	257	573
Non-life insurance companies	55	91	95	105	125
Life insurance companies	157	246	400	649	810
General pension funds	62	105	161	270	339
Labour market pension funds	20	25	34	43	39
ATP	51	89	144	247	307
LD	22	31	39	62	58
Total[1]	1,792	2,498	3,128	4,851	7,015

Columns may not sum due to rounding errors.
Source: Finanstilsynet. Hovedtal fra Finanstilsynet 2004.

4.5.1. Banks

Banks offer various forms of deposits and loans to customers. Most of the deposits are closely linked to the medium of transactions. This applies in particular to deposit accounts to which cheques or credit cards are attached. Often, such accounts also have a credit limit. These deposits are very liquid, i.e. they can be withdrawn on demand.

The basic principle of banking is leverage, that is, all deposits cannot be held in liquid form but have to be lent to agents with a savings deficit on a maturity which is usually longer than that of the deposits. In this way, banks transfer liquid deposits into longer-term lending, and they generate revenue by charging a higher interest on lending than they offer on deposits (the interest rate margin). This also implies that there is a systematic risk in banking; it would not be possible for all depositors to obtain their deposits on demand for the simple reason that banks do not keep liquid funds equal to deposits. Hence, there is a risk of a bank run where a bank turns illiquid because a too large fraction of its customers demand their deposits. To minimize the risk of such a situation, banks are strictly regulated.[5] In Denmark, there are strict rules to be fulfilled to be allowed to operate a bank.[6] The guaranteed capital of a bank has to be at least EURO 5 million. A solvency rule requires that the capital base inclusive of short-term supplementary capital at any time shall constitute at least 8% of the (risk weighted) assets. A liquidity rule requires that banks should keep liquid funds of at least 15% of deposits which can be withdrawn on demand or with notice less than one month.

Since banking rests on trust, there are further regulations to prevent that banks operate in a too risky way or become too dependent on the prospects of a few borrowers. The rules stipulate that business with one customer must not exceed 25% of the bank's capital base, and if it exceeds 10%, it has to be reported to the Financial Supervisory Authority. Moreover, the total amount of business with large customers (all with business above 10% of the capital base) must not exceed 800% of the capital base.

The banking sector has undergone substantial changes in recent years due to mergers and takeovers. In 1970 there were 236 banks, in 2003 there were only 176. Most of the larger banks are the result of takeovers and mergers. Consider the five largest banks: "Danske Bank" is the result of a merger of Landmandsbanken, Handelsbanken and Provinsbanken in 1990; Nordea is a Nordic merger of the Merita-Nord bank and Uni-bank which, in turn, was a merger of SDS, Privatbanken and Andelsbanken also in 1990; and BG-bank is a merger of Bikuben and GiroBank in 1995. Jyske Bank has remained unaffected by the mergers. Sydbank is the outcome of mergers of several local banks.

---

5.   There is also a deposit insurance scheme among banks, guaranteeing deposits up to DKK 300,000.
6.   Within Euroland, there is a formal reserve requirement stipulating that the liquid funds should exceed 2% of the sum of passives.

Structural changes have also involved other financial institutions. Until recently, the legislation has maintained very strict boundaries between various forms of financial activities and effectively restrained institutions to only operate in one business area. While the rules remain restrictive, there have been some liberalizations. During the 1980s, this resulted in the establishment of holding companies comprising financial institutions operating in different areas. As an example, insurance companies established holding companies in order to be able to operate both the traditional insurance companies and banks (e.g. Hafnia Holding, Baltica Holding and TopDanmark). Similarly, mortgage credit institutions started operating banks. Some banks have made their own mortgage credit institutions during the 1990s. Mergers across different types of financial activity have also taken place, e.g. mergers between Danske Bank and Danica, Unibank and Tryg-Baltica and BG-bank with Realkredit Danmark.

Cross-national operations are increasing in importance, and this induces institutional changes. Danske Bank has entered the market in both Norway, Ireland, and Northern Ireland, and Unibank has, as noted, been merged into the Finnish-Swedish Merita-Nord bank (Nordea).

The concentration in the market is rather strong. The two largest banks have a market share about 50% when measured in terms of the sum of deposits and the capital base of banks.

The interest rate margin - the difference between the average deposit and lending rates - has been reduced in recent years, partly as a result of the general tendency towards lower interest rates, and partly due to tighter competition between banks. In 1994, the margin between average lending and deposit rates was 6.5%, and by the end of 2005, it was 4.1%. Although there has been a slight increase in the margin recently, this development has also induced a process towards user fees in banking, i.e. customers are charged for use of various facilities and services provided by banks. Banks have also tried to minimize costs by reducing the number of branches. This has also been facilitated by increasing use of electronic means of servicing customers (home-banking, e-banking etc.). The increasing importance of electronic financial transactions is reflected among other things in the very sharp increase in the use of electronic forms of payments (credit cards etc.). In 1990, there were 66 thousand purely electronic payments by use of the Dankort with a turnover of DKK 31 billion. In 2004, there were 579 million transactions with a turnover of DKK 195 billion.

4.5.2. Mortgage credit institutions

Bonds are dominant assets in financial markets in Denmark. Bonds are issued both by mortgage credit institutions and the State. A typical bond is a long-term asset with a fixed maturity, say 10, 20 or 30 years, and it pays fixed nominal interest to the possessor. The standard bond is an annuity where the borrower pays a fixed amount (percentage of the amount borrowed) over the maturity of the loan implying a profile where the effective burden of interest rate payments is decreasing and repayments are increasing over the lifetime of the bond. A serial bond has the property that the repayment is a constant percentage through the lifetime of the bond and therefore the total payment has a decreasing profile.

The basic bonds offered by mortgage credit institutions have collateral in real property. The mortgage banks transform heterogenous assets, namely borrowing with collateral in real property, into a homogeneous product for the lender. Loans are granted within limits on maturity, loan relative to property value etc. laid down in the Mortgage Credit Act. For an owner-occupied home use for all-year occupancy, the lending limit is 80% of the value of the property, for a weekend cottage the limit is 60%. The remainder is financed by previous savings, private mortgages or bank loans. Currently, there are no rules governing the type of loan which can be offered, but a loan for an owner-occupied home cannot have a duration exceeding 30 years. In recent years a substantial product development has taken place for financing of housing, including possibilities of short-term borrowing, allowing for interest rate adjustments depending on market developments, and possibilities of only paying interest rates and no instalment for a period of time.

The use of bonds as a means of borrowing for firms has not been widespread in Denmark (except for agriculture), although some mortgage credit institutions have been specialized in loans to private companies.

Currently, there are 10 mortgage credit institutions. The principle of the operation of these institutions is that the funds for loans are obtained via current issue of bonds. This means that if a loan of a given type (repayment profile, maturity) is granted, there is an issue of an equivalent number of bonds with the same characteristics. Since there is a global balance principle according to which total repayments by borrowers should equal total payments to holders of bonds, the risk of the institution is limited to the credit risk, i.e. default on the part of the borrower. Mortgage credit institutions are subject to a solvency requirement - like ordinary banks - of 8% of their (risk-weighted) assets. The institutions are under supervision of the Financial Supervisory Authority.

The state is also an important issuer of bonds. Public-sector borrowing is based on treasury bills (maturity up to 9 months) and bonds (maturity 2, 5 and 10 years). Given the variations over the years in the public-sector borrowing requirement (see Chapters 1 and 6), it follows that there is substantial variation in the net issue. Currently, there is a budget surplus for the public sector and accordingly a negative net issue. However, the outstanding stock of state bonds is still substantial and hence, the market for state bonds is an important one. Since the maturity of state bonds is shorter than that of the mortgage credit institutions, state bonds also have the role of complementing financial markets by contributing to a more rich maturity structure.

The outstanding volume of bonds in the first quarter of 2006 has a market value of DKK 2,500 billion. Of this, 65% are bonds issued by mortgage credit institutions with collateral in houses, and the rest mainly various forms of state bonds.

4.5.3. Insurance companies and pension funds

Individuals and firms face various risks on which they would like to take out an insurance contract to reduce the consequences of adverse events. The basic principle of insurance markets is to pool risk. Take fire insurance as an example - there is a risk that your house may burn and the economic consequences to the house owner would be catastrophic; fire insurance is therefore required in order to obtain a loan at a mortgage credit institution. However, by making an insurance contract with an annual payment in return for a given compensation in case of fire, the house owner can diversify the risk. The insurance company exploits the fact that not all houses will burn. Hence, all customers pay the insurance fee, but only a fraction has to be compensated. All insurance customers are better off because they pool or share the risk that their house might burn. This principle of risk pooling underlies all forms of insurance.

Non-life insurance includes insurance for various contingencies like fire, car accidents, theft, damage and liability. Some of these insurances are mandatory. For instance, there is a mandatory liability insurance for many liberal professions like accountants, lawyers, real estate agents, etc. Others are voluntary with contracts being made on an individual basis.

Insurance companies offer standard insurance packages like a "family insurance", but also more specific products.

Life insurance makes it possible to insure relatives (husband, children etc.) against your death. A major reason for the introduction of this type of insurance is that the death of the breadwinner in a family can have drastic consequences for the rest of the family. Many pension arrangements also have an insurance element where you essentially insure against the event of becoming old. This may seem paradoxical, but the problem is very basic. Nobody knows how long they are going to live and therefore how much they need to save for their old days. Without insurance the savings requirement would be larger, because you need to save as a precaution against becoming very old. Not all will become very old and therefore this would imply "excess savings" (or bequests). By an insurance arrangement this problem can be solved. If all contribute to a given system with a right of obtaining a certain pension as long as they live, then the risk of becoming very old is diversified.

There are also a variety of pension products meeting the basic need of saving for retirement. This form of saving has been subsidized via the tax system offering a tax rebate on your pension saving, which is taxed upon withdrawal (age limitation) at a lower tax-rate (typically 40%). Negotiated labour market pension schemes have been growing in importance during the 1990s and are now rather widespread in the labour market. In 1986, the total assets in pension funds were DKK 341 billion or 55% of GDP, while in 2005, it was approximately DKK 2,200 billion or about 140% of GDP.

These pension schemes are organized such that wage earners pay a certain fraction of their wage into a pension scheme. For the LO/DA area (Chapter 4), the contribution will from 2007 be 10.8% of which the employer pays 2/3 and the employee 1/3. The contribution is accumulated on an individual account, usually combined with an insurance contract, such that the pension fund based on the accumulated contributions and their return offer a life-long pension from retirement (currently at the age of 65).[7]

In Denmark, there are more than 200 insurance companies and 30 multi-employer funds offering insurance and pension products to indi-

---

7.   In addition, there is the ATP – the Danish labour market supplementary scheme – covering all wage earners. It is a fully funded scheme, but contribution defined, i.e. pension right is not directly related to your own contributions. The LD (Lønmodtagernes Dyrtidsfond) is the result of a freeze of wage increases induced by inflation due to indexation of wages in 1977-79 which was transformed into a supplementary pension scheme.

viduals and companies. The activities can be separated into three: non-life insurance, life insurance and pensions. There is substantial concentration in the sector; within non-life insurance activities the 10 largest companies have 80% of the market measured by total premiums paid.

Insurance companies and pension funds are under strict regulation by the Financial Supervisory Authority. The different types of insurance and pension activities are not to be undertaken by the same company. The specific rules are complicated by the fact that these institutions can be organized in the form of mutuals, public limited companies or as branches of foreign companies. They operate under a capital adequacy requirement stipulating a lower limit on the capital base of the company depending on its business portfolio. There is also regulation on how the funds can be invested to prevent that too risky positions are taken which could bring the possibility of meeting its contractual obligations at stake. One important distinction is between gilt-edged assets (typically mortgage bonds, state bonds and real property) and non-gilt-edged assets (typically shares). A maximum of 50% of the funds can be invested in non-gilt-edged assets. There are a number of more specific restrictions which have to be fulfilled.

4.5.4. Other financial institutions

Investment funds offer assets which are made up as a combination of other assets. There are investment funds investing in certain types of bonds or shares, which can also be differentiated to financial assets from specific geographical areas, or specific industries. These products are of interest to small investors who due to information and transactions costs are unable to establish a diversified portfolio on profitable terms. However, via the pooling offered by investment funds such risk diversification can be attained. Moreover, investment funds are usually fairly liquid. Legal rules (including restrictions on investment policies) limit the operations of the funds.

Leasing companies offer firms the possibility of renting real capital like machinery, cars etc. Leasing has the advantage for the firm that they do not have to raise capital to finance the acquisition of capital goods and moreover, the risk associated to the resale value is eliminated.

Factoring companies specialize in managing the debtors of companies. The standard procedure is that a firm after having sold a given commodity or service invoices the buyer. This effectively amounts to providing a loan (from delivery to payment) as well as running a credit risk (will the buyer pay?). The factoring company offers to relieve the firm of these burdens by overtaking the firm's debtors. This can be attractive for small and medium-sized companies for whom it can be costly to administer debtors.

4.6. Financial markets

Important for trade in financial assets are stock exchanges. In Denmark we have the Copenhagen Stock Exchange at which it is possible to trade a variety of financial assets including shares, bonds, money market instruments as well as derivatives like futures and options (the FUTOP market).

Trade at the stock exchange is electronically enabling traders to trade from their own office. During trading dates, there is continuous trade and the stock exchange provides information on share prices, trade volumes etc.

There is a substantial amount of trade in financial assets which does not pass via the stock exchange but where the trade is based on the price quoted at the stock exchange. In this sense, one might term the stock market as a market setter or reference point for the pricing of financial assets. Note that financial institutions have an obligation to report trade to the stock exchange such that information on market developments becomes more complete.

4.6.1. The stock market

The stock market in Denmark is relatively small compared to other countries where there is a stronger tradition for organizing firms as limited corporations. The stock market is growing in importance but relative to the bond market, it is still small and liquidity is small for many stocks. Stocks for about 200 companies are traded at the stock exchange, but there are only few large companies.

Table 4.3.   Trade in share and bond markets, Denmark, 1995-2004.

	1995	1998	2001	2004
SHARES				
Market capitalization ultimo, billion DKK	381	809	738	856
Turnover, billion DKK	157	448	405	593
Average turnover rate (%)	41	55	55	69
BONDS				
Volume of bonds in circulation, ultimo, billion DKK	1871	1963	2198	2702
Turnover, billion DKK	5983	8152	5483	6946
Average turnover rate (%)	325	415	249	253

Note: Turnover rate is calculated as 100* (turnover during the year relative to capitalization end of year)

Source: Københavns Fondsbørs, Factbook, various issues.

The OMXC20 index is based on the share price of 20 shares. The shares to be included are selected semi-annually as the 20 most traded shares. The OMXC20 index is updated continuously (every minute during trading) and is used as an indicator of the general trend in the market. There is also an all-share index, OMXC, and indices for different sectors. It is possible to trade futures and options (put and call) into the OMXC20 index and some of the major stocks.

Figure 4.5 displays the development in the all-share index, OMXC, and an index for IT-stock prices. The figure shows the price hike of IT shares in 1999-2000, which by many was interpreted as a price bubble driven by an IT-hype. This was a global phenomenon, but from the middle of 2000, prices started decreasing, and in this sense the IT-bubble disappeared. Recently, there has been a general upward trend in share prices.

Figure 4.5.   Share prices – Copenhagen stock exchange - OMXC and IT index.

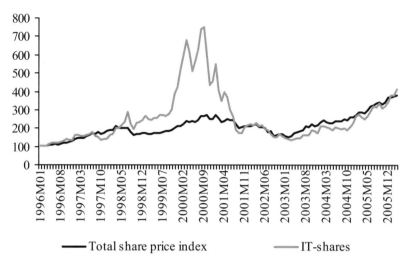

Note: Total market index given by the OMXC index.
Source: Danmarks Nationalbank: *Statistics, www.nationalbanken.dk*

4.6.2. Bonds

The Danish bond market ranks sixth among European bond markets measured in terms of both turnover and value of outstanding bonds. This reflects the strong tradition of bond financing in Denmark, cf. above. Accordingly, the liquidity in the market is very high for the major bond series, and the bond market attracts many foreign investors.

The bond prices are listed by the stock exchange, which also releases information on average rates on return on various types of bonds issued by the state, mortgage credit institutions and specialized institutions as well as an overall average. Figure 4.5 displays the interest rate development over the period 1987.1-2006.4. It is seen that the general trend was a declining interest rate. In the first half of 2006, there has been some tendency for interest rates to increase, but only moderately seen in the perspective of the decreases over the past years. It is possible to trade futures and options (call and put) in some of the major series of state bonds.

Figure 4.6. Interest rates, Denmark 1987.01-2006.4.

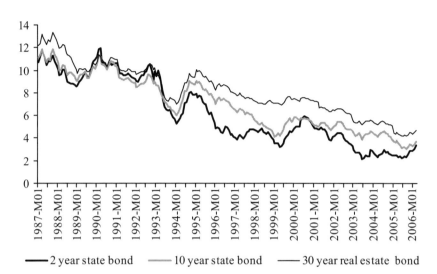

Note: 10 year state bond.
Source: Danmarks Nationalbank: Database, www.nationalbanken.dk.

The term structure of interest gives interest rates as a function of the maturity of the underlying bond. Traders often pay special attention to the term structure because it may provide information on future interest rate developments. The basic principle is the following: If you are going to buy a bond with a long maturity, and you are expecting the short-term interest to increase in the future, then the bond with a long maturity will have to trade at a price implying that the return is higher than for bonds with short maturity. Hence, if the market-expected interest rate increases in the future, the terms structure would tend to be more steep, and vice versa it becomes more flat or perhaps even negatively sloped (inverse term structure) if interest rate decreases are expected. Figure 4.7 gives an example of a term structure curve with a typical form.

Figure 4.7.   Term structure.

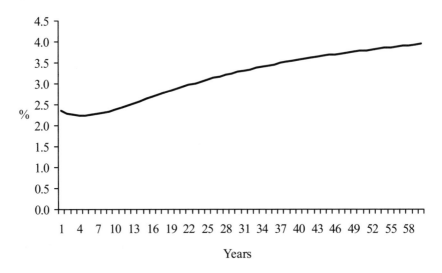

Note: Based on zero-coupon rates, which is the effective rate of return on a
         bond with only one single payment. This gives a well-defined measure of
         the effective rate of return for each maturity. This rate cannot be
         observed but is estimated. The data is for April 22, 2002.
Source: Danmarks Nationalbank.

References

Christensen, A.M. and J. Topp, 1997: Monetary Policy in Denmark since 1992, in *Monetary Policy in the Nordic Countries: Experiences since 1992*, BIS-Policy Paper no. 2.

Christensen, M. og F. Pedersen, 2003: *Aktieinvestering - teori og praktisk anvendelse*, Jurist- og Økonomforbundets Forlag.

Christensen, M., 2001: *Obligationsinvestering - Teoretiske Overvejelser og praktisk anvendelse*, 5. udg., Jurist- og Økonomforbundets forlag

Danmarks Nationalbank (The central bank of Denmark), 2003. 2 udgave: *Pengepolitik i Danmark.*

Danmarks Nationalbank (The central bank of Denmark): *Beretning og kvartalsoversigt.* Various issues.

Danmarks Nationalbank (The central bank of Denmark): *Finansiel statistik.*

Danmarks Nationalbank (The central bank of Denmark): *Monthly Review.*

Danmarks Nationalbank (The central bank of Denmark): *Statens låntagning og gæld.* Various issues.

European Central Bank: *Annual Reports.*

European Central Bank: *Monthly Review.*

European Central Bank: *The Monetary Policy of the ECB*, 2004.

Finanstilsynet (Danish Financial Supervisory Authority): *Årsberetning.*

Hoffmeyer, E., 1993: *Pengepolitiske problemstillinger 1965-90*, Danmarks pengehistorie 5, Danmarks Nationalbank.

IMF, 2006: *Global Financial Stability Report.*

IMF: *Exchange Arrangements and Exchange Restrictions.*

Jensen, P.K., 1998: *Valutareserven*, Nationalbankens Kvartalsoversigt.

Kristensen, J.P., T.A. Christensen og G.W. Pedersen, 1997: *Europæisk monetært samarbejde - fra EMS til ØMU*, Handelshøjskolens Forlag, København.

Københavns Fondsbørs (Copenhagen Stock Exchange): *Factbook.*

Lewis, K., 1999: Trying to explain home bias in equities and consumption, *Journal of Economic Literature*, xxxvi, 571-608.

Mehlbye, P.D. og Jacob Topp, 1996: *Udviklingen på pengemarkedet*, Nationalbankens kvartalsoversigt, august 1996.

Mikkelsen, R., 1993: *Dansk pengehistorie 4: 1960-1990*, Danmarks Nationalbank.

Nielsen, P.E., 1994: Monetary Policy in Denmark in the Last 10 Years, in A. Giovannini and J. Åkerholm (eds.): *Exchange Rate Policy in the Nordic Countries*, CEPR.

Wendt, P., 1998: *Penge- og kapitalmarkedsforhold.* Handelshøjskolens Forlag.

Økonomiministeriet (Danish Ministry of Economic Affairs), 1998: *Danmark uden for Euroen.*

Ølgaard, A., 1995: Pengepolitik, valutakurspolitik, monetær politik og penge- mængde-definitioner, *Nationaløkonomisk Tidsskrift,* 133.

Web addresses

www.bis.org (BIS: Bank of International Settlements "The central bank of central banks)

www.ecb.int (ECB: European Central Bank)

www.finansraadet.dk (Danish Bankers Association)

www.forsikringenshus.dk (Danish Insurance Association)

www.ftnet.dk (Danish Financial Supervisory Authority)

www.imf.org (IMF: International Monetary Fund)

www.nationalbanken.dk (The central bank of Denmark)

www.realkreditraadet.dk (The Association of Danish Mortgage Banks)

www.xcse.dk (Copenhagen Stock Exchange)

Chapter 5

The Danish labour market

The labour market is in many respects the core of the economy. It is here people find jobs and earn incomes to support themselves. It is there firms recruit the labour needed for the activities. Moreover the outcomes of the labour market are important for business cycles and growth and for political concerns over the distribution of job and income possibilities in society.

Since the labour market deals with people it is also in a number of respects different from other types of markets. In particular the institutional setting of the labour market and how it interacts with education-, tax- and social policy is very important. The latter is important since it implies that there intimate relationship between welfare policies in general and the way in which the labour market functions. It is also important because the labour market cannot be approached by a traditional competitive framework.

The close link between welfare policies and labour market institutions and policies also imply that there are wide differences in labour market structures across countries. Particular concern should therefore be taken in cross-country comparisons of labour market features since complement-arities in policies are often very important.

In this chapter we take a closer look at the Danish labour market. Both historical developments and current labour market challenges are discussed. The Chapter starts by considering the factors determining labour supply in both its quantitative and qualitative dimensions (Sections 5.1 and 5.2). The institutional settings of the Danish labour market are presented in Section 5.3. Labour market outcomes in terms of wages and employment/unemployment are addressed in Sections 5.4 and 5.5, and the Chapter ends with a discussion of labour market policies including the so-called "flexibility" policy in Section 5.6.

5.1. Labour supply

Labour supply determines the available input for market activities. It has both a quantitative and a qualitative dimension. The quantitative dimension refers to the quantity of labour supply (number of persons, working time etc.) while the qualitative refers to the qualifications (education, experience etc) of the labour force. The qualitative dimension is taken up in the next section.

The quantitative dimension of labour supply relates to "how many?" and "how much?" The labour force at a given point in time is defined as the part of the population which has a job, is self-employed or is willing to work. This means that the unemployed are also part of the labour force. The size of the labour force depends on demographics (size of the population, age and gender distribution) and the individual decision as to supply labour. The latter depends on the net benefit from working (wage, fringe benefits and psychic benefits minus taxes) compared with the net benefit from non-working (unemployment or pension benefits, the value of time not working and transfer income minus taxes). In 2004 the labour force was almost 2.9 million persons, which amounts to slightly more than 50% of the total population, cf. Table 5.1.

Table 5.1. *Labour force composition in Denmark, 1921-2004.*

	Population	Labour Force	Participation in %		Proportion of female labour force part time
			Men	Women	
1921	3,061,300	1,465,654	59	31	
1930	3,530,600	1,715,620	63	35	
1940	3,826,100	1,939,223	67	35	
1950	4,251,500	2,036,296	64	32	
1960	4,565,500	2,173,317	64	32	
1970	4,906,900	2,313,287	60	34	33
1980	5,122,065	2,745,500	61	47	33
1990	5,135,409	2,907,745	62	52	25
2000	5,330,020	2,879,997	58	50	16
2004	5,397,640	2,854,100	57	49	15
Growth 1921-2004, p.a., %	0.69	0.81			
Growth 1980-2004, p.a., %	0.22	0.16			

Source: P.J. Pedersen: *Arbejdsstyrke og Beskæftigelse 1911-1970* and Danmarks Statistik: STO, various years.

Considering the long run trend of the labour force, cf. Table 5.1 it is seen that the labour force has been increasing both in absolute terms and relative to population size up to the 1990s. An important reason for this is increased labour participation for women (see below). Since then there has been a declining trend which can be attributed to earlier retirement.

5.1 1. Labour force participation

Labour force participation is usually seen relative to the age group considered to be in "working ages", e.g. the group between 16 and 66 years. In 2004 labour force participation for men was 79.7% and for women 73.4%.

Figure 5.1. Female participation in selected OECD countries, 1960-2004.

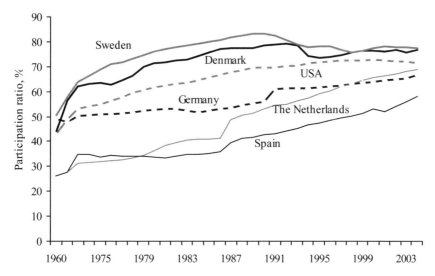

Source: OECD: *Historical Statistics* 1960-1984 and OECD: *Labour Force Statistics*.

The change in labour force participation for women is striking. All western countries used to have a low participation level for women. The turning point in Denmark came in the 1970s. Before, most female parents stayed at home with their small children and a relatively large proportion did not later join the labour market. As a consequence the female labour force participation was about 35%. However, from the 1970s and onwards this changed and an increasing share of women entered the labour market. This reflects female emancipation/and better education as well as the expansion of the welfare state. The latter both required the labour supply of women, but also facilitated it via childcare and separate taxation of men and women (see also Chapter 6). It is also noteworthy that over the years the fraction of females working part time has decreased. In 1980, 33% of all women were employed as part-time workers, while the proportion had fallen to 15% in 2004. And among women between 25 and 55 years of age it is only 8-9 percents who work part time. The reason is probably that better childcare and better educations have made part-time work relatively less attractive.

The upward trend in female participation is not unique for Denmark. Most Western countries are at different stages of this development. Age-specific labour force participation for countries and regions in Europe[1] shows that the participation for some regions around London and Paris look very much like Denmark for the later years. However, there are still differences across countries due to different norms and cultures as well as welfare arrangements (see Chapter 6).

A particular challenge related to labour force participation is the labour market integration of immigrants and their descendants, especially from low income countries. The labour force participation is in general lower, and in particular the differences for women are large. In a forward perspective the issue of labour market integration is a major challenge. While immigrants and descendants from less developed countries today constitute 4.7% of the population and 3% of the work force, this group will in 2040 constitute 12% of the population and about 10% of the work force.

Table 5.2   *Labour force participation age group 17-64, ethnic groups.*

	Males	Females
Danish Origin	0.84	0.76
Immigrants from less developed countries	0.62	0.45
Immigrants from more developed countries	0.70	0.61
Descendants from less developed countries	0.69	0.55
Descendants from more developed countries	0.79	0.75

Note: Countries divided into less and more developed countries according to UN-definition.

Source: Velfærdskommissionen (2004)

---

1.   EU Commission: Employment in Europe, various issues.

1: to give someone the political or legal rights to that they did not have before.

5.1.2. Entry and exit from the labour market

Crucial for labour supply is the average entry and exit rate from the labour market. In recent years the trend has been a later entry and earlier exit (retirement) from the labour market.

Considering labour market entry the average age of students at universities are among the highest in the OECD. Considering the average lag between leaving basic schooling (folkeskolen) and attaining a labour market relevant education is almost 5 years (Velfærdskommissionen, 2005).

While labour force participation in Denmark is high by international standards, this does not apply to the age group 60-65. Over time there has also be a decline from a participation rate for the 60 to 65 year-olds from around 90% in 1960 to about 45% This reflects the possibilities for early retirement, where in particular the Post Employment Pay (Efterløn) attainable at the age 60 is playing an important role. Public Pension (Folkepension) is available from the age 65.[2] Cross country comparisons shows that retirement decisions are affected by institutional arrangements and the economic consequences of retirement (Velfærdskommissionen (2004), OECD (2003)). The issue of retirement ages is also becoming an issue because longevity[1] is increasing. Consequently for unchanged eligibility[2] ages increased life expectance is translated into a longer period as a pensioner. While this may be desirable from an individual point of view, it is obvious from a societal view that it is not feasible[3] to do so for all. Retirement ages are for that reason being discussed in many Western European countries since the so-called "ageing problem" is shared by most countries.

5.1.3 Working hours

The quantity of labour supply depends on working hours during the week, vacations etc. In Denmark the so-called "normal hours" are set as a result of the general wage bargaining, cf. Section 5.4.4. The concept of normal hours covers literally everyone, and can be interpreted as the maximum normal hours for the majority of hourly workers and a good part of the salaried workers. Hours worked beyond the normal hours are paid as

---

2.   Lowered from 67 years of age from 2005.

1: The amount of time that someone or something live.

2: able or allowed to do it.

3: possible to work.

overtime. And jobs with less weekly hours than 28 hours are defined as part time.

Normal hours have been gradually reduced in Denmark and this follows an international trend. The main driving force is growth and increased material living standards allowing some of the gains to be taken out in the form of increased leisure (see also Chapter 8). The reduction is on average about 0.7% per year (Andersen et al., 2005). The reduction has had different causes. In the late 1960s and in the beginning of the 1970s the reduction was in the number of hours per week, then vacation was gradually increased from 4 to 5 weeks; and in the 90s the reduction happened again through a reduction of the weekly working hours from 40 to 37 hours. Vacation has been extended gradually since the first legislation about vacation appeared in 1938. Recently, we have started extending vacation from 5 to 6 weeks. According to the original law, vacation is both a right and an obligation. This gives a total "normal" working year of about 1658 hours in 2006. Normal hours in Denmark are among the lowest in the world. Only the German and the French manufacturing workers have a normal work year with fewer hours per year than the Danes, cf. Figure 5.2.

Figure 5.2. Normal hours in manufacturing in various countries, 2004.

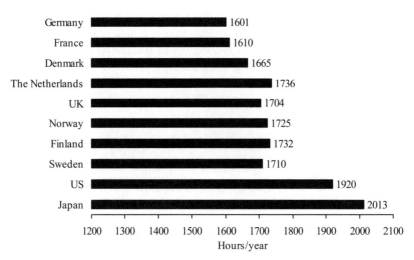

Source: Bundesvereinigung der Deutschen Arbeitgeberverbände, 2004.

5.2. Qualifications

The quality of labour supply is obviously of great importance, and it is often capture by the term human capital with reference to the qualifications, experience etc. possessed by the work force. This includes many dimensions. The most important qualification comes from the formal educational system, consisting of compulsory and formal school together with higher education and vocational training. Most of these educations are provided by the public sector in Denmark with no direct costs for the individual.

Educational levels have increased across generations which is seen from Figure 5.3. Younger generations are in general better educated than older generations. In particular a decreasing proportion does only have the mandatory public schooling, and the share with further education is increasing. However, the differences between the 40-49 years old and the 50-59 years old are of minor order.

Figure 5.3. The population according to highest educational achievement, 2003.

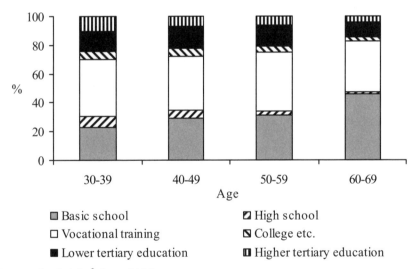

Source: Statistisk Årbog, 2005

For international comparisons, educations are usually divided into several levels. The lowest level of school is the compulsory 9 years of basic school. The next is the 10th grade (voluntary) followed by high school (gymnasium), which is another 3 years. At the same level is the apprentice training (both 12 years of education). After this follows college or non-university (nurses and teachers schools), BA, MA and PhD educations. The apprentice training is the most widespread vocational training in Denmark. About 1/3 of a youth cohort gets an apprentice training. Nowadays, apprentice training is common in Denmark, Germany, Austria and Switzerland. Workers who have served an apprenticeship are traditionally called skilled workers in contrast to non-skilled. The latter characterization does not preclude that many of the non-skilled workers actually have acquired high skills within a specific area, but skilled workers have a broad or general training which potentially make them more flexible.

Table 5.3 shows that Denmark by no means is in the top league of countries with respect to education. First, a relatively large share of the population has no further education than compulsory school. Second, a low share has upper tertiary education. This is partly compensated by a larger fraction having lower tertiary education, i.e. BA-level. International comparisons are difficult and some of the differences between the last two columns could easily be caused by differences in definitions.

Table 5.3. *Formal qualifications in Denmark compared to other countries. Percentage distribution.*

	Primary and lower secondary education	Upper secondary education	Lower tertiary education	Upper tertiary education
ISCED	0,1,2	3,4	5B	5A,6
US	12	49	9	29
Denmark	18	50	7	25
Finland	24	42	17	16
France	35	41	9	14
Germany	17	59	10	14
Norway	12	56	2	29
Sweden	18	49	15	18
Country mean	31	45	8	16

Notes: International Standard Classification of Education (ISCED) 0,1,2: Kindergarten, basic school and non-compulsory school
ISCED 3,4: Vocational training (apprenticeships) and high school
ISCED 5: Short, non university educations, college etc
ISCED 6: University educations, Master and PhD
Source: OECD: *Education at a Glance*, 2004.

The Danish classification does, however, not coincide fully with the international classification in Table 5.3. One of the problems is the classification of the non-university educations.

Additionally, there is a large element of on-the-job training, where people improve their skills by doing the job and by taking part in specific courses. Some of these are organized through the public system of educational job preparation courses (AMU courses), which are mainly targeted at ordinary wage earners. Another segment is largely privately organized. There is no statistics for the latter, but there are occasional surveys showing a huge activity in this area.

5.3. Industrial relations

The Danish labour market is thoroughly organized and historically labour market issues have been settled in centralized negotiations between representatives for employers and employees. This is sometimes referred to as the "The Danish Model". The key ingredient is that the trade unions and the employer's federation (the social partners) make agreements on most of the regulatory issues, without political interference. The social partners take responsibility for wage bargaining and wage setting. They also make agreements on normal working hours, and set rules together with the Government for labour protection with respect to overtime and work environments. An example of a difference between the Danish institutional structure and many other countries is that there is no minimum wage legislation in Denmark, but the social partners negotiate a minimum wage. The higher inclination in the EU to legislate on rules is a challenge to the Danish system.

The fact that labour market related issues are left to be determined by negotiations between the labour market organisations without political interference is the principle defining the so-called Danish labour market model. However, two important caveats should be pointed out. First, there are many examples of explicit or implicit public interference in labour market negotiations. Second, the agreements arrived at in collective bargaining are not independent of political decisions, e.g. the determination of minimum wages is not independent of the level of social assistance and unemployment benefits, pension agreements depend on the tax subsidy etc. (see below on the flexicurity model).

5.3.1 Employee organizations

About 80% of all employees are members of a Trade Union in Denmark. The high membership ratio is partly a consequence of a close connection between UI-funds and Unions though there is no direct legal connection between the two systems. However, Union membership and membership of the UI-funds are usually solicited as a joint package. Furthermore, the same persons are often involved as officials in the Trade Unions and the UI-system and administrations are also often related in different ways. Because of all these elements, potential members do often consider the joint membership as a package. One also finds high membership ratios in the 4 other countries having a similar relationship between unions and UI-funds: Belgium, Sweden, Iceland and Finland, whereas it is only about 50% in Norway, where UI is part of the welfare system. (Neumann et al, 1992).

The unions in Denmark have traditionally been mostly organized according to trade (skills and level). The pattern used to be that skilled workers (those who had served an apprenticeship) had their own union separate from the non-skilled within the same industry. To some extent this old division of members is also related to wage differentials in the sense that some unions have more low-wage members than others.

Almost all unions for workers are members of the umbrella organization, LO. Thus, LO represents about 53% of all wage earners. LO used to be the powerful overarching union being the main bargaining power on workers side, but has now handed over much of this power to member unions as part of a general decentralization on both sides of the labour market. Unions outside LO are mainly unions for supervisors at different levels, university graduates, and civil servants. The unions mainly representing low wage workers are 3F, (work-men's and work-women's trade union), FOA (public sector) and HK (retail etc). These represent among others the workers in the food industry, hospitals and retail industry, respectively.

There are no organized works councils in Denmark, though there are employee representatives on the board of most larger shareholding companies. Though these members are representing the employees they are clearly acting under the same set of norms and laws as other board members. In particular, this means confidentiality, personal integrity, and personal responsibility.

5.3.2. Employers Organizations

On the employers side there are also a number of organizations. The umbrella organization here is Danish Employers Federation, DA. DA consists of single employers and industry-wise federations of employers. Among the largest are Danish Industry, DI, and Danish Trade and Service (DHS). The degree of organization is significantly lower on the side of employers compared to workers.

5.3.3. Collective bargaining

The wage formation in Denmark used to be highly centralized with biannual wage bargaining between LO and DA and between the unions of the public employees and the Government. As a result of these negotiations, wages and planned wage hikes were agreed on for large groups of employees and were fixed for a contract period that usually ran for 2 years. However, the contracts were not equally binding for all groups of workers and employers on the private labor market. Thus, wages were fixed for employees in the private labor market under the so-called "normallønssystem" (normal wage system). The workers covered under this wage system were mainly non-skilled and women. Other groups of workers (in particular skilled workers) had wage contracts, where discrete wage increases were allowed and anticipated during the contract period.

Wage bargaining has in recent years become much more decentralized and basically leaves only non-wage issues to the central level. All wage bargaining have been moved down to lower level organizations, to the firm level or even to the individual level. As a consequence the wage setting system has over the last couple of contract periods become more and more directed towards a system where only the base pay and the lowest wages are negotiated and where the employee negotiates additional pay directly with his employer with the assistance of the union representative. This is called the minimum pay system. Thus, in 2004 22% of all contracts on the organized labour market for workers did not mention a wage at all (DA, 2005) because the contract simply stated that the wage had to be agreed on between employer and employee. As a consequence the central wage negotiations are less and less concerned with wages, while issues covering pension, working hours, and vacation are still left for central bargaining.

The result is that there are increased possibilities for agreeing on special local wage systems and for introducing new performance related pay including bonus.

While the wage setting has been decentralized on the private labour market, the public sector wage bargaining is still highly centralized with central negotiations every 2 years. However, a new wage system called "New-wage" has been introduced. It has fewer steps on the wage ladder than previous and opens up for local agreements and for various sorts of individual wage premiums related to performance and special qualifications. However, the element of individual performance related pay is still fairly small within the public sector partly due to outspread resistance from the employees. Since, the public sector has always had a career system, where promotions to some extent were and still are dependent on performance the changes may not be so big after all.

5.3.4. Industrial Conflicts

Denmark belongs to the group of countries with relatively few industrial conflicts. One of the reasons is that we have an elaborate legal system to take immediate action when conflicts arise. The major exceptions from the low level are conflicts where there is no collective agreement. This is technically the case, when contracts run out or on areas where there has been no collective contract.

The main rules of conduct for the Danish labour market are based on an agreement (contract) between LO and DA, the so-called "Hovedaftale" (the general agreement) complemented by legislation. The first contract was made in 1899 and it has been revised a couple of times since then. This contract secures the freedom to organise on both sides. Both sides have the right to use strikes and lockouts as part of the instruments to reach a collective agreement. As soon as an agreement has been reached, both sides are then obliged to "keep peace" as long as the agreement runs. If disagreement occurs, a prescribed set of rules for conduct is used. If the disagreement is caused by breach of agreement, the first step above the firm level is to involve the main organizations on both sides. If they cannot solve the dispute, it will go to the Labour Court. The Labour Court was instituted by law in 1910 and consists of judges appointed by the two sides and the Government. The verdict is final and may consist of a fine to the convicted party.

If the dispute is caused by differences in the interpretation of the general agreement, a litigation procedure is prescribed. Both sides are obliged to follow the procedures and to accept the ruling.

The effect of the system is that Denmark has seen relatively few strikes while the general agreement has been in effect (see STO). In return, major strikes may occur in connection with the bargaining process, since the strike and lockout weapons here are fully legal. However, before these weapons can be used there is a detailed procedure to be followed. If an agreement cannot be reached on a specific area, the two parties usually submit strike warnings. At the same time (or before), they will usually seek consultation at the State Conciliation Board (forligsinstitutionen). This board is run by the State but has no power to force the two sides to reach an agreement. After a successful negotiation the conciliation officer may propose a compromise with the consent of the two sides. Both sides are obliged to send the compromise to a referendum among members or to their governing boards depending on the internal rules.

5.4 Wages

The distribution of wages in the Danish labour market is shown for ordinary wage earners and for management (supervisors and up) Figure 5.4. The distribution for both groups is skewed to the right. The most common wage for ordinary wage earners is DKK 183. Half of all wages (the area between the lower and the upper quartile) lie between DKK 155 and DKK 220. The mean wage is DKK 196. The wage dispersion for the management group is substantially larger. One simple way to look at the dispersion is the distance between the two quartiles. For managers, this distance is DKK 149. while for ordinary wage earners it is DKK 65.

Figure 5.4. Wage distribution for ordinary wage earners (upper panel) and supervisors etc. (lower panel).2005.

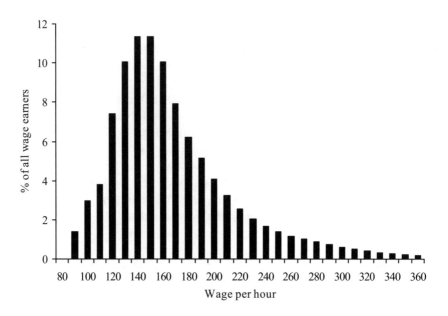

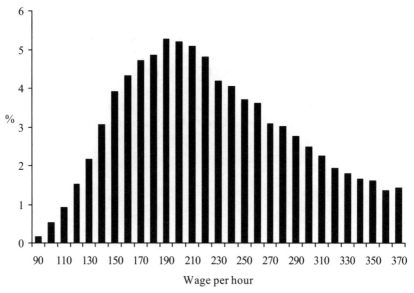

Source: Dansk Arbejdsgiverforening: *DA Lønstatistik* 2005.

5.4.1. Wage differentials between sectors and gender

Employers can in the aggregate be split between the State, the local government sector and the private sector. They differ with respect to the average wage level and with respect to wage dispersion. They also differ with respect to gender differences in pay. Figure 5.5 shows the averages, the median, and the lower and upper quartile for these two dimensions. First, all wage distributions are skewed to the right, i.e. there is a bigger tail to the right than to the left. Second, the median is highest for men and furthermore, the median is highest in the State sector for men and women, respectively. Third, private sector wages have a higher dispersion than any of the other sectors. Fourth, the wage dispersion in the upper tail in the private sector is so high that it draws the average wage upward to become the highest of all despite a somewhat lower median. This is also the case in the other sectors but to a much lesser degree. This is partly the result of the seniority-based wage system, i.e. the wage depends on the time the person has been in the job, in most of the public sector versus the less constrained wage formation in the private sector. It is also a consequence of differences in the structure of qualifications across the different sectors.

Figure 5.5. *The wage for sectors and gender in 2003. Lower quartile, median, and upper quartile.*

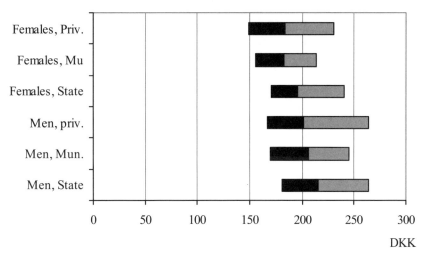

Source: Danmarks Statistik: *Statistisk Årbog* 2005.

5.4.2. Wage differentials for educational groups

Gender-specific[1] wage information for educational groups in the three sectors is shown in Figure 5.6. First, the graph confirms a strong wage progression depending on education. Second, it shows that the State is paying most for male wages for educations up to the level of tertiary non-university college. For the higher levels, men and women in the private sector get a higher wage. The local government sector is paying more modestly for all levels. Third, women receive less than men compared level by level for all sectors and all levels, though the difference is clearly largest for the private sector.

Figure 5.6.   Median wage hourly rates for educational groups in sectors and for gender. 2004.

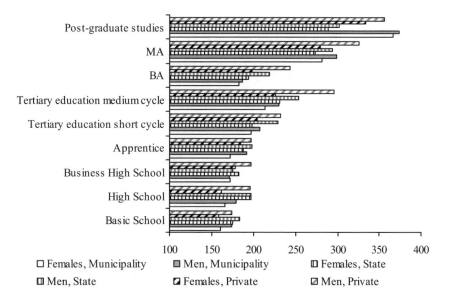

Source: Danmarks Statistik, Statistikbanken.

5.4.3. Wage growth

So far we have looked at factors that can explain the wage level in different jobs. It is clear from the above that education, gender and sector are rather important. Together with the length of general experience, these

1: the fact of being mate or female.

factors can explain a little more than ¼ of individual wages.[3] Other individual factors as specificity of education, ability, diligence and practical skills play a big role as well and these factors explain another ¼ of the individual wage. Furthermore, different firms pay different wages to otherwise equal persons because they have different capabilities of using human resources together with their physical capital and because they use different methods of remunerating their work force. That explains another ¼. Finally, there is an unexplained part.[4]

Figure 5.7. Distribution of wage growth for employees in the same firm.

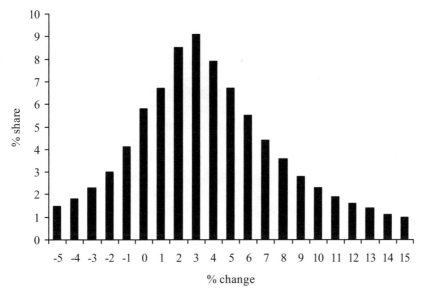

% share

% change

Source: Dansk Arbejdsgiverforening: *DA Lønstatistik*, 4th Quarter 2005.

Figure 5.7 shows the distribution of the annual wage growth measured as the wage growth for main groups of employees in identical firms and weighted with group size. The first thing to notice is the substantial dispersion.¹ A quarter of the ordinary wage earners experience a wage growth of more than 8% and another quarter experience a growth below 2% at a time when the median worker receives a 4% wage growth. The

---

3.   For an international comparison, see Harmon, Walker and Westergaard-Nielsen, 2001.
4.   See Abowd, Kramarz and Margolis, 1999.

1: the process of spreading things over a wide area or in different directions.

dispersion is slightly smaller for salaried employees. The reason is that workers get a more varying pay over time because of fluctuations in piece rates and other sorts of performance-related pay than salaried employees do.

5.4.4. Wage costs

Employment depends on the wage costs to the employer. The difference between the wage received by the worker and the wage cost of the employer is the following for ordinary employees. First, there is a mandatory contribution to vacation pay equal to 15% of the wage. Second, there is a special compensation for weeks with holidays of 2.8%, ensuring that a normal weekly wage is paid even in weeks with one or two holidays. In addition there is sickness pay and pay for inconvenience, i.e. night shift, dirty work etc. These components amount to about 3% and 4% respectively. Finally, there is a mandatory contribution to ATP (supplementary pension scheme) and on top of that comes contributions to other pension arrangements. On average this is about 8.4% and 10.8% from 2007 for most of the LO/DA area. Most of these pension arrangements are organized so that the employers part is 2/3 of the contribution while the employee pays 1/3. Altogether these wage costs sums to 34% of the paid wage. On top of these costs come indirect wage costs of 1.8% of the paid wage. These cover insurances and contributions to the apprentice system etc.

Compared to other countries these indirect wage costs are very low, cf. Figure 5.8. Most countries in Europe collect what is called social contributions at the employer level and the result is that the paid wage looks much smaller in these countries compared with Denmark, where people receive a higher wage but at the same time pay a high level of taxes which covers the same public expenditures (pension and health) as the social contributions in other countries. Again Denmark resembles the USA and the UK more than other Continental European countries. The tax burden is of course quite different, see Chapter 7. That also explains why the income tax is so high in Denmark compared with other countries with a similar welfare system.

At the same time it is remarkable that the total Danish wage costs are highest per hour. This means that Danish workers have to be more productive than workers from the other countries in order to retain competitiveness.

136

Figure 5.8. Direct and indirect wage costs for the manufacturing industry in different countries, per hour, 2004.

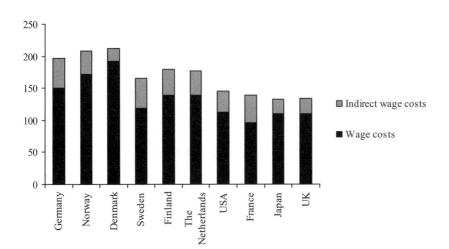

Source: DA 2005, based on Bureau of Labor Statistics.

5.5. Unemployment

Unemployment and unemployment risk are major concerns both for individuals and policy makers. Therefore unemployment is often considered the most crucial indicator of how well functioning labour markets are.

Most European countries experienced mass unemployment after the first oil crisis in 1973, see Chapter 1. Denmark was no exception as can be seen in Figure 5.9. Only Sweden and Finland succeeded for a long time in preventing an increase in unemployment, but even there they did not prevail.

Unemployment may have many causes. One is that there at the aggregate level is insufficient demand, which in turns lowers firms' labour demand. While fluctuations in aggregate demand can be an important factor for short-run changes in unemployment it is less unlikely to be the cause for persistent unemployment. This is often explained by so-called structural unemployment. Structural unemployment may be due to a number of factors: One is mismatch between demand and supply of labour across regions, skills etc.; another factor is that the structure of benefits for

1=change in price, amount, level etc.

the unemployed creates unemployment in itself because the unemployed have too few incentives to seek work; a third factor could be an effect of the wage setting implying that wages do not or only sluggishly reacts to unemployment. We conclude this section on unemployment by looking at the labour market policy.

Figure 5.9.   Unemployment in Denmark and other OECD countries 1970-2004.

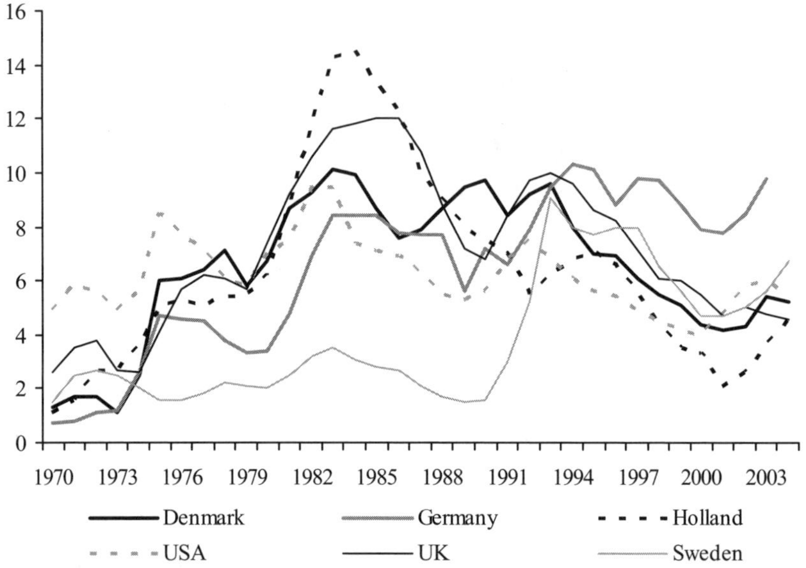

Source: Danmarks Statistik: STO – various years.

Unemployment is in Denmark measured in two different ways. One is the degree of unemployment defined as the fraction of normal hours spent as unemployed. This measure comes from the register-based UI (Unemployment Insurance)-statistics, which is based on the actual individual unemployment as reported in order to obtain unemployment benefit. This statistics has total coverage. Another measure used in Denmark and in many other countries is the Labour Force Survey collected according to EU directives and based on a survey that is carried out in all other EU-countries. The main difference is that the latter measure uses the ILO-definition of unemployment.[5] The result is that the

5.   The international statistics is most often based on the ILO definition of unemployment, which stipulates that a person is unemployed, if he does not have a job, is available for work and is actively searching. The operational definition

138   l: something that encourage you te work harder, start a new activity etc.

Danish register based unemployment tends to exaggerate unemployment measured by the Labour Force Survey.

5.5.1. Short and long-term unemployment

An annual degree of unemployment of 0.5 means that the person has been unemployed 50% of the 52 weeks. These 26 weeks can cover one long spell or may cover several shorter spells. Aggregating individual degrees of unemployment, gives total unemployment measured in full-time equivalents.

Table 5.4.   The composition of unemployment.

	1979	1985	1994	2000	2004	2004 % of persons	2004 % of unem- ployment
Total number of people	575	741	818	560	573	100,0	100,7
Less than 73 days	297	312	290	299	264	46,0	12,2
74-146 days	125	159	152	115	127	22,2	21,1
147-219 days	68	119	122	68	85	14,8	23,6
220-292 days	42	71	94	40	53	9,2	20,7
293 days and more	43	80	160	38	45	7,8	23,1
Average unemployment rate among the unemployed	0.28	0.34	0.42	0.27	0.31		
Men	0.23	0.30	0.42	0.28	0.32		
Women	0.35	0.38	0.42	0.26	0.30		
Annual rate of unemployment in percentage of the labour force	6.1	9.1	12.2	5.4	6.4		
Men	5.1	7.5	11.0	4.6	5.8		
Women	7.4	11.0	13.6	6.2	7.0		

Source: Danmarks Statistik: STO and Danmarks Statistik: SE: *Arbejdsmarked* 2005:4.

used in the Labour Force Surveys is according to EU directives for all member countries that the person is fully unemployed in the reference week, he/she has to have been looking for work within the last 4 weeks, and must be able to start working within 2 weeks.

Table 5.4 shows how unemployment in 2004 (176,000 full-time equivalents) was composed of 573,000 persons who had at least one spell of unemployment each. This means that 176,000 man years of unemployment were levied on 573,000 different persons. On average, each of these persons has been unemployed for about 4 month. However, unemployment consists of a lot of short spells and fewer long spells: in 2004, 264,000 were unemployed for less than 73 days, while 127,000 were unemployed between 74 and 147 days. Only 45,000 were unemployed more than 293 days in 2000. Because of the Danish rules for vacation pay, the last mentioned group has effectively been full-time unemployed.

5.5.2. UI benefits

In most countries, unemployment insurance is organized as a compulsory insurance for all wage earners and in some countries, the UI system is part of the social security system. In Denmark, Sweden, Finland and Belgium unemployment insurance is organized on a voluntary basis and in principle, the UI-funds are independent of the State and of the Trade Unions. In reality, some of the union officials are also involved with the UI-funds with the result that many members cannot distinguish between the two.

Historically, UI-funds grew out of the Trade Union movement like mutual health insurance. In Denmark and many other places, the first UI-funds were entirely private. Already in 1903, the Danish Government was paying a substantial contribution to the UI-funds and received some insight in their business in return. The state subsidy is now substantial. Though each member pays a monthly contribution of DKK 278 plus a contribution to administration costs which is between 0 and 180 DKK per month with an average close to 130 DKK. The members' contribution covers only a small fraction of the total costs leaving the bulk of the expenses to the State. Likewise, all changes in unemployment are absorbed by the state subsidy. In many other countries, contributions cover a larger part of the costs and usually, the UI-budget has to balance over a longer span of years allowing the budget to be negative in years with high unemployment.

In Denmark you can become member of a UI-fund when you are between 18 and 65 and reside in Denmark. In order to get UI-benefits you must have been member for more than 1 year, unless you have graduated from an education/vocational training lasting more than 1.5 years, and you have worked for more than 52 weeks within the last 3 years. Only work without subsidy and work as an UI-fund member counts in this respect. Furthermore, you have to be registered at the employment service and have to be available for work.

The benefit is 90% of the previous hourly wage (the reference wage) with a maximum of DKK 3,335 per week (2006), which is DKK 90 per hour. Benefits are taxed as other income but the 8% labour market contribution is not applied.

The structure of the Danish benefit system differs from the systems in neighbouring countries with respect to taxation, compensation structure, and length of the benefit period (see Welfare Commission (2005), Hansen (2000)). Though the replacement ratios in all countries are falling with increasing wages, the systems differ with respect to the starting point (the maximum benefit) and the slope. The most noteworthy about the Danish system is that it offers a high replacement ratio for low income groups, while it is fairly low for medium and high income groups. Another difference is that the duration period (currently 4 years) is rather long in Denmark in international comparison.

The rationale of reducing benefits over time spent unemployed is to create an incentive for the unemployed to accept a job even if the wage offer is relatively low. Similarly, the purpose of a relatively high replacement ratio is to prevent a serious reduction in income (the insurance effect), that could get the person to use resources on finding a cheaper apartment etc. However, a high replacement ratio creates also an incentive problem, because the high replacement ratio makes the income from finding a job little different from the income as unemployed. If the unemployed person is eligible to other transfer payments this problem is aggravated. It has been demonstrated that the financial incentive to be work may be modest or even absent.[6] These incentive problems are clearly more serious in Denmark than in any of the other countries because benefits for low-wage earners are high and benefits are not reduced over time as in most other countries.

In most countries the UI system is financed via taxation or special contributions from wage earners and employers. These are only rarely related to the actual short-run costs. Only the US UI system has a built-in employer contribution, which for a small part depends on the number of people made unemployed from each firm. The idea is that if a firm makes more people unemployed, it should also pay a larger contribution. The US

---

6. See Pedersen and Smith (2002).

system has been in effect in most states for more than 60 years and has been proven to lower the total level of unemployment and in particular the short-term level of unemployment, where workers are fired because of short-term lack of demand.[7] In order to give employers a similar incentive in Denmark, an employer-paid first day of each unemployment spell was introduced in 1988. This was later extended to two days. It has probably had a small effect on the so called temporary lay-offs.

5.6. Labour market policies

The Government intervenes in the labour market in different ways. Most governments have an objective of pursuing an economic policy to secure a high, sustainable employment. When the macro economic policy cannot solve the problems, most governments have programs for the unemployed with different focus on getting them back to work and measures to secure their welfare benefits. The Government also regulates work conditions and sets safety standards to protect workers and consumers. Furthermore, it seeks to "repair" market failures. Below, we give an overview of the labour market policies pursued in Denmark in recent years.

5.6.1. Labour market reforms

Since unemployment became a problem in the Danish economic policy in the 1970s, various policies have been tried to weaken the adverse effects on individuals and society. The main emphasis has been on preventing direct loss of income, maintaining the ability to work and preventing psychological problems for those hit by severe unemployment. Most labour market policies therefore focus on income maintenance. I addition some policies have aimed at diminishing the labour force. Collectively they are called "passive measures". Other policies are devoted to getting people back to work by providing training and jobs. Those are usually called "active labour market policies". Below, we present a survey of both types of policies.

In a sequence of reforms during the 1990s starting with the "Labour Market Reform of 1994" labour market policy has been changed considerably. The reforms had several ingredients[8] including: i) duration

---

7.   See Anderson and Meyer (1997).
8.   See e.g. Economic Council (autumn 2002)

of unemployment benefits was shortened considerably. ii) the formal duration was reduced from 7 to 4 years and combined with activation measures. To maintain unemployment benefits there was a requirement to participate in some type of activation after 12 months of unemployment measured over a 24 month period. The first period of 12 months is without other obligations than to search for work. The activation period can last up to 3 years. In this period, the unemployed has to be kept activated more than 75% of the time.iii). For youth, i.e. below the age of 25, the first period is only 6 months and after that the youth has the right and the obligation to take an education of at least 18 months of duration. The support during this period will be the usual student support, which is about half of UI-benefits. If the unemployed has a vocational training already, the obligation is to take job training. Non-compliance means a complete stop for all benefits. The level of sanctions is not equalled any other place in the whole system.

As a result of the reform, none of the subsidized job training periods under the labour market programs will provide eligibility to further unemployment benefits.

5.6.2. Activation measures[9]

The main activation measure is job training. The purpose is to give the unemployed an opportunity to get back into work through a job-training period at a private or public employer. The employer receives a subsidy of about DKK 60 per hour for a 6 month period and has to pay the usual wage for that particular job. Given the subsidy the private employers have to pay normal wages, whereas the public sector pays a fixed hourly wage. Furthermore, individual job training can be arranged for people who have difficulties in getting a job because of long-term unemployment or poor educational background. The ratio between private and public job training has been around 1 to 4 before and after the reform. In addition, activation can take place in so-called pool jobs (puljejob) in the public sector. These jobs can be created within areas of the public sector, where the public service may be improved. Education is another type of activation. Education can be taken at ordinary educational institutions or as courses designed for the unemployed. Another major program providing benefits for education was the leave scheme for education. This was in effect from

---

9. Rules and amounts refer to 2006, if not otherwise stated. Source: www.danmark.dk.

1994 to the end of 2000. The leave scheme for education offered paid leave from a job provided the employer gave his consent. Even unemployed could get leave for education. The benefits equalled UI-benefits and in this case educations should be approved. At first there were few constraints on the number and variety of educations, but gradually the choice became more and more constrained until the whole program was stopped.

Figure 5.10. Active labour market policies, 1980-2004.

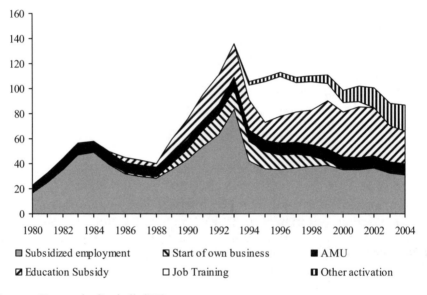

Source: Danmarks Statistik STO.

Figure 5.10 shows how the different activation programs have developed over time. It is obvious from inspection of the graphs that different activation programs have been substituting each other. It started in 1994, when a relatively big fraction of those on the short-term job offer scheme changed to the new education programs. First, they moved to the leave schemes and more recently there has been a shift to ordinary educations but with full benefits. The reasons are most likely related to the relative constraints on the choice of education and the possible duration of benefits. Various job training schemes seem to have been popular throughout the period, though a number of new measures "other activation" seem to gain in popularity. These cover integration of immigrants etc. The changing composition seems to reflect the changing labour market situation.

5.6.3. Passive measures

The passive measures consist of schemes for childcare leave, sabbatical leave, post employment pay (efterløn) and transition pay (overgangs-ydelse). The most dominating of these is the post employment pay introduced in 1979. Members of the UI-funds, who were between 60 and 67 of age, could obtain post employment pay. The first year, 48,000 went into this program and in 1999, the number had grown to 149,000. From the age of 62, more than 50% of the cohorts are now on post employment pay. In 1999, the program was supplemented with a premium if post employment pay was postponed till after the age of 62. It is now politically discussed how to reform the post employment pay in order to retain more seniors at the labour market. Transition pay was in effect from 1992-1995 and was an offer to unemployed between 50 and 60 years of age. The arrangement was that they could get 82% of the highest UI-benefit if they left the labour force permanently.

The leave scheme program, introduced in 1994, made it possible to take leave from a job because of childcare. The leave period is 8 to 52 weeks. All parents with children below the age of 9 are eligible for childcare leave. Unemployed and welfare recipients are also eligible. The benefits are 60% of the highest UI-pay. Childcare leave is to a high degree used to extend maternity leave and this has been used to levy the pressure on many municipal day-care programs. Finally, the sabbatical leave program is worth mentioning. It was in effect from 1994 to 1999 and made it possible to take leave for pure sabbatical reasons. The rules were similar to the other programs with two exceptions: the employer should give his consent and he should employ a long-term unemployed as a substitute.

The rationale of the leave schemes was undoubtedly to create temporary jobs for the unemployed and thus making it possible for more unemployed to gain a foothold on the labour market. As the total demand for workers was just about to increase in these years, this may have had some positive effects. The cost was labour shortage in some professions (nurses for example). The trend of these passive schemes is illustrated in Figure 5.11.

Figure 5.11. The passive labour market policies, 1980-2004.

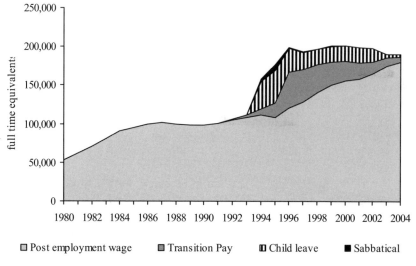

Source: Danmarks Statistik: STO.

The total effect of the different measures is illustrated in Figure 5.12. Active and passive measures (except post employment pay) have been bundled while post employment pay and open unemployment are illustrated in separate graphs. It should be noted that unemployment has been reduced but the two other curves seem to grow with the result that the total number of people under some sort of labour market related income support has not changed as much as the unemployment rate has gone down.

So even with markedly lowered unemployment and dramatically improved labour market conditions, there are still more than 300,000 person equivalents on some sort of temporary transfer payment. However, many more people are involved since most of these full-year equivalents have shorter stays in one of the programs. In addition to the direct loss of production from the number of people involved there are the resources used to activate, to train and to control eligibility. Comparing the graph for the open unemployment with the one for active and passive measures makes it clear that active and passive measures tend to grow more than unemployment in years with increasing unemployment and to fall less than the open unemployment in years with falling unemployment, i.e. an increasing trend.

Figure 5.12. The total number of people under labour market programs or openly unemployed, 1980-2004.

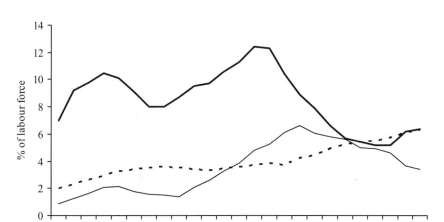

Source: Danmarks Statistik: STO.

This, of course raises the question whether these measures are efficient in the sense that they help people getting back to work. The traditional view has been to look at individual effects, where one looks at the job chances for participants compared with non-participants.[10] These individual effects should be held up against the direct costs and the costs arising from the fact that people do not search for work when they are participating in an activity.

The main programs have been evaluated at several occasions. The clearest result is with respect to the youth program which has been shown to have an impact on the unemployment of youth.[11] But the relatively high growth rate in the economy has also had a positive impact on the demand for youth in particular because an increasing total demand for labour is accompanied by an even larger demand for new entrants. Several other programs have also been evaluated. The general result is that the subsidized job training schemes in the private sector have a positive impact as long as they create a match. If the person does not stay with the employer after the training period, the effect is rather dubious. Similarly,

---

10. See Arbejdsministeriet, 2000.
11. See Jensen, Rosholm and Svarer (2003).

for the public sector jobs. It is hard to find a clear positive effect of the educational programs. At face value some of the programs look beneficial, but when taking the relatively long duration of the program where people do no search into account, most programs look less favourable.[12] A more recent result shows that a substantial effect from activation comes from the mere threat of becoming activated.[13]

5.6.4. Flexicurity

In recent years the Danish labour market has become internationally famous for the so-called flexicurity model. By the word "flexicurity" reference is made to flexible hiring and firing rules for employers and a social security system for workers. Thereby the concerns for employers over flexibility and for workers over income support. By many this has been taken as a model conducive to job creation, structural change and growth, and the fact that Denmark has a low unemployment rate by international standards is by some taken as evidence in support of the virtues of this model.

Denmark has one of the lowest levels of employment protection in Europe. In most cases, blue-collar workers can be laid off with relatively short notice. Many white collar workers and salaried employees in some occupations are by law secured a period of notice in case of lay-offs depending on tenure. (1 month per year of employment up to a maximum of 9 months). There are no laws for blue collar workers but some unions have included relatively short periods of notice in case of a layoff as part of their contract. This short or non-existing notice has been widely accepted among Trade Unions and legislators because it creates a flexible labour market that allows for the most efficient use of labour. For the Ttrade Unions, the compensating arrangement is the high and easily accessible UI-benefit.

There is no doubt that the flexicurity model has some attractive properties. However, some caution should be taken in interpreting the virtues of the model.[14] The flexicurity elements were basically unchanged over several decades, and were therefore also in place during the period from the mid 1970s to the early 1990s where there were double digit unemployment rates. The main changes which have been made over this

---

12. See Arbejdsministeriet (2000).
13. See Rosholm and Svare (2004).
14. See e.g. Andersen and Svarer (2006).

period is the introduction of the active orientation of labour market policies during the 1990s including in particular shorter duration of unemployment benefits and the activation policy. Moreover, despite the reduction in the official unemployment rate there has not been a corresponding fall in the number of persons being dependent of public transfers, cf. above. Hence, the "road back to job" has not been sufficiently strong, cf. the fact that a substantial number of people have difficulties getting back in employment if they loose their job. (Ibsen and Westergaard-Nielsen, 2005). It is also remarkable that the conditions under which people loose their job is important. Their chances of getting reemployment is higher, if they loose their job in a workplace closure or major restructuring (Frederiksen and Westergaard-Nielsen, 2006).

While flexible firing rules is conducive for job creation it also has some other effects. One is that it causes a higher job turnover in the labour market. Danish turnover is as high as 27 per cent on average (Ibsen and Westergaard-Nielsen, 2005).[15] It is somewhat higher among young people and in particular for people who have only been employed for less than 2 years and lower for older people with longer tenure. However, it does not differ widely between occupational groups. By contrast, young workers tend also to carry the burden of turnover in countries with stricter employment protection in the sense that employers try to avoid employing young people on a permanent basis. In several EU countries the unemployment rate of youth is more than 20 per cent while it is only about 3 per cent for Danish youth. Of course, there are other reasons for this, the most important being the Danish apprentice system. But one may conclude that higher employment flexibility (and higher turnover) in Denmark does not lead to higher unemployment. Moreover, the combination of flexibility and social security leads to less concern about job security in Denmark than in e.g. the UK.[16]

---

15. Turnover is measured as the mean value of the proportion of all employees, who are not at the workplace the following year and the proportion who are new at the workplace.
16. See Kristensen and Westergaard-Nielsen (2004).

References

Abowd, John, Francis Kramarz, and David Margolis (1999): High Wage Workers and High Wage Firms, *Econometrica*, 67:2, 251-333.

Andersen, T.M., and M. Svarer, 2006; Flexicutiry Flexicutiry - den danska arbetsmarknadsmodellen, Ekonomisk Debatt, 17-29.

Andersen, T.M., H. Linderoth, V. Smith and N. Westergård-Nielsen, Beskrivende Dansk Økonomi, Handelsvidenskab, 2005.

Anderson, Patricia, Bruce Meyer (1997): *Unemployment insurance takeup rates and the after-tax value of benefits*, QJE 112: 913-937.

Arbejdsministeriet (Ministry of Labour): *Effekter af Aktiveringsindsatsen*, København, 2000.

Bundesvereinigung der Deutschen Arbeitgeberverbände, 2004.

Christensen, Jørgen Peter & Jørgen Estrup (1970): Strukturændringer på det danske arbejdsmarked i 1900-tallet i *Vækst og Kriser i dansk økonomi i det 20 århundrede*, Skrifter fra Aarhus Universitets Økonomiske Institut, nr. 27.

Danmarks Statistik (Statistics Denmark): SE: *Arbejdsmarked*.

Danmarks Statistik (Statistics Denmark): Statistisk Årbog 2005. (Statistical yearbook).

Danmarks Statistik (Statistics Denmark): STO.

Dansk Arbejdsgiverforening (Danish Employers Confederation): *DA Information*.

Dansk Arbejdsgiverforening (Danish Employers Confederation): *DA: Lønstatistik* 2005.

Dansk Arbejdsgiverforening (Danish Employers Confederation): *Wage statistics*.

Det Økonomiske Råd. Dansk Økonomi, various issues.

Ehrenberg R. and R. Smith: *Modern Labor Economics, theory and public policy*, Addison-Wesley, 2005. Textbook.

European Commission: *Employment in Europe*.

European Commission: *Employment performance in the Member States*. Employment rates report 1998.

Frederiksen, A. and N. Westergaard-Nielsen, Where did they go? Labour Economics, 2006.

Hansen, H.: Elements of Social Security. A comparison covering: Denmark, Sweden, Finland, Austria, Germany, The Netherlands, Great Britain, Canada. The Danish National Institute of Social Research 00:07.

Harmon, C., I. Walker and N. Westergaard-Nielsen: Introduction in Harmon, C., I. Walker and N. Westergaard-Nielsen (eds.), *Education and Earnings in Europe*, Edward Elgar, 2001.

Ibsen, R. and N. Westergaard-Nielsen: Job Creation and Destruction over the Business Cycles and the Impact on Individual Job Flows in Denmark 1980-2001, Journal of German Statistical Association, Vol 89.2, 2005.

Jensen, P., M. Rosholm, and M. Svarer, The response of Youth Unemployment to Benefits, Incentives and Sanctions, European Journal of Political Economy, Vol 19, p 301-316, 2003.

Kristensen, N., and and N. Westergård-Nielsen: Does Low Job Satisfaction Lead to Job Mobility? IZA, discussion paper, 1026, 2004.

Ministerie van Sociale Zaken en Werkgelegenheid: *Unemployment Benefits and Social Assistance in seven European Countries*, Den Haag, 1995.

Neumann, G., P.J.Pedersen and N. Westergaard-Nielsen: *Long-run international trends in aggregate unionization, European Journal of Political Econonomy* 7, pp 249-274, 1991.

OECD: *Education at a Glance*, 2005.

OECD: *Historical Statistics* 1960-1984.

OECD: *Labour Force Statistics* 1973-1993.

Pedersen, P. J. and N. Smith (2002), Unemployment traps and financial disincentives to work, *European Sociological Review* vol 18, no. 3. pp. 271-288.

Pedersen, P.J.: Arbejdsstyrke og Beskæftigelse 1911-1970. *Socialt Tidsskrift* 53:2.

Rosholm, M. and M. Svarer, Estimating the Threat Effect of Active Labour Market Programmes, Working Paper, 2004-06, Dept of Economics, University of Aarhus.

Smith Nina: Economic incentives to work (in Danish) in N. Smith (ed.), *Work, Incentives and Unemployment*, Aarhus University Press. 1998.

Velfærdskommissionen, 2004, Fremtidens Velfærd -- kommer ikke af sig selv.

Velfærdskommissionen, 2005, Fremtidens velfærd – sådan gør andre lande, Analyserapport.

Westergård-Nielsen, N.: 20 Years of Labour Market Policies in Denmark in S. Ilmakunnas and E. Koskela (eds.), *Labour Market Institutions and Employment*. VATT Publishers, Helsinki 2001.

Web addresses

www.da.dk (Danish Employers Confederation)
www.danmark.dk (Rules, transfer income and eligibility)

Chapter 6

The Danish welfare model

6.1. Introduction

Denmark has a large public sector, also in international comparison (cf. Chapter 1), and this is considered an integral part of the so-called Danish welfare model. In the policy debate there is a strong perception that this model has some unique characteristics, and the general public and all political parties in Danish Parliament agree that the Danish welfare model or welfare society should be maintained, although there is obviously disagreement on many specific issues.

The term "welfare society" is loose, and it is commonly understood in broad terms as encompassing the norms, institutions and rules in society aiming at correcting the outcome of an unregulated market economy and in particular aiming at a more egalitarian outcome. Although the public sector is an essential and large element of the welfare state it is misleading to equate the two, since the objectives of the welfare society go beyond the activities of the public sector in a narrow sense (therefore the term welfare society may be more appropriate than the welfare state).

The size and structure of the public sector is always a controversial political issue since it raises fundamental questions concerning the balance between market forces and public intervention. The welfare societies which have been developed in industrialized countries reflect the political compromise between markets and public intervention (the third way), and different routes have been followed in different countries, depending on institutional heritage, the local power balance, and other factors.

It is useful to distinguish between three different types of welfare societies or models, namely the liberal, the corporatist and the universal model.[1] The different models are distinguished by the weight given to the

---

1. This distinction was introduced by Esping-Andersen (1990).

153

market, the civil society (family, church, friends, private organisations etc.) and the state in the allocation and distribution of economic resources.

In the liberal welfare model the state plays a residual role in the sense of providing the ultimate floor in cases where the market or civil society does not suffice. State-provided benefits are modest, and the concern about work incentives plays a dominant role. The corporatist or continental European model relies on status and the family as the backbone of society and therefore also as providers of social services. In its modern form private insurance schemes play a crucial role, and they are mostly tied to labour market status. The activities of the state tend to be directed towards families rather than individuals. Finally, the universal or Scandinavian model has the state as a central provider of social services. The rights are universal and defined at the individual level and the activities of the state are financed by general taxation. The level of services provided meet the needs and requirement of most, and the social safety net ensures various forms of income in the case of social events like unemployment, sickness and inability to work but also for education, retirement and pension. In the sense the model is extended.

Obviously, no country can be classified unambiguously as belonging to one of these prototypes of welfare models, but it is clear that this classification captures important differences between e.g. the welfare model in the USA, the UK, Germany and Denmark. Cross-country data on the relative size of the public sector also give an indication of the welfare models adopted in various countries (see Chapter 1 and Section 6.4).

Traditionally, the choice between state and market has been perceived to be mainly a question of efficiency vs equity. The market mechanism is taken to function efficiently, and to the extent that its outcome is judged politically unacceptable, public intervention may be justified to obtain more equitable outcomes, although it comes at a cost in terms of efficiency. If this perception fully captures all relevant aspects, the issue of the extent of the welfare state would basically be a political question of where to place society on the trade-off between efficiency and equity. Moreover, it would imply that cross-country comparisons should reveal that economies with large public sectors or more egalitarian structures should be less efficient. This may show up in lower growth rates or other readily available measures on economic performance. However, despite numerous empirical studies it has not been possible to identify such clear links,[2] reflecting that the issue is more complicated.

---

2. See e.g. Agell, Ohlsson and Thoursie (2006) and Fölster and Henrekson (2006) for a recent exchange of views on this issue.

Economic theory makes it clear why no such simple conclusions can be made. Public intervention may be justified in the presence of market failures, in which case it can contribute to enhancing efficiency. Such failures can take many forms like imperfect competition, incomplete information, incomplete market structures and various forms of transaction costs. Market failures in the provision of insurance are particularly important in a discussion of the welfare state since many public sector activities can be interpreted as social or implicit insurance, that is, the public sector offers services and transfers if various contingencies are realized in a citizen's life. Modern economic theory has shown that this applies not only to public services, transfers and taxation but also more generally to various institutional arrangements, e.g. in the labour market. The provision of social insurance also poses problems in the usual way of interpreting many public sector activities as fulfilling a redistributive purpose. Indeed, there is redistribution in an ex-post sense when we know the contingencies facing people, but in an ex-ante sense they also perform an insurance function - individuals know that these mechanisms are available if they come to need them. This shows that the traditional distinction between public sector activities aiming at correcting market failures and those aiming at redistributive objectives is problematic. Measures aiming at correcting market failures may also often imply more redistribution. This explains why we cannot expect to find simple relations between the public sector size and various measures of economic performance. We have to consider the effects at a more disaggregate level, that is, what are the specific expenses and how are they financed. As an example the effects on economic performance of public expenses may differ considerably depending on whether they are used on education or to subsidize housing.

Likewise macroeconomic policy or stabilization policy should be interpreted in this broader context. The motive for such policies is to reduce the risks associated with business cycle fluctuations, and to avoid the economic and social costs associated with unemployment. Such policies are thus intimately related to the objectives of the welfare society, and they can be interpreted as providing social insurance.

However, despite the fact that strong arguments for public intervention can be made on efficiency grounds there is a reason for concern. Even when such policies exist in theory, they may be difficult to implement in practice, since the ideal policy may require very detailed information on how the economy functions. Moreover, the problem is complicated by the fact that the role and importance of market imperfections change over time. As an example private insurance markets are much more sophisticated today than fifty years ago. In addition political power can be misused in the sense that policy intervention is not always motivated by a desire to correct various forms of market imperfections, but rather driven by specific interest groups or bureaucratic and other forms of rent-seeking activities.

The following sections take a closer look at the public sector as part of the Danish welfare model. Section 6.2 considers the public sector size and structure by characterizing the public sector along three different dimensions, namely, by type of transactions, functions and sectors. Section 6.3 deals in more detail with transfers as a core activity of the welfare society. The financing of public sector activities through various forms of taxation are considered in Section 6.4, while Section 6.5 deals with the public sector balance and debts. Finally, Section 6.6 shortly discusses some of the challenges the public sector is facing.

6.2. Public sector size and structure

With regard to the public sector it is essential to make a distinction between the following three roles, namely, that of *organising, providing* and *financing* particular services or activities. In some cases the public sector has all three roles, while in others it might only have the organising role, e.g. by making certain types of insurance mandatory. In the latter case the state relies on the market for financing and provision, but still the market is not left on its own. In some cases the state may use only the financing instrument to achieve its goals, e.g. by providing subsidies for certain activities or by levying taxes on specific services or commodities. The Danish welfare model has the public sector in a central position along all three dimensions, that is, in organising, financing and providing various services and transfers to the public.

In 2004 total public sector expenses were DKK 794 billion, which amounts to 55% of GDP,[3] the number of public employees was 970

---

3.   While it is customary to see total expenses relative to GDP as a measure of the relative size of the public sector there are a number of problems in such comparisons. As an example the measure of the relative size of the public sector is critically dependent on whether transfers are taxable income or not. Other things being equal the transfer payments are larger in a system which has transfers as taxable income (as the Danish) compared with a system in which they are exempted from taxation. Hence, gross figures may exaggerate differences in public sector size.

thousand, constituting 36% of total employment (see Section 2.7 on public utilities). To understand the functions and structure of the public sector it is useful to split total expenses according to real economic, functional and sectoral dimensions, cf. Table 6.1.

Table 6.1. Public sector expenses, billion, DKK, 2004.

Type of transaction		Function		Sectoral	
Consumption	386	General activities	102	State	479
Transfers	375	Society and social purposes	592	Social funds	26
Capital accumulation	27	Business related activities	52	Counties	87
Capital transfers	6	Non-allocated according to function	49	Munici-palities	203
Total	794	Total	794	Total	794

Source: Danmarks Statistik (STO, 2005). Rows may not sum to total, due to rounding errors.

6.2.1. Types of transaction

The distribution of public sector activities according to type of transaction or real economic purpose corresponds to the distinction typically made in macroeconomic analysis to capture how the resource allocation is affected. The distinction is between direct public consumption, transfers of various forms to households and firms, public investments and capital transfers (includes interest rate payments). Public consumption and transfers are roughly of the same size (49% and 47% of total expenses, respectively), while capital accumulation and transfers are not very important quantitatively.

Figure 6.1 shows the development in the distribution of public sector expenditure according to types of transaction. The growth in public consumption was strong during the 1950s and 1960s, but it levelled off during the mid 1970s and it has since remained fairly constant. The growth in transfers took off in the mid 1970s and kept growing more or less steadily until the start of the 1990s and subsequently it has decreased slightly. This development can be grossly summarized by saying that public sector growth was first driven by public consumption and subsequently by transfers. Although there are differences in the precise timing, most industrialised countries have experienced similar developments although as noted already (see Chapter 1), the relative size of the public sector differs across countries.

Figure 6.1.   Public sector expenditure relative to GDP 1970-2004.

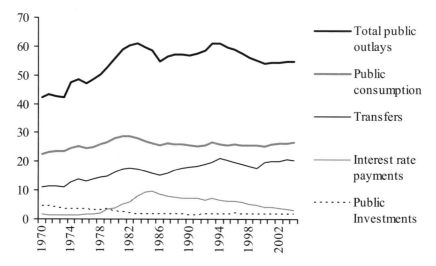

Source: Danmarks Statistik (STO).

Public consumption reflects activities of the public sector which in general have the purpose of supplying the population with various services and opportunities, like e.g. health care and education. These are also sometimes denoted in-kind services since they reflect a choice on the part of society to let certain activities be supplied via the public sector. In the Danish case there is a large universal element, that is, everyone has access to these services. Obviously, some of these services are very close substitutes to private goods, and there are of course possibilities of acquiring additional services in the market, some of which are even subsidised (e.g. private schools). In other areas like health care there has been much opposition to allowing for supplementary market solutions (e.g. private hospitals). There are, however, exceptions to this like dental services, which are left voluntary and with private financing, though with public subsidies.

It is worth noting that of the DKK 386 billion in public consumption in 2004, DK 257 billion were wage payments, and of the remaining difference most is expenses to materials used by public employees. Accordingly, the public sector plays a large role not only in organising and financing, but also in providing services to the public. Outsourcing of activities organised by the public sector is not widespread in Denmark, although there is some, and recently more use has been made of outsourcing. It is currently vividly debated whether outsourcing can improve the efficiency in supply so as to make room for either cost reductions or quality improvements.

Transfers is another major item on the budget and since this is essential to the welfare state, they will be treated in more detail in Section 6.3.

Public investments are largely infrastructure investments, and they have for many years remained at about 1-2% of GDP. Interest rate payment reflects the development both in public debts and in interest rates. Since the public sector increased its debt during the 1970s and into the 1990s, there have been increasing interest rate payments, but they have been gradually reduced since the mid 1980s, partly due to a debt reduction and partly due to falling interest rates, see Section 6.6.

6.2.2. Function

Considering public sector activities from a functional perspective, that is, according to the purpose of these activities, we can make a distinction between on the one hand classical public sector activities (administration, infra-structure, military, police and the system of justice) and on the other hand activities more identified with the welfare state (education, health care, and transfers of various sorts).

Considering the quantitative importance of these broad categories of functions we find that general activities amount to 12% of total expenses, but the bulk of expenses goes to what in national accounts is termed society and social purposes (75%), while expenses to business constitute a small fraction (7%), cf. Table 6.1. Expenses not allocated to a function are e.g. interest rate payments.

For the activities considered here, the public sector obviously has the organising and financing role. The expenditures reflect welfare ar-rangements available to all via the public sector and without (except in few cases) means testing and they are predominantly publicly financed, i.e. via general taxation. This reflects the universal welfare model adopted in Denmark.

Figure 6.2 makes it possible to see in more detail the activities involved under the heading of society and social purposes.

Figure 6.2. Functional distribution of expenses of society and social purposes, 2004, %.

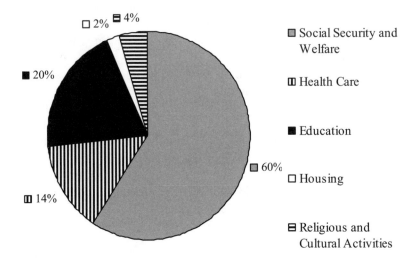

Note: Distribution of total expenses DKK 592 billion 2004.
Source: Danmarks Statistik (ST0, 2005).

It is seen that the largest burden rests on social expenditure which include both transfer payments (see below) and expenditure on various forms of welfare activities. This shows that broadly interpreted social insurance is a core activity of the public sector. Two other important areas are education and health care, which are of course also central to a welfare society.

Note that these numbers only give direct expenditure incurred by the public sector. There are other ways to benefit certain areas, take housing as an example. In the case of owner occupied there is a subsidy due to the combination of deductibility of interest rate payments, and low taxation of the rent generated by housing (tax expenditure), and for rental housing there are subsidies to the financing of housing as well as benefits from rent subsidies and controls (see Section 7.5).

6.2.3. Public sector structure

Finally, we can make a sectoral decomposition of public expenses to capture the institutional structure of the public sector. Geographically there is a three tier system with the state comprising the whole country, which in turn is divided into 16 counties,[4] and 273 municipalities. In addition there are social funds responsible for the administration of e.g. unemployment insurance. While the state is naturally responsible for general government activities like military, the legal system, administration etc., the counties are responsible for hospitals and parts of education (high schools), while the municipalities are responsible for the remaining majority of public activities. Considering how the provision of activities is distributed we find that municipalities are responsible for 43% of total public expenses, while the state directly administers 37%, counties 13% and social funds 6.7%, cf. Figure 6.3.

Figure 6.3.   Public expenditure – sectoral decomposition. Provision and financing, 2004.

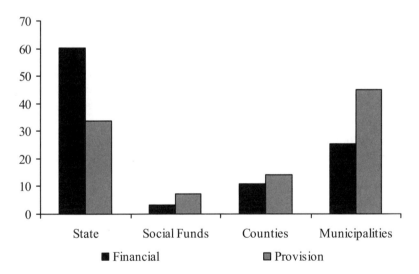

Source: Danmarks Statistik (STO, 2005).

These figures give a misleading picture of the role of the municipalities as organisers and financiers of public activities. Many activities are regulated

---

4.   Including Copenhagen and Frederiksberg Municipalities.

by the central government, and the municipalities are left to administer these systems with no or very limited discretionary powers. To see the importance of this, Figure 6.3 also gives figures indicating the financial burden resting on the various entities in the public sector. It is seen that the bulk of expenses are taken care of by the state (63%) while municipalities only pay 24%, counties 10% and social funds 3%. Hence, we find that the state has 63% of the financing and only 37.3% of the provision, while municipalities have 23.7% of the financial burden, but 43% of the provision.

This separation of financing and provision requires some financial compensation to municipalities, and it has two elements. First, there is a financial arrangement with the state which involves block grants as well as full or partial refunding of expenses to various tasks regulated by the central government. Second, there is an inter-municipal redistribution scheme which redistributes contingent on both the tax base and the expenditure needs in various municipalities. This is in accordance with the universal welfare model adopted in Denmark, based on general taxation (see Section 6.5), and with widespread redistribution also across regions.

The current institutional structure of the public sector is the result of a wide-ranging municipal reform from 1970, which founded the basic principles applying today, although there have been some changes since. The relation between the different layers in the public sector reflects many concerns. First, decentralisation allows municipalities to tailor their activities to the preferences of their constituency, whereas centralised solutions tend to be standardised and less flexible. Second, a decentralised system allows less risk diversification and more heterogeneity among otherwise similar groups in society, which runs counter to basic objectives in the welfare state. Third, a centralised system may be more cost effective to the extent that there are substantial fixed costs or economies of scale involved in many public sector activities. Fourth, a decentralised system may imply inefficiencies to the extent that there are substantial externalities involved among municipalities. An example is the decision to accommodate refugees, where most agree that society is responsible for housing, but most municipalities are reluctant to allow them to settle in their particular area. Finally, the decentralised solution may allow for more institutional competition which can be important for flexibility and adaptability in the public sector.

6.3. Transfers

Transfers of various forms are core elements in the social insurance provided by the welfare state. Alongside the design of the taxation system (see Section 6.5) this is the main channel through which economic opportunities are reallocated across individuals and time.

In 2004, public expenditure on transfers to households constituted DKK 261 billion, which amounted to 18% of GDP. As can be seen from Figure 6.1. transfers relative to GDP were steadily increasing up to the mid 1990s, and subsequently there has been a small reduction. Of the total transfers to households about 80% served to substitute for loss of income, while the remaining include a variety of transfers like child allowances (3% of total transfers), allowances to families with children (5%), housing subsidies (4%), study grants (4%) etc. In most cases transfers are defined at an individual level without any consideration of family status.

Figure 6.4. Transfers compensating loss of income, 2004.

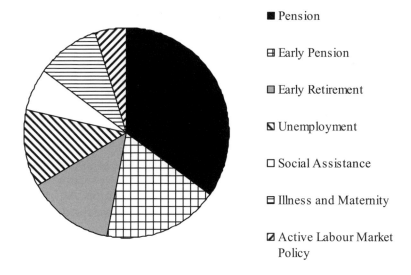

- ■ Pension
- ⊞ Early Pension
- ▣ Early Retirement
- ◩ Unemployment
- □ Social Assistance
- ▤ Illness and Maternity
- ▨ Active Labour Market Policy

Note: 2004 DKK 151 billion.
Source: Danmarks Statistik (STO, 2005).

The various forms of transfers substituting loss of market income are central to the welfare society, and the relative importance of the various forms of such transfers can be seen from Figure 6.4, and Table 6.2 shows the number of recipients of the various types of transfers. It is apparent that the public sector has resumed a larger responsibility for transfers over the years. This reflects the social insurance implied by these welfare arrangements and the fact that unemployment increased to a permanently higher level in the mid 1970s (see Chapters 1 and 5), but it also reflects that welfare ambitions have increased.

Table 6.2.   Recipients of transfers, 1000 persons.

	1970	1980	1990	2004
Pensions	568	677	700	723
Unemployment	24	159	211	150
Social Assistance	41	116	137	103
Illness[1]	37	69	74	123
Active labour market policy	.	.	.	69
Early retirement	.	54	101	191
Early pension	205	236	250	265
Total	875	1,311	1,475	1,625

1. Including maternity in 2004.
Source: Danmarks Statistik: STO 1998 and SE: Sociale forhold, sundhed og retsvæsen 2005:21.

The strong universal element in the Danish welfare model also applies to transfers.[5] The clearest examples are the social assistance scheme and the public pension, both of which are a citizen's right. The base pension in the public pension (folkepensionens grundbeløb) is given conditional on age,[6] and is therefore a genuine universal transfer. Supplementary benefits (housing, medicine etc.) are, however, means tested. Social assistance ("kontanthjælp") is the floor provided by the welfare society to individuals who are unable to support themselves due to unemployment (and who are without unemployment insurance), illness or loss of supporter. There is an activity requirement attached to claiming such assistance and it is vaguely dependent on family income/wealth. Unemployment benefits are not fully universal since membership of a UI-fund is required (see Chapter 5 for details), but via the financing there is a substantial collective element.

---

5.   In many European countries pursuing a continental welfare model, previous income and labour market status are crucial determinants, like the fact that the unit is often the family rather than the individual. The latter implies that the transfers may depend on the income of the spouse etc.

6.   Recently the base pension has been made contingent on your labour income as a pensioner, and hence it is no longer fully universal, but it remains unconditional on wealth.

Despite the large collective element in social insurance there are also examples of publicly organised but privately provided and financed insurance schemes, that is, mandatory private insurance, e.g. fire insurance for house owners and car insurance for car owners.

The case of pensions is interesting since it brings forth different ways of organising social insurance, and also some of the structural changes taking place within the welfare state. Currently, the pension system involves three different models or principles. First, there is the public pension with a strong universal element – everybody is entitled to a base pension and it is fully financed via general taxation. Second, there are collectively bargained pensions which are labour market related and involve some public subsidisation, and finally there are private pension arrangements which also involve some subsidisation via favourable tax treatments. Hence, even if there is a universal public pension there is quite some differentiation in pension coverage across the population which is related both to labour market status (including income) and to individual decision-making.

Finally, it is important to stress that important welfare activities are related to the labour market and they are collectively negotiated, namely, aspects like minimum wages, working hours, wage structure, etc. The fact that labour market related issues are left to be determined by negotiations between the labour market organisations without political interference is the principle defining the so-called Danish labour market model (see Chapter 5). Two important caveats should be pointed out. First, there are many examples of explicit or implicit public interference in labour market negotiations. Second, the agreements arrived at in collective bargaining are not independent of political decisions, e.g. the determination of minimum wages is not independent of the level of social assistance and unemployment benefits, pension agreements depend on the tax subsidy etc.

6.4. Tax burden and the structure of taxation

The welfare model adopted in Denmark has the public sector in an important role, and its universal structure implies that most welfare state expenses are financed via general taxation. With an extended welfare state follows a relatively high tax burden measured as total tax revenue as a percentage of GDP.

Considering the trend in the tax burden it obviously follows the trend in public sector expenditure, although the two need not be tightly linked year by year (see Section 6.6). The general trend for OECD countries has been an increasing tax burden, and the average level increased from 28% of GDP in 1970 to 36% in 2003, see Table 6.3. Denmark has followed this trend. Denmark usually tops alongside Sweden in international comparisons of tax burdens, which reflects the role given to the public sector in the welfare models adopted. In contrast USA has a tax burden in 2003 which is about the same size as in 1970, and which is somewhat below the average among industrialized countries. This is consistent with the discussion in Section 6.1 pointing to the various welfare models and modes of financing chosen in different countries. Note, that the importance of institutional differences applies to comparison of the tax-to-GDP ratio. The tax burden will be much higher if social security benefits are subject to taxation, but it can be downward biased by taxes which increase GDP measured in market prices.

Table 6.3.   Taxes and duties as percentage of GDP in market prices.

	Personal income taxes		Social security contribu-tions[1]		Taxes on goods and services[2]		Other taxes[3]		Total taxes	
	1970	2003	1970	2003	1970	2003	1970	2003	1970	2003
Denmark	19	26	2	1	15	16	3	5	39	48
EU (15)[4]	9	10	7	12	11	12	3	7	30	41
USA	10	9	4	7	5	5	7	5	27	26
OECD[4]	8	9	6	10	10	12	4	5	28	36

2) Labour market contributions and subscriptions.
2) General sales taxes and excise duties.
3) Other income and profit taxes, taxes on wealth, real property etc.
4) Unweighted average.
Source: OECD (2005): *Revenue Statistics* 1965/2003.

The structure of taxation in Denmark differs in important ways from that of most other countries, cf. Table 6.3. Personal income taxes make up a larger part of tax revenues, and social security contributions a much smaller part than in other countries. Moreover, the relative importance of taxes on goods and services is high in Denmark. This is a reflection of the Danish welfare model, and the idea that everyone should contribute to the financing of welfare state activities through general taxation. Given the important role of personal income taxation, sub-section 6.4.1 explains the main principle in more detail.

Indirect taxes in the form of taxes levied on goods and services are also an important source of revenue. For Denmark the Value Added Tax (VAT) makes up about 2/3 of taxes on goods and services while excise duties make up the rest. VAT is a tax on the firm's value added, which in practice means the difference between the sales price and the costs of materials, that is, VAT is added to the consumer price (excluding VAT). The VAT rate is 25% which is the highest in Europe. It is a flat rate applying to all goods, in contrast to all other countries which have differentiated VAT rates (typically with lower rates on e.g. food).

Denmark has a long tradition for levying excise duties on tobacco, alcoholic beverages, and vehicles in particular. The tax on cars[7] is an interesting example of tax incidence. The tax on cars is about 300% of the pre-tax price. This has two implications. First, the average age of the stock of cars in Denmark is somewhat higher than in other countries. Second, car prices before taxes are among the lowest in Europe. The reason being that car producers bear some of the tax burden to avoid that car prices for consumers become too high.

Other important forms of taxation include taxes on corporate income and property etc. The Danish corporate tax rate (28%) has been lowered several times since the peak in 1986 (50%), and the decline has followed a general trend towards lower corporate taxation (see Section 6.7). The property tax rate of owner-occupied flats and houses is 1% of the value based on general public assessment of real property.[8] A county land tax of 1% and a municipal land tax[9] of 1.56% (average 2005) are also based on public assessment of real property. The property value tax as well as the land tax are part of local government tax revenue. In Table 6.3 these taxes are included in the entry "other taxes", and it is seen that they contribute only a small share of general government revenue.

6.4.1. Personal income taxation

The current system[10] of taxation of personal income is based on a distinction between two forms of income, *personal income* and *capital*

---

7. The registration fee has recently been changed from weight tax to Green Owner's Tax. The Green Owner's Tax is calculated on the basis of the fuel consumption of a car.
8. The tax rate is 3% of the value exceeding about DKK 3 million.
9. The municipalities are free to determine their own land tax.
10. Introduced with the tax reform in 1987. A second tax reform in 1994 introduced labour market contributions.

income, cf. Box 6.1 with separate rates of taxation. Personal income comprises wages, salaries, social security benefits, income from self-employment etc. In personal income there is a deduction for payments into pension funds (taxed upon withdrawal) and of labour market contributions.

Box 6.1.

1. Personal income	
	Wages, salaries, fees etc.
	Social security benefits
	Income from self-employment
	Other personal income
÷	Pension fund contributions
÷	Labour market contributions (LMC)
2. Capital income	
÷	Interest payments
	Interest revenues
	Other capital income
3. Income deductions	
	Some transportation expenditure
	Unemployment insurance, union fees etc.
	Deduction for being gainfully employed
1+2-3	Taxable income

Capital income is current income from capital assets, and the tax code includes rather complicated rules for how various forms of capital income enter the calculation of taxable capital income. Taxation differs between positive and negative (net) capital income taxation. While negative capital income is taxed (effectively deducted) at a low rate (currently 33%), positive capital income is taxed at the rate for personal income, and thus at a higher tax rate. One reason for this structure is to avoid the tax loophole which otherwise would arise by converting personal income to capital income. Capital income for all taxpayers as a whole is negative, because deductible interest payments are about four times as large as taxable interest revenues.[11]

Taxable income is the sum of capital income and personal income minus income deductions. Deductions in personal income and capital income are thus also deductions in taxable income. Table 6.4 shows the tax rates and corresponding income concepts in the year 2006.

Table 6.4.   *Personal income taxation. Tax rates and income concepts. Denmark 2006.*

	Tax rates	Income limits DKK 1,000	Income concepts
LMC[1]	8.0	0	Income[5]
Municipal + County	32.7[2]	38.5[4]	
Church	0.737[2]	38.5[4]	Taxable income
State			
Basic tax rate	5.48	38.5[4]	Personal income
Medium tax rate	6	265.5[4]	+ positive (net)
Higher tax rate	15	318.7	capital income
Tax ceiling	59[3]		

1) Labour Market Contribution.
2) Average.
3) Income tax to the state, municipality and county may not exceed 59%. Including LMC, the tax ceiling is 62.4%. Including church tax, the tax ceiling is 63.1%.
4) The income limits are changed every year, and the unused part of 38,500 and 265,500 can be transferred to the spouse.
5) Net profit of personally owned business, fees, wages and salaries etc., without any deductions.
Source: www.skat.dk.

Income taxes are calculated as income minus deductions multiplied by the relevant tax rate. The Danish tax system is progressive since the overall tax rates rise with income.[12] Counties and municipalities have some

---

11. The current tax rate of investment income in pension funds (voluntary and mandatory) is 15%. The Danish tax system also includes a special tax on capital gains.
12. A *proportional tax* yields a constant share of income no matter how high the income is, a *regressive tax* yields a falling share of income with rising income, and a *progressive tax* yields a rising share of income with rising income.

leverage over their tax rates. The sum of the average municipal and county rate in 2006 was 32.7% varying from 27.5% to 35.6%.[13] Municipal, county, and church taxes are calculated on the basis of the taxable income while taxes to the state are calculated on the basis of personal income plus positive (net) capital income.

Table 6.5.   Marginal tax rates and distribution of tax payers in Denmark, %.

	1986	1998	2006
Marginal tax rates			
Lowest rate	48	45	43
Intermediate rate	62	51	49
Top rate	73	62	63
Full-time employed, average rate	58	54	52
Distribution of tax payers[1]			
Lowest tax bracket	35	9	37
Intermediate tax bracket	51	54	23
Highest tax bracket	14	37	39

3) Full-time employed.
Source: OECD: *Economic Surveys. Denmark,* July 2000, p. 87 and Finans-ministeriet (2004): *Fordeling og incitamenter,* p.13. www.skat.dk.

Tax reforms have been undertaken relatively frequently, with recent major changes in 1987, 1994, 1998 and 2003. A concern for the reforms was to reduce marginal tax rates. Table 6.5 reports the marginal tax rates for selected years to give some indication of the changes implied by tax reforms. It is seen that marginal rates have been lowered by the reforms, although the 1998 Tax Reform increased the marginal tax rate for high income groups.[14] Decreasing income tax rates have to a great extent been financed by broadening the tax base, especially by reducing the taxable value of negative capital income (the majority of house owners have a negative capital income because of mortgage interest payments)[15] from 48-73% in 1986 to approximately 33% in 2006, cf. Tables 6.4 and 6.5.

---

13.   Source: www.skat.dk. Denmark has 14 counties and 275 municipalities, a very decentralised structure of the public sector for a small country like Denmark. In 2007, a reform will reduce the number to 5 respectively 98.
14.   The 1998 Tax Reform raised the tax ceiling from 58% to 59% and introduced the specific pension contribution of 1%. In 2004, the contribution was suspended.
15.   From 2002, negative capital income (net) is only deductible in the tax base for the municipal tax.

However, because of the reduced taxable value of deductions many taxpayers' income passed the threshold for paying the highest marginal tax rate. The income level which implies that one reaches the top bracket is now only just above the income of the average production worker. As a result, a large proportion of taxpayers are now paying about 63% in tax at the margin, cf. Table 6.5. The 2003 Tax Reform introduced an income deduction for being gainfully employed (2,5% of income, max DKK 7300 in 2006) and increased the medium tax rate income limits considerably. Therefore, the distribution of tax payers is very much different in 1998 and 2006, see Table 6.5.

Low-income earners may, however, also have a very high implicit tax rate, in some cases much higher than 63% because they not only pay more tax when their income goes up, but also lose part of their social benefits (unemployment benefits, family benefits, housing benefits etc.). The implicit tax rate which combines the increase in taxation with the reduction in social benefits as income rise may even exceed 100%.[16]

One way to assess the overall tax burden resting on labour is to consider the so-called tax wedge giving the difference between the cost of labour for employers and the real purchasing power of wages for employees. This is an important measure of the distortions that taxation creates by making a difference between the cost of labour to firms, and the compensation workers get. Thus, the wedge includes not only personal income taxes and social security contributions, but also indirect taxes.

The Danish tax wedge - about 60% in 2003, cf. figure 6.5 – is in line with some of the other European countries, but much higher than the wedge in UK, Ireland and United States.

16. In 2006, the implicit tax rate is estimated to be 70% or more for about 10% of taxpayers aged 18-66 year. Source: Finansministeriet (2004), p. 199.

Figure 6.5. The tax wedge on labour, selected countries 2003, %.

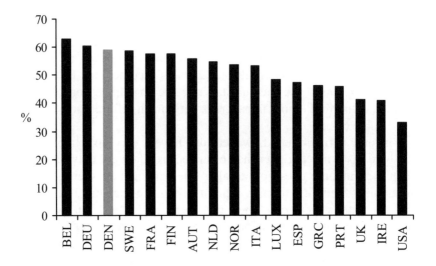

Note: Calculated for an average product worker. Data for Ireland, Portugal, Norway and USA apply to 2001

Source: Velfærdskommissionen (2005)

6.4.2. Redistribution of income

A major objective of the welfare state is redistribution. Redistributive elements arise via transfers, compensating loss of income, and progressive elements in personal income taxation. To shed some light on how much redistribution is achieved via taxes and transfers Table 6.6 shows the net payments per person in households across different income groups. Evaluated in net terms there is redistribution, groups with low income are net recipients and groups with high income are net contributors. Note that a positive net payment in total reflects that government consumption expenditure has to be financed, that is, taxes are not only financing transfers.

Considering the contributions to redistribution through taxes and transfers one finds that transfers are very much declining in income varying from 2% of total income in the high income group to 75% in the low income group. The fact that there is a relatively small transfer income for household income below DKK 150,000 is caused by the fact that those households mostly consist of only one person, in many cases a student.

Table 6.6.   Household income and net payments to general government, 2001-2003, DKK 1,000/household.

Income brackets	Less than 150	150-299	300-499	500-799	Above 800	Total
1 Income	28	110	312	588	1047	366
2 Transfers	88	108	78	45	26	74
1+2 Total income	117	218	390	633	1073	441
3 Direct taxes[1]	31	60	115	202	371	139
4 Indirect taxes[2]	24	36	51	76	105	55
3+4-2 Net payments to general government	-34	-117	89	232	450	120
Net payments per person in household	-34	-78	42	80	145	57

1) Income taxes etc.
2) Production taxes (value added tax, excise duties etc.).
Source: Danmarks Statistik: SE: *Indkomst, forbrug og priser*, 2005:7.

Direct taxes are increasing in absolute terms in the income level, but relative to total income the contribution is almost the same for all income groups (range from 27% of income in the low income group to 35% in the high income group). This suggests that the progressive element in personal income taxation contributes little to redistribution. A reason being that deductions are also increasing in income, and hence in net terms the progressiveness is not very strong.

Indirect taxes are seen to be decreasing relative to income, and they are therefore not contributing to equalization of income, they are said to be degressive. Note that the table does not include information on the distributional profile of public services, where low income groups tend to be benefiting more than high income groups.

Finally, it is worth pointing out that Denmark is ranked as one of the most equal countries in the world (cf. Chapter 1), and Denmark is often singled out as a country with one of the world's highest income levels per capita, and the most equal distribution of income. It is particularly noteworthy that the distribution of income has not become more unequal for quite some years. However, since 1997 the distribution of income has become slightly more unequal.[17]

6.5. General government financial balances and gross debt

Public sector spending and taxation do not necessarily match in each single year. The difference between current revenue and expenditure gives the current surplus of the general government sector, or equivalently gross savings. The overall surplus is obtained by deducting capital outlays (net).[18] If in surplus this equals the net lending of the general government sector, and if in deficit it equals net borrowing. Net lending/borrowing results in a corresponding decrease/increase in general government debt.

Figure 6.6.   General government net lending as a percentage of GDP, 1979-2005.

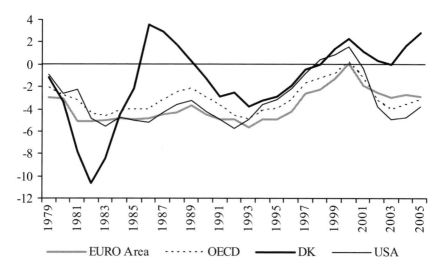

Source: OECD Economic Outlook Database.

Net lending varies considerably over the years. During the 1970s the government was running systematic deficits. In the mid 1980s there was

17. Finansministeriet (2004): Indkomstfordelingen 1983-2002 og set I et livsper-spektiv. www.fm.dk.
18. Capital transfers, gross fixed capital formation, changes in inventories, and acquisition of non-financial non-produced assets (net).

some improvement and a short spell of years with a surplus, subsequent to which net lending has taken yet another U-turn. Currently, the government is running a surplus and debt is being reduced (see also Chapter 1). The swings in public sector net lending are a widespread phenomenon. Figure 6.5 shows net lending, in per cent of GDP, for Denmark, USA, EU and the OECD area. Note that the latter two display less variability since they are calculated as country averages. During the second oil crisis (1979/80) net lending became more negative for almost all OECD countries because of the drop in economic growth rates. After 1990 growth rates improved in the OECD countries, and so did the general government financial balances. The reverse development took place after 2000. The budget surplus means that Denmark has a more favourable position for public finances than most other European countries.

One important reason for variations in public sector net lending is automatic budget response to changes in economic activity. If economic activity is increasing, the tax revenue of the public sector will increase, and some expenditure (e.g. unemployment benefits) decrease. Therefore, there will be a tendency that public balances move with the business cycle such that they improve in periods with high activity and deteriorate in periods with low activity. Figure 6.7 gives some indication of this budget sensitivity to the business cycle, and in a cross-country comparison one finds as expected that countries with larger public sectors tend to have more budget sensitivity than countries with smaller public sectors. The automatic budget reaction has some favourable effects. During a recession the tendency for public expenses to increase and taxation to decrease works to stabilize aggregate demand in the economy and therefore to prevent that a business cycle downturn becomes too severe, and oppositely in a business cycle upswing. Therefore, automatic budget reactions are often termed automatic stabilizers. Automatic stabilizers are an important aspect of the welfare state since they work to stabilize income of households and therefore to provide a form of social insurance.[19]

The automatic stabilizers are as the name suggests automatic, that is, responses which automatically follow when the activity in the economy changes. Another reason for changes is so-called discretionary policy

---

19. Automatic stabilisers are estimated to be relatively strong in Denmark, see OECD Economic Studies No. 30. The general government includes the central government, local governments, and social security funds. The great variation in the general government's net lending can to a very large extent be attributed to fluctuations in central government's net lending.

changes, where policy makers make explicit decisions to change tax rates, unemployment benefits, public consumption, public investments etc. The motivation for such changes can be many, but they will in general affect the level of activity in the economy. This can in itself be a motive for discretionary fiscal policy changes to affect the business cycle development (see Chapter 1).

Figure 6.7.   Automatic stabilizers and the size of public sector, selected countries

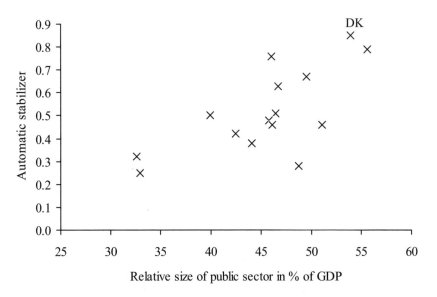

Note: Automatic stabilizers measured by the sensitivity of the budget balance measured relative to GDP to a change in GDP.
Source: Andersen (2004)

In discussions on fiscal policy it is therefore important to have a measure on how changes in fiscal policy affect the level of activity in the economy. This measure is termed the fiscal effect, and it gives the change in GDP after one year caused by the adopted discretionary fiscal policy changes. A positive/negative fiscal effect is tantamount to a fiscal expansion/ contradiction policy. Of course, policy changes normally have effects for several years. Therefore, the fiscal effect is only a rough measure of the immediate effects of discretionary fiscal policy.

There are some interesting observations to make on fiscal policy over the last years. The government tightened fiscal policy from 1982 (negative fiscal effect in 1983-1986), which, however did not result in a period of low growth in the private sector. This was partly because the budgetary squeeze was followed up by a fixed-exchange rate policy (see Chapters 1 and 4), which contributed to a marked fall in interest rates, and which via rising property values made private consumption and investments increase. In 1993-94 a fiscal expansion was used as part of the so-called kick-start strategy to improve the business cycle situation and reduce unemployment. The fiscal effect was positive in 1993 and 1994, part of the fiscal expansion was implemented via the 1994 tax reform which was underfinanced in the first years.

Figure 6.8.   Fiscal effect: First year output effects of discretionary fiscal policy changes.

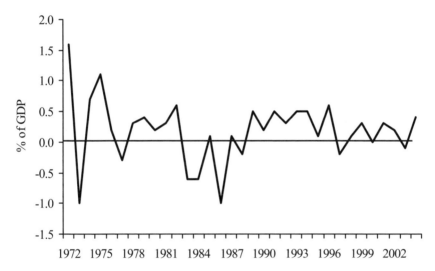

Source: Ministry of Finance *Finansredegørelse* 2004, p. 246.

Returning to the overall stance of public finances we find that a long period in which the government has been in a net-borrowing position (cf. Figure 6.6) has caused an increase in public debt. Substantial increases in public debt levels have been observed since the end of the 1970s in almost all OECD countries,[20] including Denmark, see Table 6.7. Denmark's debt-to-GDP ratio is below the Euro Area average as well as below the OECD average. Due to a considerable consolidation in recent years, the debt level in Denmark has been reduced below the average for other industrialised countries, cf. Table 6.7.

Table 6.7. *General government gross debt as a percentage of GDP.*

	1980	2005
Denmark	45	50
Euro Area	36	79
USA	45	64
OECD	43	79

Source: OECD Economic Outlook Database.

Developments in public sector deficit and debt levels have been much in focus because the Maastricht treaty leading to the Economic and Monetary Union stipulates that budget deficits are not to exceed 3% of GDP, and debt levels are not to exceed 60% of GDP (see Chapter 4). This has influenced fiscal policy during the 1990s in Europe, and there has been a general tendency towards consolidation of public finances. While Denmark has decided not to join the Economic and Monetary Union, it is part of the economic policy pursued to fulfill the fiscal norms to signal that the Danish decision on the common currency is not motivated by a wish to run a more lax fiscal policy. The current position of EU countries with respect to the budget norms can be seen in figure 6.9.

---

20. However, institutional factors make international comparisons of debt unreliable. If the general government sector is defined according to national accounting principles, it follows that general government debt in profit enterprises is ignored. However, parts of the debt in these enterprises is included when general government debt is estimated on the basis of the accounting statistics of the general government sub-sectors. OECD estimates are based on the national account principles.

Figure 6.9. Budget balance and public debt for EU countries, % of GDP 2005.

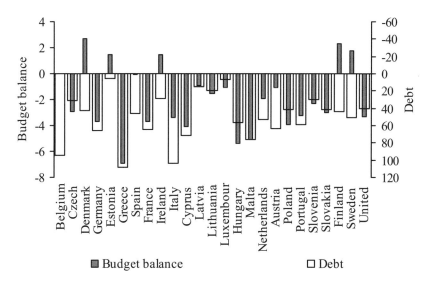

Source: Eurostat

6.6. Challenges to the welfare state

The public sector is always in the centre stage of economic policy debates because of the amount of resources absorbed by the sector, and because of the ongoing debate on the dividing line between markets and the public sector. This debate is currently affected by two major challenges facing the welfare state.

Demographic changes induced by lower fertility are causing a change in the age structure of the population. This is a change affecting all industrialized countries. Current Danish demographic projections imply a gradual decrease in the population of 5% between now and 2070 (from currently 5¼ mio. to less than 5 mio. in 2070). Public finances do not depend on the absolute size of population but on the composition of population between age groups being net-beneficiaries and net-contributors. The projection implies that the number of persons in the age group 15 to 64 will fall by 10 per cent from 2002 to 2040 and by 16 per cent to 2080. In the same two periods the number of old aged (65+) increases by 52 per cent and 47 per cent, respectively. Figure 6.10 gives the projection for the dependency ratio, and it is seen that is reaches a new and higher level. This is mainly driven by the fall in fertility and increasing longevity.

Figure 6.10. Demographic dependency ratio – Projection.

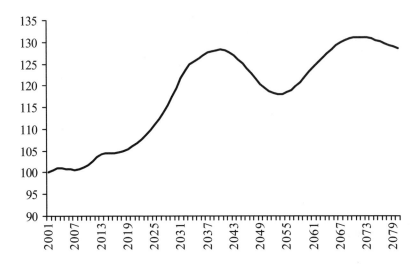

Note: The figure gives the ratio of young (below the age of 15) and old (above the age of 64) to the working age population (age between 15 and 64)
Source: Velfærdskommissionen (2004).

These demographic changes will affect public finances significantly. The reason is basic. There will be more people in age groups primarily being net-beneficiaries of the welfare state, and there will be fewer people in age groups being net-contributors to the welfare state. Figure 6.11 gives a projection for public sector expenditures and revenues given the demographic changes in figure 6.10. It is should be noted that the projection is made under the assumption that current welfare arrangements are maintained, i.e. there is no room for any improvement. The message of the figure is clear, in the medium to long run current welfare arrangements can not be finances. Hence there is a need for a reform to ensure fiscal sustainability of the welfare systems. Should this be financed by an increase in the already at the outset high tax burden? Would it be possible to find areas to save within the public budget, so as to make room for this increasing expenditure? Will the public debt have to increase? Will we have to retire later? Or will we be forced to make cuts in what the welfare state offers to elderly citizens?

Figure 6.11. Public expenditures and revenues.

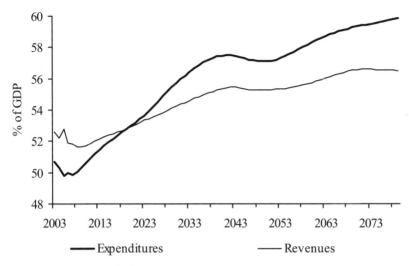

Source: Velfærdskommissionen, 2004

International integration (see Chapter 3) is also creating a challenge to the public sector. This has two dimensions. First, international integration may imply more risk and more rapid structural changes which increase the need for welfare state activities in general. Second, the financing of welfare state activities through taxation may be more difficult since tax bases become more mobile. Since – other things being equal – there is a tendency to choose the location offering the lowest tax rate, there is a risk that tax revenues will be eroded. One example of this is border trade and e-commerce, where customers in both cases can reduce or perhaps even evade paying taxes to the Danish tax authorities. With the globalization of capital markets (see Chapter 4) the possibilities of taxing capital income are deteriorating. If tax bases become more mobile there is also an incentive for governments to try to use taxation (and perhaps some forms of public expenditure) to attract firms to locate in their country. One instrument would be to offer lower tax rates, e.g. corporations. If some countries start doing this other countries will have to follow suit since they would otherwise lose companies. In corporate taxation one finds an example of this. About 15 years ago the average corporate tax rate in

Europe was 50%, whereas today it is approaching 30%.[21] This can be seen as an example of counter-productive tax competition between countries. They lower tax rates to gain competitiveness, but they all do so, such that in the end the relative position is unchanged, but tax rates and thus revenue has been reduced. Another example is that implementation of The Single Market involved the removal of border controls as from 1/1-1993 for private individuals, which meant that people could now bring goods for personal use from one EU country to another. In order to prevent an unintended rise in cross-border trade, duties on beer and wine were reduced in mid 1992 in Denmark.

Very important questions arise on how to design tax systems in an environment in which there is more international integration, and what the scopes are for international cooperation between countries (e.g. within EU) to avoid the negative side effects of competition. Large differences in taxation, combined with free access to foreign markets, will result in tax-based movements across borders, which is not optimal from an economic point of view. Economic optimality requires, for example, that the factors of production are used in those countries where, ceteris paribus, they produce at the lowest social costs, and not just transferred to countries with the lowest tax level.

---

21. See Sørensen (2000). Note that the reductions in rates are partially recovered through broadening tax bases.

References

Adema, W., 2000: Revisiting Real Social Spending Across Countries: A Brief Note, OECD Economic Studies, 30, 191-197.

Andersen, T.M. and T.D. Schmidt, 1999: "The Macroeconomics of the Welfare State", ch 9 in T.M. Andersen, S.E. Hougaard Jensen and O. Risager, Macroeconomic perspective on the Danish Economy, MacMillan Press Ltd.

Andersen, T.M., 2000: Danmark som velfærdssamfund, Frydenlund Grafisk.

Andersen, T.M., 2004, Velfærdssamfund – Økonomiske aspekter, Arbejdsnotat 2004-2, Velfærdskommissionen, www.velfaerd.dk.

Angell, Jonas, Henry Ohlsson and Peter Skogman Thoursie, 2006: Growth effects of government expenditure and taxation in rich countries: A comment. European Economic Review, 50, 211-218.

Christoffersen, C., M. Paldam, and A. Würtz, 1999: Public Versus Private Production. A Study of the Cost of School Cleaning in Denmark http://www.econ.au.dk/afn/abstr99/22.htm.

Danmarks Statistik (Statistics Denmark). Skatter og afgifter. Oversigt.

Danmarks Statistik (Statistics Denmark): SE: Indkomst, forbrug og priser.

Danmarks Statistik (Statistics Denmark): Statistisk tiårsoversigt (STO).

Danmarks Statistik: SE: Indkomst, forbrug og priser, 2005:7.

Danmarks Statistik: SE: Sociale forhold, sundhed og retsvæsen 2005:21.

Danmarks Statistik: Statistisk tiårsoversigt (STO).

Esping-Andersen, G., 1990: The Three Worlds of Welfare Capitalism, Policy Press.

Finansministeriet (2004): Fordeling og incitamenter.

Finansministeriet (2004): Indkomstfordelingen 1983-2002 og set i et livsperspektiv.

Finansministeriet (Ministry of Finance): Finansredegørelse, Various issues (available from: www.fk.dk).

Fölster, Stefan and Magnus Henrekson, 2006: Growth effects of government expenditure and taxation in rich countries: A reply. European Economic Review, 50, 219-221.

Hansen, H. 2000: Elements of Social Security, A Comparison Covering: Denmark, Sweden, Finland, Austria, Germany, The Netherlands, Great Britain, Canada. The Danish National Institute of Social Research, 00:17.

Huizinga, H.P. and S.B. Nielsen, 2000: "The Taxation of Interest in Europe: A Minimum Withholding Tax?", in S. Cnossen (ed.): Taxing Capital Income in the European Union, Oxford University Press.

Knudsen, L.K., T. Larsen, N.J. Mau Pedersen, 2001: Den Offentlige Sektor, Handelshøjskolens Forlag (5. udgave).

Martinez-Mongay, C., 2000: Effective Tax Rates. Properties and Comparisons with other Tax Indicators, Economic Paper 146, European Commission, Directorate-General for Economic and Financial Affairs.

Mortensen, J.B. og O.J. Olesen, 1991: Privatisering og deregulering, København.

OECD (2005): Revenue Statistics 1965/2003.

OECD: Ageing in OECD Countries – A Critical Policy Challenge, Social Policy Studies No. 20, 1996.

OECD: Economic Outlook.

OECD: Economic Studies.

OECD: Economic Surveys. Denmark, July 2000.

OECD: Revenue Statistics.

Pedersen, L.H. and Peter Trier, 2000: Har vi råd til velfærdsstaten? DREAM working paper 2000.6. To be downloaded from: http://www.dst.dk/dst/120.

Plovsing, Jan (2000): Socialpolitik, Copenhagen Business School Press.

Regeringen (The Danish Government), 2000: Et bæredygtigt pensionssystem, (available from www.oem.dk).

Regeringen (The Danish Government), 2001: En holdbar fremtid – Danmark 2010 (available from www.fm.dk).

Smith, N. m.fl. 1998: Arbejde, incitamenter og ledighed, Rockwoll Fondens forskningsenhed.

Søndergård, J., 2000: Velfærdsstatens udvikling i det 20. århundrede og perspektiverne for det 21., Nationaløkonomisk Tidsskrift, 138, 24-39.

Sørensen, P.B., 2000: The Case for International Tax Co-ordination Reconsidered, Economic Policy 31, 429-472.

Velfærdskommissionen, 2004, Fremtidens velfærd kommer ikke af sig selv, Analyserapport, København, www.velfaerd.dk.

Velfærdskommissionen, 2005, Fremtidens velfærd – sådan gør andre lande, Analyserapport, Københvan, www.velfaerd.dk.

Velfærdsskommissionen, 2006, Fremtidens velfærd – vores valg, Analyserapport, København, www.velfaerd.dk.

Økonomisk Råd (Council of Economic Advisors), 1997: Dansk Økonomi Efteråret 1997, Kapitel 2, Løn, Skat og Fordeling. (available from: www.dors.dk).

Økonomisk Råd (Council of Economic Advisors), 2000: Dansk Økonomi Foråret 2000: Kapitel IV Sundhed - En opgave for velfærdsstaten (available from: www.dors.dk).

Web addresses

www.akf.dk (Institute of Local Government Studies – Denmark)
www.danmark.dk
www.dst.dk (Statistics Denmarks)
www.europa.eu.int/comm/eurostat
www.fm.dk (Ministry of Finance)
www.oecd.org (OECD)
www.oem.dk (Ministry of Economic Affairs)
www.sfi.dk (National Institute of Social Research)
www.skat.dk
www.skm.dk (Ministry of Taxation)
www.sm.dk (Ministry of Social Affairs)
www.sourceoecd.org (through university libraries)
www.statistikbanken.dk
www.worldbank.org (World Development Indicators)

Chapter 7

Rules and regulations

7.1. Introduction

In a decentralized market economy, the allocation and distribution of economic resources depends on the functioning of markets. A benchmark case is that of perfect competition, in which prices adjust to equalize demand and supply, and where no demander or supplier has any influence on price determination. In a wide range of situations, competitive markets will achieve an efficient allocation of resources, that is, it is not possible to suggest a reallocation which will improve the situation for some agents without deteriorating it for others.

Perfect competition can not be taken for granted. Market power prevails when a single or a group of demanders or sellers can exert an influence on the price or other conditions to their own benefit. One definition of market power is when producers are able to charge a price exceeding average production costs. In this case, there clearly is an inefficiency and price signals are distorted since the demanders pay a price which exceeds the costs of producing the commodity in question. Market power can be created through mergers or collusions between groups of suppliers or by successful strategic behaviour for instance via product differentiation. Barriers to entry are crucial for maintaining market power, since entry of new firms otherwise would take place in areas with high profitability and thus erode the market power of incumbent firms. An important policy issue is to ensure that markets function competitively, and policy proposals are often made[1] to improve the competitive process. Free and unregulated markets do not, however, automatically ensure perfect competition. The legal framework is important to stipulate for rules of contract formation and to deal with problems in case of breach of

---

1. See DORS (2005), Chapter II and Konkurrencestyrelsen (2005) for a recent discussion of Competition problems and competition law issues.

contract. This is not sufficient in itself sufficient to eliminate imperfect competition as there is a strong incentive to try to establish market power. The Competition Act and the competition authorities play a crucial role and Section 7.2 considers evidence on imperfect competition and explains the instruments used in competition policy.[2]

While the case of perfect competition and the implied efficient allocation of economic resources in many cases is a useful benchmark it can not be used in the presence of externalities. The presence of externalities implies that some effects are not properly captured by market mechanisms. An externality is a cost or a benefit, connected with the production or the consumption of a particular good, which accrues to agents not involved in the market for the good, i.e. agents other than sellers or buyers. Externalities can be both positive and negative. An important example of a negative externality is pollution where a given production activity affects the environment in a harmful way. Private produces do only take private costs into account and they may differ from the social costs. The presence of externalities gives a rationale for rules and regulation to correct for market failures in the price system Energy and the environment are important areas with externalities, which have affected economic policies significantly in recent years, and where various forms of rules and regulations play an increasingly important role. Section 7.3 reviews issues in energy and environment policies.

Even if a competitive market ensures efficiency, the outcome may be considered unjust and therefore politically unacceptable. This is an important rationale for welfare state activities (see Chapter 6) where the public sector has taken a substantial direct role in allocating and redistributing resources. Welfare objectives can also be pursued via rules and regulations for market functions. The agricultural sector is an important example of how price interventions and income support schemes have been used to affect the economic situation of farmers and the domestic supply of agricultural products. Agricultural policy is an EU-policy area, and Section 7.4 takes a closer look at the policy and its effects. The housing market is another market which is heavily regulated among other things because the quantity and quality of housing are considered essential objectives of the welfare state. Section 7.5 considers housing policy in more detail.

---

2. See Lipczynski, J, Wilson, J. & J. Goddard (2005) for a textbook discussion of competition, firm strategy, competition Policy.

7.2. Competition policy in Denmark

The basic principle in Danish competition law is that restricted practices and abuse of market power is prohibited, and that the burden of proof rests with market participants (firms). In the past anti-trust laws were based on a control principle in the sense that no form of market agreement (except resale price maintenance) was prohibited a priori, and that the authorities had the burden of proof in documenting that market power was exerted.

The law has been revised several times and the current law from 2005 reflects a full adoption of the Danish law to international standards. The act has two fundamental rules: a ban against agreements that distort or restrict competition and a provision against abuse of a dominant position in the market. The prohibition principle means that agreements and behavior not in accordance with the rules are illegal. Consequently, the firm risks being fined and sentenced to pay compensation to violated parties, e.g. other firms. In comparison with earlier practice, the Danish competition authorities have used the law to establish a more offensive strategy against agreements restricting competition or abuse of dominant positions in the market, see "Konkurrencenyt" or the annual publication "Konkurrenceredegrelse".[3]

The prohibition against certain anti-competitive agreements follows from §6 in the Competition Act stating that 'Any conclusions of agreements between undertakings etc., which have as their direct or indirect object or effect to restrict competition shall be prohibited'.[4] Examples of prohibited actions include

- Determination of binding purchase or selling prices or any other trading conditions;
- Limitation or control production, markets, technical development, or investments;
- Market sharing or sources of supply;
- Applying dissimilar conditions to equivalent transactions with trading parties, thereby placing them at a competitive disadvantage;
- Making the conclusion of contracts subject to acceptance by the other parties of supplementary obligations which, by their nature or

---

3. See the website of The Danish Competition Authorities, www.ks.dk. All publications can be downloaded free of charge.
4. Consolidated Act No. 785 of 8. August 2005, part 2 §6.

according to commercial usage, have no connection with the subject of such contracts;

- co-ordinate the competitive practices by two or more undertakings through the establishment of a joint venture; or
- determine binding resale prices or in other ways try to make one or more trading partners not to deviate from recommended resale prices.

A similar but stricter set of rules exists for dominating firms, Competition Act §11, which says that '*Any abuse by one or more undertakings etc. of a dominant position is prohibited*'. However, the law does not specify under which conditions a firm has a dominant market position. First of all the market has to be defined in the dimensions of geography and product. How large is the market and which substitute products (from the demand as well from the supply side) should be included in trying to determine the relevant market? Having defined the relevant market firms in possession of market shares above 40%, which has been held for some time, would normally be considered as dominant.

In 2000, the Competition Act was supplemented with rules on mergers between firms. In fact, Denmark was the last EU country to impose effective control on mergers by law. The rules apply to mergers with an aggregate sale on the Danish market of at least DKK 3.8 billion. The competition authorities may attach terms and conditions and orders to its approval of a merger in order to secure pre-merger competition on the market. The most important tools of the legal authority are to require the merged firm to dispose of an undertaking or parts of an undertaking, assets or other proprietary interests or to grant third-party access to e.g. infrastructure. [5]

However, the merger control in Denmark is still rather liberal compared with the other EU countries. In Sweden the limit is as low as DKK 2.6 billion and in Ireland the corresponding limit is as low as DKK 190 million. The relationship to EU competition laws is regulated by a "one-stop-shop"- principle meaning that potential violations of the competition rules are tried by only one authority, i.e. either the Danish or the EU competition authorities.

---

5. §12e. The merger rules are specified in §12 in the Competition Act. By now several merger cases has been decided by the competition authorities with requirement. E.g. MD Foods-Arla and Danish Crown-Vestjyske Slagterier-Steff Houlberg, should sell of part of their capacity as a condition for the mergers. Like vice the mergers in the financial sector e.g. Nykredit-Totalkredit were only approved with terms and conditions.

7.2.1. Indicators of imperfect competition in Danish industries

A number of indicators point to imperfect competition in a number of industries. The most simple indicator of the intensity of competition is the product market concentration rate, which is defined as the turnover of the four largest domestic firms in per cent of the total domestic turnover for the same industry, see Box 7.1. The overall concentration rate include imports in the market turnover (which lowers the simple concentration measure), and this measure has been fairly stable over the recent years, i.e. around 40% for service industry, 23-24% in construction industry. But the concentration index has fallen slightly for manufacturing firms – from 36% to 32 since 1992, which e.g. may reflect the openness of the sector and globalization in general, see Konkurrencestyrelsen (2005). These average figures conceal, however, substantial variations in the concentration rate across industries.

Based on an evaluation using indicators for lack of competition, see Box 7.1, Konkurrencestyrelsen identified 53 industries where competition seems to be imperfect.[6]

It is seen that competition problems are widespread across the private business sector. In manufacturing, lack of competition is prevalent in the food, beverages and tobacco industry and in the building material industry. The former industries are characterized by high concentration, low mobility in market shares with excessive market power as a consequence. The latter, i.e. the building material industry, is characterized by only little competition from abroad. Thus, national traditions in building and building methods serve as an effective barrier of entry for foreign firms producing building materials. In addition, the minimum efficient production scale (i.e. the existence of large- scale advantages in production for incumbent firms) and a relatively high minimum capital requirement for potential domestic entrants might serve as an effective barrier for entry. Therefore, the building material industry can display prices above average and high earnings, without necessarily being effective.

---

6.   The Danish Council of Economic advisors to the government analyse competition problems in Denmark in DORS (2005), chapter 2. They find that more competition in terms of a reduction of the mark-up's on the product- and labour markets in Denmark potentially could affect GDP positively by nearly 6% in the long run. A similar experiment for the EU area would benefit the Danish GDP by 9% - stressing the importance of sufficient competition.

Box 7.1.   The competition authorities' criteria for identification of industries showing signs of insufficient competition.

The extent to which there is insufficient competition can be judged by considering the following 10 indicators in combination with an overall judgement of the market situation, see Konkurrencestyrelsen (2005).

1. The product market concentration rate (CR4), which is defined as the turnover of the 4 largest domestic firms in the industry in per cent of total industry turnover on the Danish market (4-firm concentration ratio), must be above 80%. CR4 is calculated for 600 different industries.

2. The import 'corrected' product market concentration rate (CR4), which is defined as the turnover of the 4 largest domestic firms in the industry in per cent of total industry turnover plus import on the Danish market, must be above 50%. CR4 is calculated for 600 different industries.

3. The degree of competition is reduced because of public regulation.

4. The entry rate of new firms to industry is less than 3% (in manufacturing industries) and less than 8 percent in service industries.

5. The Index of market share mobility at firm level is below 10% per year.

6. The variation in firm productivity within the industry is 25% above average in all industries.

7. The industry return on assets is 50% higher than average in all industries.

8. The industry's wages corrected for education and other characteristics of the employees are 15% above wages in the furniture industry

9. The price level of the particular Danish industry must be at least 3% higher than the corresponding average of EU9-countries.

10. Judgment by the competition authorities

Note that only industries with a total domestic turnover of at least DKK 500 million and at least 600 employees are considered.

Konkurrencestyrelsen (2005) pp 62-66.

Looking at the services industries, high concentration and high prices are the indicators mainly pointing towards competition problems. Thus, public transportation is characterized by high concentration and regulation but as a consequence of effort in order to deregulate, e.g. air transportation and ground transportation, the competition problems have been diminished within recent years.

Table 7.1.   Industries showing signs of insufficient competition, 2005.

Industry	O	K	IK	T	M	SP	L	A	P	V
Mining and quarrying										
Extr. of crude petroleum, natural gas etc.	*	*	*	*	*		*			
Mfr. of food, beverages and tobacco										
Production of meat and meat products (pigs and cows)				*	*				*	*
Production of meat and meat products (poultry)		*	*	*	*				*	
Processing etc. of potatoes		*		*	*				*	
Manufacture of sugar	*	*	*	*	*				*	
Breweries	*	*	*						*	
Mineral water plants etc.	*	*	*	*					*	
Mfr. of dairy products		*	*	*	*				*	*
Mfr. of tobacco products	*	*	*	*	*				*	
Mfr. of paper products; printing and publishing										
Publishing activities, excl. newspapers	*				*	*	*		*	*
Publishing of newspapers	*						*	*		
Mfr. of chemicals and man-made fibres etc.										
Mfr. of refined petroleum products		*	*	*	*		*			
Mfr, of industrial gases		*	*	*	*		*			
Construction materials and mineral products										
Mfr. of plates, pipes, bars and profiles of plastic				*						*
Cement factories		*	*	*	*					*
Mfr. of asphalt, roofing felt and rockwool		*	*	*	*					*
Mfr. of locks and hinges				*	*				*	*
Mfr. of electric switches, relays, fuses etc.	*			*	*			*		
Retail trade										
Dispensing chemists	*			*	*				*	
Electricity, gas and water supply										
Production and distribution of electricity	*				*	*			*	
Manufacture and distribution of gas	*	*	*				*		*	
Steam and hot water supply	*				*	*			*	
Collection and distribution of water	*				*				*	
Transportation										
Transport via railways	*								*	
Taxi operation	*								*	
Scheduled air transport	*						*		*	

	O	K	IK	T	M	SP	L	A	P	V
Charter flights, taxi air services		*	*	*	*		*		*	
Cargo handling in connection with sea transport, harbour	*			*		*				
Airports etc	*	*	*	*	*					
Shipping business				*		*			*	*
Financial intermediation										
Monetary intermediation	*						*		*	
Financial leasing	*					*	*		*	
Other financial intermediation	*					*	*		*	
Financial institutions	*					*	*		*	
Life insurance	*						*		*	
Pension funding	*					*	*		*	
Non-life insurance	*					*	*		*	
Other activities auxiliary to financial intermediation	*						*		*	
Activities auxiliary to insurance	*					*	*		*	
Personal services										
Legal activities	*			*			*			
Medical activities	*							*	*	
Dental activities	*							*	*	
Other health care activities	*									
Other services										
Wholesale of pharmaceutical goods and nursing requisites				*	*	*	*		*	*
Postal services	*			*					*	
Development and selling of real estate		*	*	*	*		*			
Letting of real estate	*			*		*	*			*
Gambling and betting activities	*							*		
Motor vehicle repair and services				*					*	
Refuse dumps and refuse disposal plants	*			*	*				*	
Technical testing and analysis	*		*			*	*			
Motion picture and video distribution		*		*	*		*		*	*
Radio and television activities		*	*	*	*	*	*		*	

Konkurrenceredegørelse 2005 pp 64-66

Note: O: High public regulation, K: High market concentration, IK: High import corrected market concentration, T: Low entry rate to industry, M: Low market share mobility, SP: Large productivity variation within industry, L:High wage premiums, A: High return on assets. P: High prices, V: Subjective evaluation by the Competition Authorities.

Note that the indicators discussed above yield useful information, but of course they do not specify the precise causes and consequences of insufficient competition in each particular industry.

It is clear from the table that many industries have relatively high prices compared to other countries, EU9. For some industries this may be due to public regulation.[7] Thus, 37 of the 53 industries included in the table are to some extent regulated industries. This includes e.g. the markets for newspapers, books and magazines, pharmaceuticals, communication, public transportation, teaching and childcare (the latter two not included in the list). These are all examples of markets or industries where prices are politically determined or subject to other forms of public regulation.

Finally note that higher wages is a potential reason for higher Danish prices. Comparing Denmark with EU9 the table shows that higher wages is a problem in mainly the service industries most likely because of less competition from outside.

Evaluating the Danish competition policy and regulation against other member countries,[8] OECD (2005) finds that Denmark holds a top-7 position among OECD countries with respect to overall product market regulation. However the OECD index of regulation may favour Denmark because industry specific regulation rules are not included in the measure. Still OECD concludes that state regulation and entry barriers have declined since 1998, where a similar comparison of countries took place.

This result is in line with the aim of the competition strategy in Denmark 'More competition – higher Growth' which was launched by the Danish Government in 2002.

7.3. Energy, the environment and sustainable development

Natural resources and environmental issues play a large role in public debates due to a concern for both the sufficiency of resources and sustainability of the environmental assets. This is an area where externalities play an important role which may induce overuse of natural resources and a depletion of the environment. This is complicated by the fact that some of the negative implications develop over time, i.e. future generations will have to bear some of the consequences of current activities. This makes the issue of regulation much more complicated than in most other areas.

The concern for environmental and natural resources gained ground during the golden growth period in the 1960s (see Chapters 1 and 8). In

---

7. In general, public regulation causes higher prices in three ways. Firstly, by hampering competition, secondly by politically determined higher prices and thirdly by increased costs imposed on the business sector by the public.
8. OECD Economic Departments Working paper no 419. See KS (2005) pp 55-58 for a brief overview of the OECD results.

the famous "The Limits to Growth" (Meadows et al., 1972), it was predicted that within a time span of less than 100 years, society will run out of important resources causing a collapse of the economic system.[9] The message was that the observed development was not sustainable. Since then, issues of natural resources and the environment have played an important role. This is reflected in energy and environmental policies in single countries, but also in international initiatives. The latter is reflected in the Brundtland Commission (1987) which defined a sustainable development as a development that meets the needs of the present generation without compromising future generations' ability to meet their needs. However, sustainability was not precisely defined.

This chapter takes a closer look at regulation in relation to natural resources and the environment. Focus is on the scarcity of natural capital since it has been on the economic/political agenda both in relation to the oil crises and the debate on the greenhouse effect (global warming).

7.3.1. Natural capital and sustainable development

Natural capital provides three kinds of returns: resource consumption, waste assimilation and amenity services.

The relation between resource consumption and sustainable development depends on the type of resource. Some resources are *non-renewable*, inasmuch as there is only a given quantity, which diminishes with consumption (oil, metals, etc.). If non-renewable resources cannot be substituted by other resources and they are indispensable it follows that the development is not sustainable.

Other resources are *renewable*, since they over a certain period of time, can regenerate, e.g. fish stocks, trees, etc. In this case, resource consumption is sustainable as long as consumption does not exceed the quantity that is replaceable.

Finally, there are *inexhaustible* resources, which, no matter how much they are consumed, are continuously available, e.g. sun and wind. Hence,

---

9. At the end of the eighteenth century, T.R. Malthus focused on resource scarcity. According to Malthus, there is an underlying tendency for population to grow in a geometric ratio. However, food production can only increase at a constant rate per annum. Therefore, famine and disease caused by malnutrition will put a brake on population increases, and a considerable part of the world population have to live at subsistence level. Since 1798, the standard of living has risen due to industrialization and technological progress and the rising GDP per capita has reduced the fertility rate. Obviously, Malthus was wrong.

the very long term, sustainable development requires that non-renewable resources are replaced by inexhaustible and renewable resources.

Often economic activity and resource consumption result in *pollution*, which is analogous to the consumption of environmental capital, e.g. increased levels of CO_2 in the atmosphere, increased levels of nitrate in drinking water etc. To put it bluntly, nature functions as a waste sink. Using nature as a waste sink has a negative effect on both resource consumption and amenity services. For example, pollution of rivers, lakes and seas affects fish stocks negatively, thereby reducing earnings in the fishing industry. The user of the resource seldom takes these effects into account, i.e. there is a negative externality and this gives an argument for public intervention.

Amenity services include walks in the forest, the prospect of clean streams and rivers, fresh air, birdsong, the variety of species and so on. In other words, nature has a creative as well as a life-supporting value. Amenity services are often public (collective) goods and the consumption cannot be individualised[10] and thus charged for. The market mechanism cannot get used to determine how much of the goods to "produce". Amenity services provide a clear case of market failure.

The presence of external effects in terms of pollution and depreciated amenity services gives a rationale for public intervention. However, what should be the specific criterion on which to base this intervention. While it is easy to agree in broad terms that the development should be sustainable, it is more difficult to provide a precise definition in a specific case. The literature distinguishes between three different forms of sustainability, which lead to quite different policy views. These three definitions are:

Weak sustainability. Subsequent generations should achieve a level of well-being at least as great as the present generation. There is, in principle, no difference whether the fulfilment of needs is met via natural capital or other forms of capital. *Strong sustainability.* The value of natural capital should not decrease. The definition leaves no room for physical capital substituting natural capital.

Environmental sustainability. The physical flows of individual resources should be maintained in a strict interpretation. The strict interpretation of sustainability would lead to total economic breakdown and in reality, the concept is meaningless from an economic point of view. On the whole, sustainability is difficult to define and make measurable.

---

10. This refers to the so-called *free-rider* problem. The individual consumer cannot be prevented from enjoying the good even though he/she does not pay for it.

An important question is which instruments should be used in regulating natural resource use and pollution. The increasing focus on these issues has led to intensified efforts to use legal/administrative and economic instruments in the environmental policy. Legal/administrative control instruments employ bans/approval/orders/emission standards, etc. with accompanying sanctions for violations and agreements/information of various kinds. Economic instruments include taxes, subsidies etc. To attain given goals, use of quantitative restrictions may seem most useful. If the consumption of a resource has to be reduced, we can calculate quantitative restrictions which will ensure that this objective is reached. In practice, there are a number of important problems. First, to ensure that quantitative restrictions are not violated, we have to set up a (costly) administrative system to control the agents upon which the restrictions are imposed. Second, the quantitative restrictions will usually be calculated on the basis of the existing production level or number of firms, so what do we do if the number of firms increase or decrease. Third, quantitative restrictions tend to be proportional, i.e. everybody has to reduce their use by a given percentage. This does not in general yield an optimal solution, since the marginal effects on the environment may be different for different production units. In many cases, a price regulation, i.e. a tax, is much better since it overcomes the problems raised above. The intuition is straightforward, the case for intervention arises because of externalities not taken into account by private agents, in other words the price they pay is too low. Hence, by levying a tax it is possible to make the price match better the true social costs of a given activity.

The measure discussed here is passive in the sense of taking the initial situation for given. A more dynamic perspective is taken by measures aiming at *cost-saving technological advances* which allow for production technologies being less harmful for the environment or for the use of resources that could not previously be exploited, e.g. underwater oil deposits. Technological development also increases the possibilities of replacing/substituting one natural resource with another.

It is important to point out that it is possible to contribute positively to the return from natural capital via the expenditure side and to use resources directly on the natural capital. Fry can be released in lakes and seas, trees can be planted, resources can be increased via recycling, pollution can be reduced by means of sewage disposal plants, cleaning up of toxic dumps, etc.

Finally, it is important to note that substantial information problems often arise not only in respect to knowledge about the environmental issues but also in respect to valuation of these issues (what is the value of having the option to go for a walk in a nice non-polluted forest?). This is in particular made difficult by the fact that inter-generational issues are at stake. Therefore it is not in general possible to measure the trend in total natural capital in monetary units, but there are some exceptions where natural resources are sold on market conditions. Considering these markets can be a useful starting point for assessing whether the resources are becoming more and more scarce indicating an unsustainable development.

7.3.2. Resource prices

Scarcity can be measured as the price of natural resources in relation to hourly wages.[11] Raw material prices have fallen drastically in Denmark in relation to hourly earnings between 1958 and 1972, after which the oil crises in 1973/74 and 1979/80 led to relatively rising prices, cf. Figure 7.1. Since crude oil is the most important international natural resource, the oil market is dealt with more thoroughly. Similar trends are found for other countries, see e.g. Nordhaus (1992). The conclusion is, therefore, that natural resources have become less scarce in relation to the factor of production *labour*. Less and less work is needed to acquire a unit of natural resources. There does seem to have been a temporary reversal of this trend around 1970, however, when oil and raw material prices stopped falling, but in the 1980s and 1990s they fell again.

These developments have been influenced by political developments in the Middle East and by the attempts of the organisation of petroleum exporting countries (OPEC) to control the market. The so-called first oil crisis was caused by the outbreak of war between Israel and Arab countries in October 1973 where the Arab states within OPEC used the "oil weapon" as a means of retaliation. Production was cut back, and countries regarded as being particularly pro-Israeli were boycotted. Even though the production cutbacks were modest in a global context, prices practically went through the roof and the first oil crisis (energy crisis) was a reality. The second oil crisis towards the end of the 1980s was due to political upheaval in Iran (late 1978) and the Iran/Iraq war in mid-1980 pushed prices up even more. These oil crises had an extensive effect on energy consumption in the oil importing countries, see next section.

---

11. The relative oil price trend is often measured by deflating the oil price with a price index for the West's exports of industrial products. The relative price trend then shows the trend in purchasing power of a barrel of oil in the export markets.

Figure 7.1. Raw material price index/hourly earnings[1] and the crude oil price/hourly earnings in Denmark since 1958.

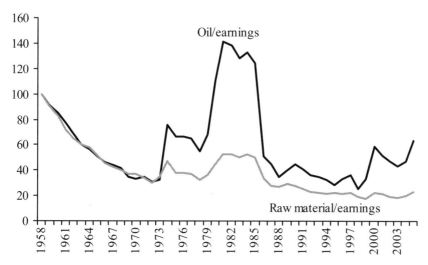

1) Manufacturing.
Source: Danmarks Statistik: SÅ, STO and www.statistikbanken.dk.

To maintain a high oil price, OPEC has tried to implement a traditional cartel policy to reduce supply. Thus, in March 1982 OPEC set quotas for how much oil individual member countries could produce. New quotas have come and gone since then. These agreements could not prevent the price of oil from falling in relation to hourly wages after the second oil crisis, see Figure 7.1. However, since the beginning of 1999 there have once more been considerable increases in oil prices due to the Iraq-crisis and increasing demand caused by high growth rates in China etc.

It is worth stressing that the oil crises were not caused by an alarming fall in global oil deposits indicating an unsustainable development. Consider the R/P rate that measures oil reserves in relation to oil production and thus shows how long reserves will last with unchanged production and no discovery of new reserves. Proved reserves are reserves that are known and economic to recover today. Since 1960, the R/P rate for proved oil reserves has fluctuated between 30 and 42 years and in recent years, it has been over 40 years.[12] Certainly, we are not running out of oil in the foreseeable future.

---

12. www.opec.org. *Annual Statistical Bulletin* and www.bp.com. *Statistical review of world energy.*

The reserves are very unequally distributed across countries. OPEC countries possessed 74% of proved reserves at the end of 2004.[13] However, in 2004 OPECs share of global production was only 41%. In a global context, Denmark is a small oil nation having only 0.1% of global oil reserves (R/P rate 9) and 0.5% of oil production.

7.3.3. Energy consumption

Energy consumption per capita is higher in Denmark than in OECD Europe but much lower than in the United States, see Table 7.2. In 2002, energy intensity in Denmark was two thirds of the OECD average. The reduction in energy intensity in Denmark since the first oil crisis has been achieved as a result of the expansion in combined heating and power plants (CHP), structural changes away from energy-intensive industries to less energy-intensive service industries and better insulated buildings etc.[14]

Table 7.2.   Total primary energy supply (TPES) per capita and energy intensity in OECD countries.

	Toe[1] per capita		Energy intensity[2]	
	1973	2002	1973	2002
Denmark	3.95	3.67	0.24	0.14
OECD Europe	3.08	3.41	0.26	0.18
United States	8.19	7.97	0.43	0.25
OECD Total	4.17	4.67	0.32	0.21

1) Ton of oil equivalent, defined as 10^7 kcal.
2) Toe per thousand 95 US$ PPP.
Source: IEA Databases. World Energy Statistics and Balances. Economic Indicators.

Table 7.3 reveals very significant changes in Denmark's energy consumption by energy source compared with other OECD countries. Denmark has achieved a marked reduction in dependence of oil since

---

13.   www.bp.com. *Statistical review of world energy* June 2005.
14.   Standards on energy efficiency are incorporated in the building code and energy plans are mandatory for all buildings when they are sold.

1973.[15] In Danish power stations, oil has been replaced especially by coal. Danish natural gas supplies were made available in 1984 and because of energy policy being increasingly influenced by environmental considerations, coal is now gradually replaced by natural gas and renewable energy sources in electricity generation.

Table 7.3.   Total primary energy supply by energy source in OECD countries, %.

	Denmark		OECD Europe		United states		OECD Total	
	1973	2002	1973	2002	1973	2002	1973	2002
Coal	10	21	30	18	18	24	22	21
Oil	89	43	54	38	47	39	53	40
Gas	-	23	10	23	30	23	19	22
Nuclear	-	-	1	14	1	9	1	11
Other[1]	1	12	5	7	4	4	5	6
Total supply	100	100	100	100	100	100	100	100

1) Hydro, renewables etc.
Source: IEA Databases. World Energy Statistics and Balances.

In 2004, renewable energy sources (wind, solar power, biomass including waste, etc.) contributed about 15% of total primary energy consumption[16] – a high share compared with other OECD countries, and Denmark's energy plan (Energi21) aims to increase renewable energy to 35% of energy consumption by 2030.[17] Moreover, energy consumption is to be reduced by 15% from 1994 to 2030 compared with an increase in consumption of 20% in the absence of plan initiatives.

Denmark has been self-sufficient with energy since 1997. In 2004, Denmark produced 119% more oil and gas than consumed and here, the production of energy in the North Sea has played a substantial role.[18]

---

15. In the 1960s, Denmark had a rate of growth in oil consumption of about 12% p.a., considerably more than other industrialised countries. Source: Paga and Birol (1994), and *Energistatistik.*
16. Source: *Energistatistik 2004.*
17. Ministry of the Environment and Energy: *Climate 2012* p.59
18. Energistyrelsen: *Energistatistik 2004.*

7.3.4. The greenhouse effect

An important issue related to pollution and the environment is the greenhouse effect. Atmospheric gases, so-called greenhouse gases (GHG), trap solar heat reflected from the earth's surface preventing it from escaping into space. Most important gases are water vapour and carbon dioxide (CO_2) and less important are methane, nitrous oxide and ozone. As a result of fossil-fuel burning in the past hundred years, the concentrations of CO_2 have increased in the atmosphere by about 30%. A clear connection between the concentration of CO_2 and climate changes has not been established so far. Even though the average global temperature has increased by about 1/2 °C over the last century, this is not outside the variations observed in the past.

However, most of the scientific community agrees that global warming will occur due to human activities. Climate change is expected to cause sea-level rise, possible flooding of low-lying areas, melting of glaciers and sea ice, changes in rainfall, changes in the incidence of climate extremes etc.

Estimates of damage costs often concern a doubling of the CO_2 concentration in the atmosphere in relation to pre-industrial level involving a temperature increase about 2.5°C in the second half of the century. This doubling will entail global costs less than 2% of GDP, but with much higher costs in the subtropics and tropics while some people in temperate and polar climates will gain from mild warming.[19] However, the estimates are very questionable. Because of the possibility of much larger costs, many are of the opinion that governments, on the basis of the precautionary principle, should take steps to reduce emission now.

Such a step was taken in Kyoto in December 1997 when a Convention on Climate Change was held under the framework of the United Nations. The outcome of the conference was the Kyoto Protocol where the participating countries (OECD countries except Korea and Mexico[20]) agreed to reduce their overall emissions of six greenhouse gases by at least 5% below 1990 levels between 2008 and 2012. The United States is required to reduce emissions by 7%, the European Union by 8% and Japan by 6%. Burden sharing was agreed by the EU member states in 1998 leaving Denmark with 21% as reduction target.

---

19. Bruce et al. (1996), Nordhaus (1998), www.unfccc.org, and www.ipcc.ch (see Climate Change 2001: Working Group 2: impacts, Adaptation and Vulnerability).
20. Developing countries did not have to come up with reductions.

According to projections, worldwide CO_2 emissions will increase by 35% (reference scenario) between 1990 and 2010.[21] The corresponding figure for OECD countries is 25%. Clearly the policies taken up are not adequate to fulfil the reductions called for in the Kyoto Protocol.

Table 7.4. CO_2 emission data, 2003.

	Denmark	EU(15)	US	OECD	Non-OECD
CO_2 emission/GDP[1]	0.36	0.34	0.55	0.45	0.55
Tonnes CO_2/capita	10.43	8.50	19.68	11.08	2.22
Share of global emission; %	-	13	23	51	49
% change 1990-2003	11	6	18	16	26

1) Kilogrammes CO_2/USD using 2000 prices and purchasing power parities.
Source: IEA: *CO_2 Emissions From Fuel Combustion* 1971-2003. 2005 Edition.

CO_2 emission per capita is relatively high in Denmark compared with the EU(15) while CO_2 emission/GDP is about the same, see Table 7.4. In the United States, emissions are very high compared with other OECD countries and emissions have increased considerably since 1990. Obviously, it will be very difficult for the United States and many other countries to fulfill the KP obligations. In December 2005, the Kyoto Protocol has not yet been ratified by US and the participating countries disagree on how to implement the agreement.[22]

Emissions of CO_2 in Denmark fluctuate markedly from year to year because of weather and variations in electricity trade. Adjusted for these factors, CO_2 emissions have fallen by 16% from 1990 to 2004, very much different from the figure in Table 7.4.[23]

Carbon taxes were introduced for households in 1992 and for industry and commerce in 1993. The effectiveness of carbon taxes is undermined by applying different rates to room heating and heavy and light processes in industry. Economic efficiency would best be served by applying a carbon tax uniformly across all sectors, but this approach would penalise industries competing in international markets.

---

21. IEA: *World Energy Outlook* 2004. 2005 Edition.
22. The Kyoto Protocol's "flexibility mechanisms" (tradable permit system, credit for emission reductions achieved by projects in countries without emission limits etc.) have been debated intensely.
23. Energistyrelsen: *Energistatistik 2004.*

7.4. Agricultural policy

Intervention in the agricultural sector is substantial and affects both price formation for agricultural products and income determination for farmers. This implies that the agricultural sector is heavily subsidized. According to an assessment by OECD, total transfers to EU farmers amounted to USD 320 (DKK 2.522) per capita in 2002 or an income support of more than USD 11.000 (DKK 87.000) per farmer, see Table 7.5. Intervention in agricultural markets is an example of international cooperation on rules and regulation since EU has a common agricultural policy (CAP). The agricultural sector is also an example of a sector in which there are restrictions on international trade, i.e. there is free trade of agricultural products within the EU but not between the EU and other countries. The following explain the basic principles of regulation in the agricultural sector.

7.4.1. EU's common agricultural policy (CAP)

The overall goals of the common agricultural policy is 1) to increase agricultural productivity, 2) to ensure a fair standard of living for the agricultural population, 3) to stabilize markets and guarantee supplies and 4) to ensure reasonable prices for consumers. It is obvious that it is not always possible to meet 2) and 4) at the same time.

The CAP is based on a price support model, which defines a corridor for the price with a maximum price, the *target price*, and a minimum price, the *intervention price*, cf. Figure 7.2. If the market price is between these two limits, the market is left to itself. To prevent the market price from falling below the intervention price, the EU acquires to its surplus stocks in periods with low demand or large supplies. To prevent that the price exceeds the target price, surplus stocks are reduced and if depleted, there is import.

Since the price corridor typically implies a price in excess of the world market price, the CAP cannot be maintained without restrictions on imports. To this end, EU levies duties on the imports of agricultural products, and they are determined at a level such that the import price (inclusive duties and transport costs to the EU's intervention centres) is equal to the target price. Since the world market price typically fluctuates, this means that import duties vary over time, being high when world market prices are low and vice versa.

A special problem arises in cases where there is permanent excess production within EU, i.e. there is systematic intervention to prevent the price from falling below the intervention price. In this case, the surplus stocks will continue to grow, unless the surpluses can be exported. But since the EU price is higher than the world market price, this is only possible by subsidising exports via so-called *export restitutions*.

Figure 7.2.   The Basic Price Model.

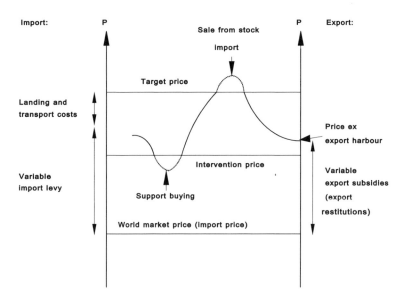

The preceding has outlined the general principles, but the precise implementation varies substantially across different agricultural products. For example, there have been differences in how well or automatically the intervention mechanism has worked (for some products, e.g. pork, there has been no intervention) and therefore in the price support given to various products. In particular, cereals and milk and dairy products have benefited from the schemes, while this is not the case for so-called "grain products" (pork, eggs and poultry).

Intervening in price formation creates additional problems when prices are maintained at a level where production tends to exceed demand within the EU. This problem started to develop during the 1970s and became quite visible in the early 1980s. The CAP came to imply not only higher prices for agricultural products to the dis-benefit of all consumers, but also an increasing burden on the EU budget caused by export restitutions etc.

This led to quantity restrictions to reduce production. An example is the milk quota introduced in 1984 implying that farmers are liable to a high levy if they produce beyond their quota. In 1992, to put a brake on overproduction, the EU carried out a radical reform of the CAP, the Macsharry reform. The reform involves arable area payments as compensation for reducing important intervention prices by about 30% and set-aside payments for land not in cultivation.[24] The beef producers were compensated for price reductions by a rise in payment per head of beef cattle. Because price is replaced by direct payments, the Macsharry reform moves a major part of the burden of the CAP from the consumer to the taxpayer. Moreover, while the distortions caused by the CAP became less visible in the form of surplus stocks, the use of quotas implied efficiency losses since they do not ensure that production takes place at the most efficient farms.

The Agenda 2000 CAP reform reduced intervention prices further, for some products up to 20%. The 2003 CAP reform introduced a single payment scheme to be implemented from 2005. According to this scheme, farmers will be allotted payment entitlements based on amounts received during the period 2000-02. As a result, producer support will, to a great extent, be independent on actual production and consequently, trade distortions will be reduced. All in all, market price support has been reduced and the farmers have been compensated by direct payments. In Denmark, price index for agricultural sales decreased 2% during the period 1993-2004 while price index for domestic supply increased by 19%.[25]

The enlargement of EU with Eastern European countries has created problems for the EU, since agricultural prices in these countries are considerably below the EU level. The ten new member states brings large amounts of land and labour into the EU agricultural sector but less than 10% increase in the value of production due to low productivity.[26] Of course, one may expect productivity to rise in the future. Maintaining the price support system would then pose a major financial burden on the EU budget.

Another critical issue is the role of agricultural products in the process towards more free trade. The CAP has clearly been for the benefit of EU farmers at the expense of EU consumers and farmers in other countries

---

24. Small farmers can receive arable area payments without being required to set aside farmland.
25. Source. www.statistikbanken.dk and Landbrug 2004.
26. Agricultural Policies in OECD Countries 2005 p. 86.

(primarily low-income countries). A GATT treaty from 1993 made fundamental changes in the CAP necessary, among other things, because of its rules for market access.

The GATT treaty contains, among other things, rules for market access. Market access is to be ensured partly by converting all non-tariff border-protection measures, including the EU's variable import levies, to fixed customs tariffs (tariffication), which are to be reduced. In reality, this neutralises the basic price model's import mechanism, leaving only the intervention price. Furthermore, a number of export subsidies including EU's export restitutions must be reduced. Currently, agricultural support is negotiated in WTO. Still, one of the main issues is to reduce trade distortions made by agricultural policies. To a great extent, the CAP reforms meet the requirement for reducing trade distortions.

7.4.2. Agricultural support

The subsidies to the agricultural sector can be evaluated by the producer support estimate (PSE), which is an indicator of the monetary value of gross transfers from consumers (market price support) and taxpayers (budgetary payments) to agricultural producers, see Table 7.5. The market price support is calculated as production volume multiplied by the difference between the domestic producer price and the world market price. Budgetary payments are direct payments as arable area payments, set-aside payments, support for modernization etc. %PSE is PSE as a percentage of gross farm revenue. For 2002-04, the average value for the OECD area is 30, meaning that 30% of gross farm revenue are producer support. For EU, 34% of farm revenue derives from support. Table 7.5 shows that many countries substitute the agricultural sector substantially, e.g. Japan, Norway and Switzerland. The case of New Zealand is particularly interesting since they have liberalized their agricultural sector and almost eliminated all subsidies.

Table 7.5. Producer Support Estimate (PSE), by country.

	%PSE			PSE, 2002		
	1979-81	1986-88	2002-04*	Per hectare[1] USD	Per farmer USD '000	Per capita USD
EU	36	41	34	730	17	336
United States	15	22	17	94	16	350
Japan	60	61	58	9,028	21	566
Norway	69	71	71	2,526	45	638
Switzerland	64	78	71	3,197	32	836
Australia	9	8	4	2	3	93
New Zealand	18	11	2	7	1	48
OECD	29	37	30	182	11	320

1) Of agricultural land.
Source: OECD: Agricultural Policies in OECD Countries: Monitoring and
    Evaluation 2004 and 2005, and OECD: Agricultural Policies, Markets
    and Trade 1995.

The support to farmers paid by consumers can be seen from Table 7.5. The subsidies in EU are slightly higher than the OECD average. On top of the support reported in the table, the consequences of an inefficient allocation of resources both within countries (quotas, arable land set aside etc.) and between countries should be added, because there is not free trade concerning agricultural products. This suggests that there could be substantial welfare gains from a global liberalization of agricultural markets. Ingco (2004) estimates a gain corresponding to 0.8% of global GDP. Finally, it should be noted that the subsidies to the agricultural sector do not imply that current farmers have high incomes, because the subsidies tend to be capitalized into higher land prices meaning that new farmers pay for support to the farmers when buying a farm.

The level of producer support was lower in the new member states (NMS) than in the EU(15), see Table 7.6. Notice that PSE increased substantially in Czech Republic and Hungary during the period 1995-2003 while the opposite was the case in Poland. The lower level of PSE in the NMS was mainly due to lower domestic market prices compared to EU. By reducing intervention prices, the CAP reforms are important with regard to integrating the NMS in the EU agricultural policies.

Table 7.6. Producer Support Estimate (%PSE) in the EU.

	1995	2003
EU(15)	36	36
Czech Republic	11	29
Hungary	13	28
Poland	16	8
NMS (10)	...	24[1]
EU(25)	...	33[1]

1) 2004. Ten new member states (NMS).
Source: OECD: Agricultural Policies in OECD Countries: Monitoring and Evaluation 2005.

7.5. Danish housing policy

Quantity and quality of housing are essential to welfare and therefore the housing market has had a crucial policy concern to ensure an adequate supply of dwellings available at reasonable prices. The housing market consists of rented houses and owner-occupied houses. In total there were 2.6 million houses in 2004. 1.3 million families lived in rented and 1.3 million in owner-occupied housing.[27] The Danish housing standard is fairly high by international standards, see e.g. Velfærdskommissionen (2006).[28] Thus, the number of persons per house has decreased from 3.1 in 1960 to 2.2 in 2004 and at the same time the average size of the house has grown from 92 square meter to 110 square meter. In comparison with EU15 – countries Denmark is found on a 7th position concerning number of houses per capita, but on a 1st position when it comes to per capita size of the houses. At the same time the quality of the Danish Houses is better or at least in the line with the EU15 countries.[29]

To some extent the relatively high Danish housing standard can be explained by regulation and subsidies to the housing market. The regulations and subsidies concerns nearly all kind of houses, i.e. owner occupied houses, rented houses etc. and DORS (2001) found that the total value of direct and indirect subsidies to housing amounted to DKK 30 billion in 1999. Direct rent subsidy was around DKK 9.0 billion, subsidies to investment in non owner occupied housing 5.0 billion. The largest

---

27. See Danmarks Statistik: www.Statistikbanken.dk
28. Velfærdskommissionen (2006): Chapter 12.
29. Velfærdskommissionen (2006): p. 649.

(indirect) subsidy comes from in-optimal taxation of owner occupied houses – DKK 15 billion per year.[30]

The market for rental housing is regulated in various ways. First, there is the legal framework offering tenants substantial protection in the form of strict rules for dismissing tenants. Second, there is a rent regulation in the form of so-called cost-based determination of rents. However the rent control dates back to the First World War and it was introduced to prevent rents to increase too much in a period with substantial inflation. While the rent control was well-motivated when it was introduced and has served the purpose of keeping rents at a reasonable level, there is no doubt that in many cases the rent structure of today is arbitrary, see e.g. DORS (2001), Chapter 3.

The regulation has implied that rents can not adjust to clear the market, i.e. quantity rationing often prevails implying that individuals or families cannot rent an apartment even though they are willing to pay the going rent. In particular for older apartments, the regulations have kept rents substantially below the market clearing level. The situation on the housing market is sometimes characterized in the way that there is a "lottery" in the rental market. The allocation of people across apartments often depends on personal relations to the landowner more than anything else. This may create a lock-in effect where people tends to stay in large apartments even if they do not need them and low mobility and inefficient allocation of persons in apartments is the result (e.g. old people living in large apartments at low rents, and young families living in small but relatively expensive apartments). DORS (2001) finds that the total value of this "lottery-gain" sums up to nearly DKK 8 billion in 1999 for the tenants – measured in terms of rent difference in a situation where the market for rented houses was allowed to clear.

Another and equally important distortion caused by the rent regulation is the decrease in the supply of apartments. With low rents and limited possibilities of increasing the rent over time, there is little incentive for private entrepreneurs to build apartment buildings. In order to increase the supply of apartments, various subsidy schemes have been introduced over time for building societies (social and co-operative housing). Tax relieves have also been used to get pension funds to invest part of their capital in

---

30.   The computations of DORS (The Council of Economic advisors) are in line with Velfærdskommissionen (2006), suggesting that the total subsidy (exclusive of direct rent subsidies amounts to DKK 21-24 in 2005. According to their computations owner occupied houses was subsidized with DKK 11 billion in 2005.

apartment houses. Building societies can obtain state-subsidized loans and direct subsidies to lowering the rent. The annual direct subsidy from these arrangements sums up to nearly DKK 6 billion in 2005, see Velfærdskommissionen (2006).

Another consequence of many years of rent control has been maintenance problems, because house owners had little incentive to maintain and improve apartment housing. Various state subsidies have been introduced to overcome some of these problems, but recently the Danish Government has reduced funds for such renewal programmes and in 2005 the State support amounted to DKK 0.6 billion per year of which sum half is received by private landlords. According to OECD (1999), DKK 100 billion are needed for further urban renewal. Because of the rent control, however, the responsibility for urban renewal has gradually become a financial burden for the public sector in Denmark.

An alternative to the rental market is owner-occupied housing in which the prices are determined by market conditions. Still, the market has been subsidized. Acquiring a house can essentially be compared to acquiring a capital good which period by period produces a service, housing. The Danish tax rules implies that the costs of finance - borrowing (see Chapter 4 on mortgage credit institutions) is needed to acquire the house, i.e. interest payments - are deductable in your taxable income. The value of this deduction has changed over the years (see Chapter 6) and during recent years, it has been substantially reduced to a current level of about 33%. However, the house produces a service which potentially could be sold in the market. Thus the house could be rented to someone else paying a rent. But the owner of the house and the user of the service happens to be the same person for a owner-occupied house. Therefore this service should be taxed, as if the house was rented to someone else. The practice has been to impute a value of the housing service provided by the house, which currently simply is a percentage of the last public valuation of the house. The statutory rate is a 1% tax of the house value per year up to DKK 3 million, hereafter 3% (see however below in the "tax freeze").[31]

The imputed value (and consequently the tax) is generally below the market value of the service for two reasons. Firstly the public valuation of the house is normally below the true value of the house. Furthermore in 2005 house owners are (in most cases) allowed to use the 2001/2002 public valuation of their house in calculating the tax. Secondly, combining

---

31. There are a number of minor exceptions to this rule, the most noteworthy being the discount for retired people.

a tax rate on capital income, which is 33% with the 1% house tax it is implicit assumed that the service from the house is 3% (1% equal to 3%*0,33). Therefore an implicit subsidy is given to owner-occupied housing, because the interest rate on e.g. long term bonds which can be used to finance the house currently is higher - around 5.5% in 2005/06.[32]

While the taxation of the user value of housing has always been politically controversial, it is justified on economic terms. Note that capital gains on owner-occupied housing are not taxed in Denmark as is the case in e.g. Germany and Sweden.

Both the rental and owner-occupied segments of the housing market have thus been subsidized. While such subsidies were justified in the past due to shortage of housing and lower housing standards, it is questionable whether there is the same justification for subsidizing housing today.

The market for owner-occupied housing often attracts attention because prices can vary substantially over time usually driven by variations in the costs of financing house acquisitions and income. It turns out that the income elasticity of housing is rather large, i.e. most people wants larger and better housing concurrently with improvements in income. Moreover house prices vary substantially with the business cycle. Since wealth in housing is one the most important assets for most people, it also follows that non-human wealth varies substantially over the business cycle. Figure 7.3 shows the development in the real housing price from 1968 until 2004. It is seen that the real prices have been cycling but in the long run, there is a reasonable smooth development. The latter is due to the fact that the stock of housing can be affected by building activities (see Chapter 2) and it turns out that the investment activity follows the real price and the business cycle development rather closely. However, in the short run house prices vary substantially since it takes time to build a house and since the flow of new houses is relatively small relative to the stock.

Focusing on the latest 5 years house prices have increased significantly suggesting that the mechanism described above has not been completely at work. However there are several important factors behind the upturn in house prices that started in 1992. Firstly interest rates decreased significantly and reach the lowest level in 50 years in 2005. Secondly, it became popular to finance houses by using short terms bonds with lower interest payments. Moreover, taxation of the user value of housing is

---

32. See Velfærdskommissionen (2006), DORS (2005) and Schmidt (2002) for a more detailed discussion of taxation of houses in Denmark.

frozen by using house values from 2001/02. Finally business cycle conditions have been promising for longer sub periods since 1992. Naturally all these factors stimulate housing demand.

Figure 7.3.   The real price on owner-occupied houses, 1968-2004.

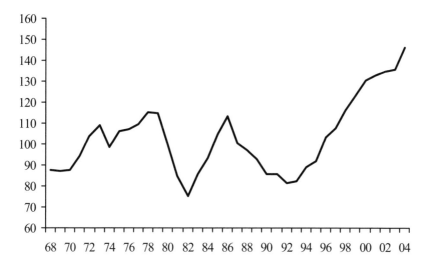

Source. Danmarks Statistik: Statistikbanken and STO various issues.

In general the figure illustrates that the variations in housing prices also reflect an element of lottery in the housing market since the timing of entry or exit from the housing market can have dramatic effects on wealth. This is reinforced by the fact that the rental market is not a flexible alternative to owner-occupied housing. Moreover, transactions costs are substantial in the housing market implying that there can be substantial lock-in effects there as well.

In sum, there are substantial frictions and distortions in both the rental and owner-occupied segments of the housing market. Since the motivation for the regulatory framework of the housing market no longer seems relevant, proposals are often made in the policy debate that time is ready for a more thorough reform. In particular, focus has been on the distortions caused by subsidization of both rental and owner-occupied housing. However, strong interest groups are attached to both segments of the market, and it has been difficult to gain political support for radical changes in the housing market. Velfærdskommissionen (2006) has 11 suggestions in order to reform the Danish Housing market. The proposals include e.g. suggestions to make rent determination in the rental market less regulated over a 20-30 year times span in order to allow rents to reflect quality, size and other characteristics, which normally in a free market affect the setting of rents of housing. Furthermore, the taxation of the user value of housing for owner occupied houses should be increased to 1.5%[33] (instead of 1%) and the exceptions to the taxation should be removed, meaning that e.g. the actual value of the house (instead of the 2001/2002 house value). For the social and co-operative housing sector the rent setting should be deregulated and public support should be more targeted (instead of being general as is the case today).

Velfærdskommissionens proposals are in line with DORS (2005), i.e. The Council of Economic Advisor. They further suggest that capital gains from selling houses should be taxed by using the tax percent for capital income (33%), see also OECD (2006), who discuss the needs for major reforms in the Danish housing policy.

Earlier proposals to deregulation of the Danish housing market include extension of property rights in social and co-operative housing, i.e. making stakes tradable. This would result in extended competition with the owner-occupied housing for all social classes and increased mobility on the housing market in general, see OECD (1999) and OECD (2000).

Concerns about social balance are often mentioned as a reason for maintaining a regulated and subsidized housing market. However, it is a question whether the social aim could be better achieved by separating social and housing policies, so that social objectives are addressed via social policy and not the housing policy, since the latter will distort the market and cause inefficiencies. Furthermore, Velfærdskommissionen (2006) and DORS (2005) even show that – contrary to the intensions of the housing policy – high income groups clearly obtain the largest benefits from the regulation and subsiding of the Danish housing market.

---

33.   1.5% corresponds to the tax of a return on 5% (5%*0.33=1.5%).

References

Bruce et al. (1996): Climate Change 1995. Economic and Social Dimensions of Climate Change. Contribution of Working Group to the Second Asessment Report of the International Panel on Climate Change.

Brundtland-kommisionkommissionens rapport om miljø og udvikling. Vor fælles fremtid. Mellemfolkeligt Samvirke,1987.

Danmarks Statistik (Statistics Denmark): SE: Byggeri og Boligforhold, various issues.

Danmarks Statistik (Statistics Denmark): STO: Statistisk Tiårsoversigt.

Danmarks Statistik: Landbrug 2004.

Danmarks Statistik: Statistisk årbog (SÅ).

DORS (2001): Danish Economy (Spring 2001). The Council of Economic Advisors, Copenhagen 2001.

DORS (2005): Danish Economy, (Fall 2005). The Council of Economic Advisors, Copenhagen 2005.

Energistyrelsen: Energistatistik.

IEA: World Energy Outlook 2005 Edition.

Ingco M. (ed.): Agriculture and the WTO: Creating a Trading System for Development. World Bank 2004.

International Energy Agency (IEA): CO2 Emissions From Fuel Combustion 1971-2003. 2005 Edition.

Konkurrencestyrelsen (2005): Consolidated Act No. 785 of 8. August 2005 (The Act of Competition).

Konkurrencestyrelsen (2005): Konkurrenceredegørelse 2005.

Konkurrencestyrelsen (Danish Competition Authority): Konkurrencenyt.

Lipczynski, J, Wilson, J. & J. Goddard (2005): Industrial Organisation - Competition, Strategy, Policy. Second Edition, Pearson Education, 2005.

Meadows et al., (1972): Limits to growth.

Ministry of the Environment and Energy: Climate 2012.

Nordhaus (1998), see Climate Change 2001: Working Group 2: impacts, Adaptation and Vulnerability. www.ipcc.ch.

Nordhaus, W.D.: Lethal Model 2: The Limits to Growth Revisited. Brookings Papers on Economy Activity, 2:1992.

OECD (1999): Economic Survey 1998-1999: Denmark, 1999.

OECD (2000): OECD Economic Surveys: Denmark, Paris 2000.

OECD (2005): Product Market Regulation in OECD Countries1998 to 2003, Economic Departments Working paper 419. Paris 2005.

OECD (2006): OECD Economic Surveys: Denmark - Volume 2006 Issue 7, Paris 2006.

OECD: Agricultural Policies in OECD Countries: Monitoring and Evaluation 2004 and 2005.

OECD: Agricultural Policies, Markets and Trade 1995.

OECD: IEA Databases. World Energy Statistics and Balances. Economic Indicators.

Paga, E and F. Birol: An empirical analysis in development countries, Annex, OPEC Review Spring 1994.

Schimdt, J. (2002): Beskatning af boliger – hvorfor og hvordan?, Samfundsøkonomen, nr. 1, 2002.

Velfærdskommisionkommissionen (2006): Analyserapport januar 2006 "Fremtidens velfærd velfærd - vores valg", Copenhagen 2006.

Web addresses

www.bp.com. (Statistical review of world energy).

www.dors.dk (The Council of Economic Advisors)

www.ens.dk (Energistatistik)

www.europa.eu.int/comm/eurostat

www.fao.org

www.foi.dk

www.ipcc.ch

www.ks.dk (The Danish Competition Authorities)

www.landbrug.dk

www.oecd.org

www.oem.dk (The Ministry of Economics and Business Affairs)

www.opec.org (Annual Statistical Bulletin)

www.sourceoecd.org (through university libraries, IEA database)

www.statistikbanken.dk

www.unfccc.org

www.velfaerd.dk (Velfærdskommissionen)

www.worldbank.org (World Development Indicators)

Chapter 8

Growth, innovation and education

8.1. Introduction

During the last century, Denmark has experienced a significant economic growth. Since 1900 the economic growth rate has been 2.75% on average,[1] which corresponds to a 15-fold increase in the production level! The main driving force for growth is increasing productivity.

Economic growth creates room for a higher material standard of living. In quantitative terms consumption of goods and services can be increased, and in qualitative terms new opportunities are offered in terms of better qualities and new products and opportunities. The latter includes a choice as to whether the improvements should all be taken out in terms of higher consumption or whether part should be taken out in the form of leisure. Economic growth is usually also associated with improved health status and increase focus on purposes not directly registered in the material output measures, e.g. higher quality of care for elderly people and schooling systems, less pollution and cleaner environment, safer roads and traffic systems with fewer fatal accidents etc.

The aim of this chapter is to review the economic growth of the Danish economy. The next section provides a descriptive analysis of the overall economic growth in Denmark during the last 30-40 years. Growth accounting as a way to decompose the growth process is introduced in Section 8.3, and the important role of 'total factor productivity' is highlighted. Sections 8.4 to 8.6 deal with factors explaining 'total factor productivity', e.g. investments in R&D (8.4), innovation (8.5) and human resources, i.e. the educational level of the labour force (8.6). Finally reflections on knowledge, growth and the role of ICT investments end the chapter (8.7).

---

1. The Danish Ministry of Economic Affairs (1999).

8.2. Growth developments

The traditional indicators for economic growth are real GDP or real GDP per capita. The former showing the change in the total level of production or valued added, and the latter the effects seen relative to the average person.

It has become commonplace to consider a real GDP growth rate of 2.5-3.0 the 'normal' growth rate for modern market economies. Denmark is no exception to this rule. Over the period from 1960 to 2004, the average annual growth rate has been 2.6%.[2] Concentrating on per capita GDP growth gives a picture of potential growth in the material standard of living, i.e. the growth in per capita consumption. In total, the Danish population has grown by 16% since 1960, amounting to 0.4% annually and thus, the per capita GDP growth has grown by 2.3% p.a. However, there are periods with high and period with low growth, cf. the discussion in Chapter 1. In the period 1960 -1973 growth was as high as 4.2% p.a., while it was 1.3% for the period 1974-1981, only 1% for the 1987 -1993 it was only 1% p.a.

Differences in growth rates across countries and various sub-periods since 1970 can be seen from Table 8.1 It is seen that the Danish growth experience is not quite similar to the growth pattern for comparable countries. Thus, in the 1970s and 1980s the majority of the other OECD countries experienced higher growth rates than Denmark. On the other hand, the average Danish growth rate during the 1990s has been higher than in many other OECD countries, but still lower than the US growth rate which continued to be on a high level during this period.

The importance of considering both GDP growth and growth in GDP per capita is also seen from the table. The difference arises of course when population growth is a main cause for the increase in activity. As an example the growth rates for the US are somewhat different when comparing GDP growth rates to growth rates for GDP per capita.

The last two columns introduce the concept of 'trend growth rates'. The trend growth rate is computed from data which have been corrected for cyclical variations across countries.[3] Therefore, trend growth rates give a more accurate picture of the long-run tendencies of the economies.

---

2. See Danmarks Statistik (1995) and Danmarks Statistik (2005).
3. Trend series are calculated using an extended version of the Hodrick-Precott filter, see e.g. Andersen et al (2005) chapter 10 for a brief introduction to the HP-filter.

Except for Denmark, Norway and the US, the trend growth rates suggest a slowdown in economic growth in the 1990s as compared with the 1980s. Finally, it should be noted, that the variability of trend growth rates across countries is lower than the variability of actual growth rates, indicating that the business cycles in the 1980s and the 1990s were not fully synchronized.

Table 8.1.   Growth performance in selected OECD countries, 1970-2003, percentage average annual rates of change.

	Real GDP growth			Per capita real GDP growth			Trend growth of real GDP per capita[2]	
	1970-80	1980-90	1990[1]-2003	1970-80	1980-90	1990[1]-2003	1980-90	1990-2000
USA	3.2	3.2	2.9	2.1	2.2	1.8	2.1	2.3
Japan	4.4	4.1	1.2	3.3	3.5	0.9	3.3	1.4
Germany	2.7	2.2	1.4	2.6	2.0	1.1	1.9	1.2
Netherlands	2.9	2.2	2.3	2.1	1.6	1.7	1.6	2.0
Belgium	3.4	2.1	1.9	3.2	2.0	1.6	2.0	1.9
Denmark	*2.2*	*1.9*	*2.1*	*1.8*	*1.9*	*1.8*	*1.9*	*1.9*
Finland	3.4	3.1	1.8	3.1	2.7	1.5	2.2	2.1
Norway[2]	4.2	1.5	3.2	3.6	1.1	2.6	1.4	2.0
Sweden	1.9	2.2	1.9	1.6	1.9	1.6	1.7	1.5

1) 1991 for Germany.
1) Mainland only
2) Data covers 1990-2000.
Source: OECD (2005c), (2003a), Table 1.1.

While the growth in per capita GDP is most often used as an indicator of the development in material welfare across countries it is important to note that growth also create new opportunities, cf. the introduction. One is that the growth potentials of an economy may be allocated into non-material improvements, which are not directly included in the GDP measure, i.e. it is not registered in the output figures of the National Account. Examples of non-material welfare improvements are shorter working hours and more leisure time, safer methods of production, protection of the environment etc. As the mixture of pure economic growth and other social goals caused by the growth potential of the economies can vary significantly across countries, cross-country growth analyses have to be made with care.

8.3. Sources of growth

8.3.1. Theories of economic growth

There are a number of theories trying to explain the mechanisms underlining economic growth.[4] Traditional growth theory, see Solow (1957), focus on capital accumulation as a fundamental factor behind economic growth. Capital growth increases production capacity. Consequently, savings and net investments in physical capital become crucial for economic growth. Economic growth is therefore mainly explained by increased use of input factors like capital, labour, and sometimes raw materials, energy etc. However, accumulating capital or increasing the labour force does not have a sustained effect on growth because of the law of diminishing returns (i.e. the more use of an input factor in production, the lower the marginal product of that factor). Therefore, the traditional growth theory predicts that in the long-run output per capita (or per worker) will stay constant and will be produced at a constant capital/labour relationship.

Successive technological progress affecting the productivity of capital and labour can, however, create room for economic growth in output per capita. Therefore, the question of what determines productivity of capital and labour is crucial in growth theory.

More recent theories of economic growth focus on endogenous factors that can explain sustained growth.[5] There are several directions of what has become named as 'endogenous growth theory'.[6] One direction focuses on education and knowledge as key factors in determining productivity development. By extending the concept of capital with *human capital* there will be a continuous growth in these models as the educational level increases. Furthermore the production of new knowledge and education (human capital) depends on the existing stock of knowledge and of existing human capital. Accordingly, the theories predict that an economy

---

4.　See The Council of Economic Advisors (1997) pp. 220-224 for a brief introduction to/review of the economic theory of growth.

5.　'Endogenous growth factors' means that these factors are dependent on the level of growth. The theories are denoted 'Endogenous Growth Theories', see for instance Romer (1986) and Grossman & Helpman (1991). The production factors 'education' and 'knowledge' are often denoted 'intangible growth factors'.

6　See e.g. Andersen (2005).

with a high level of knowledge and a large stock of human capital will create more new knowledge and human capital than economies with a lower level of overall human capital.

Another direction of the newer growth theory focuses on externalities being created by knowledge diffusion, which is seen as an important growth factor. Diffusion most easily takes place when R&D is non-excludable, which means that it is not possible for the inventing firm to prevent other firms from using the new knowledge being created, i.e. the R&D is said to be non-excludable. However exploitation of knowledge created elsewhere depends on the firms own knowledge stock.

There are several reasons to assume that the knowledge stock affects the production of new knowledge. Thus, new knowledge can (by definition) be created by investment in Research and Development (R&D). However, the ability to undertake R&D depends positively on the existing level of R&D. In general, new knowledge can be generated via learning-by-doing processes which are typically related to new investments or organizational changes within the firm. The ability to absorb and use new knowledge in internal learning-by-doing processes depends on the existing general level of knowledge.

Furthermore, the ability to absorb external knowledge created by other agents depends on the general knowledge already within the particular firm or society (absorption capacity). If a firm or an economy has a low level of absorptive capacity because it is lagging behind with respect to technological development, the firm or the economy may not be able to exploit the knowledge which is created by other firms or economies. Consequently, mainly firms or economies with a high technological level (i.e. high levels of past investments in R&D and education) are able to exploit the potential gains from 'knowledge diffusion' which is a very important endogenous growth factor.

In recent years social capital has also been suggested as being important for economic growth, in particular in explaining why some countries have been able to initiate a growth process and others have not., see e.g. Putnam (1995). The term social capital is covering aspects like culture, values, norms thrust, institutions etc. and it is therefore difficult to quantify. Moreover it is being debate to what extent the causality runs from social capital to growth or in the reverse, see e.g. Durlauf (2002).

8.3.2. Growth accounting

Growth accounting is a technique for decomposing the observed growth into separate factors that cause growth, see Box 8.1. Table 8.2 shows the growth accounting of the private business sector in Denmark during the period 1988-2000 conducted by the The Danish Ministry of Economics and Business Affairs (2004).

Table 8.2.   Decomposition of growth performance, Denmark 1988-2000.

	Average annual growth, %		
	1988-1995	1995-2000	1988-2000
Gross value added	2.1	3.4	2.6
Capital	1.0	1.2	1.1
Labour, quality	0.3	0.2	0.2
Labour, quantity	-0.7	0.9	-0.1
Total factor productivity	1.6	1.1	1.4

Note: The gross value added in fixed prices is used as the output measure. Source: The Danish Ministry of Economics and Business Affairs (2004), table 31 page 78.

The growth accounting may be done using different measures of production. If a gross production measure is raw materials and intermediate goods should be included as an extra input, because increased usage of raw materials and/or intermediate goods affects gross output separately. If the starting point instead is gross value added only primary factors of production should be included in the analyses because in that case account has already been taken of usage of raw materials and intermediate goods. The decomposition in 8.2 is in accordance with the principles presented in Box 8.1, see equation 3. In both cases the growth accounting explains growth in value added.

The figures in each section of Table 8.2 should be read vertically. The first column covers the entire period 1988-1995, so the average increase in real gross value added for the Danish economy is 2.1%. 1.0% of this increase is caused by extended use capital equipment. The growth contribution from the quantity of labour is negative, equal to -0.7, reflecting lower labour input due to changes in labour force participation, working time etc. On the other hand the quality of labour, which includes the influence from formal education, contributes 0.3 per year to the overall growth. Finally, the 'unexplained' part of the output growth (2.1-(1.0-

0.7+0.3) = 1.6) is due to increases in total factor productivity, TFP, representing the overall productivity development of the Danish economy when controlling for changes in capital and labour inputs.[7]

A comparison across periods of the growth contribution from labour, capital and TFP shows that, TFP has been the single most significant force behind the economic growth. However, note that the growth contribution from extended capital use also is an important growth factor, which may be due to vintage effects of capital, i.e. the latest and most efficient technology is embodied in new machinery and equipment.

Box 8.1. Growth accounting.

Growth accounting is a useful tool for decomposing the overall economic growth into its sources. Basically, the overall economic growth is caused by increases in labour and capital inputs. In addition to capital and labour growth, however, the productivity could increase, meaning that more output can be produced for a given input of labour and capital. This 'residual' growth factor is normally denoted as TFP. The starting point in growth accounting is the production function

(1) $Y = A*f(K,L)$

where Y is output (measured as value added), K is capital input and L is labour input (hours). A is a measure capturing overall productivity. Assuming a simple form of the production function, i.e. a Cobb-Douglas function, where $Y = A*K^{\alpha}*L^{\beta}$, the basic formula in growth accounting can be written as

(2) $\Delta Y/Y = \alpha\Delta K/K + \beta\Delta L/L + \Delta A/A$

where the growth in output, $\Delta Y/Y$, is explained by growth in capital, $\Delta K/K$, growth in labour input, $\Delta L/L$, and productivity growth, $\Delta A/A$. The parameters α and β are assumed to be constants measuring output elasticities of capital and labour, respectively. α and β are the percentage increases in output for a one percent increase in capital or labour. (2) can be used to measure average production increases by its sources. Next, rearranging (2) gives

(3) $\Delta A/A = \Delta Y/Y - \alpha\Delta K/K - \beta\Delta L/L$

$\Delta A/A$ represents all other (residual) factors except for capital and labour which explains the growth in Y. $\Delta A/A$ is denoted 'total factor productivity'. Growth

---

7.   The most frequently used concept of productivity is labour productivity, which can be calculated directly from value added and labour time series. In opposition to TFP, labour productivity assigns all changes in output to labour. Except for situations with declining capital, labour productivity computations result in higher figures than corresponding TFP calculations.

in total factor productivity can be interpreted as caused by changes in factors affecting the efficiency of K and L, e.g. changes in the educational level of the labour force, technical progress, increases in the general level of knowledge, improved organizational skills etc.

(3) is used for calculating the TFP-growth either at the macro level of the economy or at the sub-sector level. Assuming that markets can be described by perfect competition and profit maximizing and that production takes place under the assumption of constant returns to scale, α and β can be approximated by the corresponding factor income shares (rent and wage shares). Thus, knowing the annual growth in capital and labour and the rent and wage share out of total factor income, TFP can be calculated as a residual from equation (3). This is also called Solow-residuals.

This calculation is, however, not without problems. Measurement errors in capital, labour and output growth plus errors stemming from non-fulfillment of the assumptions behind the computations will affect TFP directly. Even if all inputs, factor shares and output are measured correctly, the resulting TFP growth will rely on the level of aggregation of the factors of production. Noting that e.g. labour input is heterogenous and may consist of various educational groups, estimation of (3) at the disaggregated input level will normally result in lower TFP growth compared with estimations based on more aggregate information on labour inputs. Accordingly, comparing growth accounting analysis/total factor productivity from different sources has to be done carefully.

8.3.3. Productivity growth in an international perspective

Has the Danish productivity performance been similar to the experience of other countries? According to Table 8.3, the Danish productivity performance has - as was the case for the overall actual growth rates in Table 8.1 - differed from many other OECD countries. In the 1980s, Denmark had the lowest growth in TFP among the OECD countries included in the table, i.e. only 0.6% p.a.[8] In addition, Denmark had a quite modest economic growth compared with the other OECD countries (except for Norway). However, in the 1990s the situation is completely reversed. Denmark now belongs to the group of countries with the largest growth in GDP as well as growth in TFP, see Section 1.7.

Table 8.3 also includes data on the labour productivity growth, which is defined as growth in GDP per man hour. As expected, the labour productivity growth is higher than the growth in TFP, because the measure

---

8.   The only country having a similar TFP growth was Norway with a TFP growth slightly above the Danish level.

of labour productivity assigns all output growth to labour, irrespectively of the basic source of productivity increase, e.g. investments in new and more efficient machinery. Looking at the 1980s, however, Denmark had a relatively better labour productivity performance compared with its TFP performance, and it remained at a high level for the rest of the 1980s. Consequently, the modest productivity performance in Denmark in the 1980s and better performance during the 1990s is probably due to negative effects from a long period with stagnating investments in the 1970s and early 1980s. The investment rate[9] rose significantly from 1983 an onwards. Time lags in the productivity effects of the capital investment of the 1980s may be an important element in explaining the relatively high productivity growth in the 1990s.

Table 8.3. *Productivity growth in the business sector in selected OECD countries, 1980-98. Average annual growth rates, %.*

Annual growth rate, %	1980-1990			1990-1998[1]		
	GDP	Labour produc- tivity	TFP	GDP	Labour produc- tivity	TFP[4]
USA	3.2	1.1	0.8	3.0	1.4	1.1
Japan	4.0	2.7	1.6	1.4	1.8	0.7
Germany[2]	2.2	1.8	1.1	1.4	2.1	1.0
France	2.4	2.4	1.6	1.4	1.7	0.9
Denmark	*1.9*	*1.7*	*0.6*	*2.3*	*2.9*	*1.8*
Finland	3.1	3.4	2.2	1.5	4.0	3.1
Norway[3]	1.5	1.4	0.7	3.1	2.2	1.9
Sweden	2.1	1.8	0.9	1.1	2.8	1.7

Labour productivity is defined as GDP per employee.
1) 1991-1998 for Germany.
2) Western Germany for 1980-1990.
3) Mainland only.
4) 1990-1997 for USA, Japan and Norway, 1990-1996 for Sweden.
Source: OECD (2000a), Table 10.

Figure 8.1 shows the simple relationship between productivity growth and economic growth for two sub-periods 1980-90 and 1990-98. Using data

---

9. Gross investments in per cent of value added. The investment rate within the Danish manufacturing sector declined from 18.7% in 1974 to a minimum of 11.3% in 1983. However, the economic upturn after 1983 caused investment to rise significantly, to 20% of value added in 1986. During the rest of the 1980s, the investment rate was above 16%, see www.statistikbanken.dk.

for the business sector, the figure clearly illustrates the correlation between TFP growth and economic growth.[10] Countries having significant TFP growth also possess the highest economic growth. However, as noted above the causality might go in the opposite direction.

Figure 8.1. *Business sector GDP growth and growth in total factor productivity, OECD countries, 1980-90 and 1990-98 (per cent annual change, trend series).*

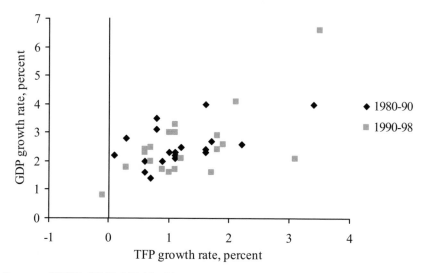

Source: OECD (2000a) Table 10.

Finally note that growth is often associated with openness and international integration. For a discussion of the causes and effects of further international integration or globalization see Chapter 3. International integration may through various channels affect productivity. The main productivity drivers coming from more trade openness are more efficient allocation of resources (countries may specialize in products they can produce effectively), economics of scale (larger markets allows large scale production), higher incentive to invest in R&D and innovation (larger markets gives higher pay off to investment in R&D, which is

---

10. When simple linear regression is used on the data included in the figure (except outlier values for Ireland), a positive relationship between TFP and GDP can be estimated at the 5% level of significance. Including the observation for Ireland, the relationship becomes very significant, i.e. at the 1% level of significance.

normally considered to be risky), more competition (international competition drives up firm's productivity), new technology embodied in goods (investment in new capital goods gives access to the latest technology) and productivity gains via foreign direct investments.

Figure 8.2 illustrates the co-variation between export growth and growth in GDP. The outlier in the northeast corner of the figure is South Korea – perhaps the most obvious example of an economy where the economic growth has been export-led. The figure clearly documents a close relation between trade and growth.

Figure 8.2   Real export growth and GDP growth in 24 OECD countries, 1960-2003.

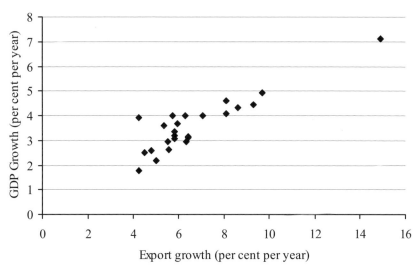

Note: For some countries the time period is shorter: New Zealand 1962-2003, France 1963-2003, Switzerland 1965-2003, Denmark 1966-2003, South Korea 1970-2003. The Pearsons coefficient of correlation is 0.79.

Source: OECD (2005c) and own computations.

8.4. Research and development

Given the importance of TFP growth which factors are driving it? Of course development of new products and cost saving technologies together with international trade has been a crucial factor in TFP growth. However, introduction of new products or new production technologies is basically the result of investments in R&D, either by the firm itself or by other firms. Therefore R&D is an important factor behind economic growth.

Not all firms need invest in R&D. A firm may (by buying the necessary information or a license to a patent or equipment etc.) apply new production technologies or knowledge in general which have been developed by other firms having undertaken R&D, i.e. the R&D producing firm. In that case, the firm using R&D is defined to be innovative, see Section 8.5 where innovation is discussed in more detail. Furthermore, a firm without R&D investments may benefit from the R&D conducted in other firms via knowledge diffusion between firms. The knowledge diffusion process typically works via human capital and thus labour mobility but also R&D cooperation between firms or informal networks. Knowledge diffusion or spillover effects coming from R&D may also arise from public investments in R&D. A notable part of total R&D is performed by public institutions (mainly universities) or through R&D cooperation between private and public firms.

Box 8.2.   Definition of research and experimental development.

Research and experimental development (R&D) comprises creative work undertaken on a systematic basis in order to increase the stock of knowledge of man, culture and society, and to use this stock of knowledge to devise new applications, see the Frascati-Manual, OECD (2004). The R&D concept includes (I) basic research, (II) applied research and (III) experimental development:

(I) Basic research is experimental or theoretical work undertaken primarily to acquire new knowledge of the underlying foundation of phenomena and observable facts, without any particular application or use in view.

(II) Applied research includes experimental or theoretical research in order to acquire new knowledge which is directed primarily towards practical purposes.

(III) Experimental development is systematic work, drawing on existing knowledge gained from research and/or practical experience that is directed to produce new materials, products or devices, to install new processes, systems and services, or to improve those already produced or installed substantially.

8.4.1. Danish R&D expenditure

According to the Danish R&D statistics, the Gross Expenditure on R&D (GERD) was approximately DKK 37 billion in 2003 or 2.6% of GDP, see

Figure 8.3. Comparing with the early 1970s, GERD has been on a rising trend and the average real R&D growth rate has been 5.1% p.a., which is clearly above the GDP growth. The increase in GERD took off from the beginning of the 1980s.

Figure 8.3. R&D expenditure by performing sector, Denmark, 1973-2003, 2003-prices.

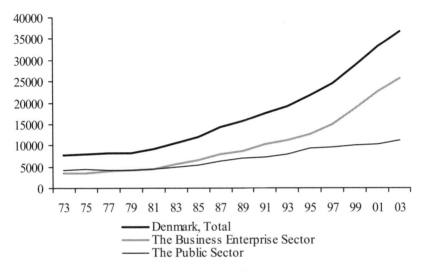

Source: *Danish R&D Statistics*, www.cfa.au.dk various issues.

In addition, Figure 8.3 illustrates that the R&D performed by the business sector has increased faster than publicly performed R&D.[11] Thus, from 1973 to 2003 the Business sector Expenditure on R&D (BERD) in real terms grew by 6.5% p.a., while the corresponding growth rate for public R&D amounted to only 3.2%. In 2003, BERD was DKK 25.6 billion, amounting to 70% of GERD.

In comparison with other OECD countries the growth of GERD has been relatively high in Denmark, although starting from a low level, cf. Figure 8.4. The growth rate was 1.1% in 1981, and 2.6% in 2003. A similar development is seen only for Sweden and Finland.

---

11. Public R&D institutions include higher education institutions, hospitals, museums, public libraries, government financed R&D institutions and private non-profit R&D institutions.

Figure 8.4.   GERD in per cent of GDP, various countries, 1981-2003.

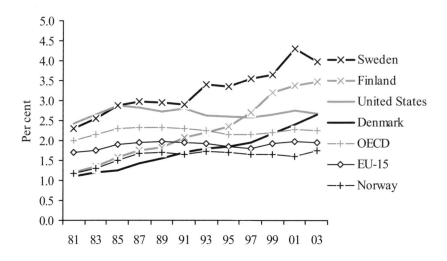

Source: OECD (2005a): MSTI various issues and Eurostat:
epp.eurostat.cec.eu.int

In recent debates on R&D the so-called Barcelona R&D Target plays an important role. In order to make Europe the most competitive and knowledge based economy of the world the EU head of states set the strategic goal in 2000 that European R&D should be increased to 3% of GDP by 2010. The Ministers recommended that public performed R&D should count for 1% of GDP and consequently the private sector R&D should reach 2% of GDP by 2010. Taken together Figure 8.4 and Figure 8.5 clearly demonstrates that while this target may seem within sight for the private sector it looks impracticable for the public sector R&D to reach 1% by 2010. To reach that target that would require an average real growth rate of 5.8% in the public budgets designated for R&D![12]

8.4.2. R&D and productivity growth

The growth accounting in Table 8.2 showed that TFP was the single most important factor behind the overall economic growth. Therefore, it is

---

12. See Velfærdskommissionen (2006) chapter 10 for a review of the Danish R&D status in international comparison.

important to identify factors affecting TFP. In this sub-section we take a closer look on the relation between R&D and productivity.

The theoretical argument is straightforward. The more funds a firm chooses to invest in R&D, the more R&D-based knowledge will be accumulated within the firm. Using this knowledge in the production process, the firm will be able to produce superior products in a more efficient way than other firms. Furthermore, the individual firm can take advantage of knowledge coming from other firms' R&D, the more R&D intensive it is in itself, i.e. the absorptive capacity with respect to use other firms knowledge is affected by the firm's own technological status. The influence of knowledge spillovers depends on the importance of R&D cooperation, informal networks between firms and human resource mobility, which again depend on the number of educated people carrying knowledge embodying R&D, etc.

Studies of the productive influence of R&D can be divided into micro and macro data-based analyses. Macro-based analyses have the advantage of internalising all spillovers and other externalities. Micro-based empirical studies usually give more precise measures of the direct relationship (between R&D and productivity) which is investigated because micro data include less "noise" than (composite) macro data.

There are a few *macro* analyses on the importance of R&D including data for Denmark. The Council of Economic Advisors (1997) finds a positive but weakly significant relationship between R&D investments and TFP growth over the period 1981-93 for a cross section of all OECD countries. Focussing exclusively on Denmark Bentzen & Smith (2000) find a significant rate of return to R&D. Using time-series data for the Danish business sector for a long time period, 1973-1997, it is found that R&D investments most likely affect TFP with a time lag of two years. A number of similar studies exist for other OECD countries, see OECD (2000b) for an overview.[13]

The most clear evidence on the productive effects of R&D stems from analyses using micro (firm) data, see OECD (2000b) for an overview. In these analyses, the direct influence from R&D on the firm's output is measured. Accordingly, accumulated R&D is normally added as an extra capital input parallel to other inputs - labour and other physical capital - in the production function. The majority of the international literature suggests that the output elasticity[14] of R&D typically is in the

---

13. OECD (2000b) pp. 118-120.
14. An output elasticity of R&D of e.g. 0.15 means that a 1% increase in the R&D capital increases output by 0.15%.

neighbourhood of 0.10-0.15. With regard to Denmark, the experience is in line with other countries. Thus, Smith et al. (2004) using data for 1995 and 1997 find that the output elasticity of R&D capital for Danish manufacturing firms is 0.09-0.12. In addition The Council of Economic Advisors (2003) finds a positive influence of R&D on firms output and furthermore there seems to be evidence of positive R&D spillovers from other firms within the industry the firms belongs to.

In conclusion of this section, the empirical evidence is in favour of the hypothesis that R&D investments are important for TFP growth.

8.5. Innovation

Despite the importance of R&D it is a fact that only 20% per cent of the private companies are engaged in R&D activities, meaning that they use economic or human resources for R&D activities. Consequently, during the 1980s policy makers and scientists have become interested in the connection between economic growth and other strategies for innovation that firms can choose.

Innovation is a more wide concept than R&D. According to OECD (2005)[15] innovation is the implementation of a new or significantly improved product (good or services), or process or a new marketing method or a new organisational method in business practices, workplace organisation or external relation. To be considered an innovation it is a minimum condition that the product, the process, the marketing method or organisational method must be new or at least significantly improved to the firm. E.g. a firm is said to be innovative during a particular period when it upgrades its capital equipment, upgrades its human capital by acquiring knowledge from other agents within the economy or promotes new products or designs. If the firm begins to advertise this may be a marketing innovation if advertising is a new marketing tool for the firm.[16]

---

15. The Oslo Manual: Guidelines for collecting and interpreting Innovation Data, 3rd edition OECD (2005b) p 46.
16. Until 2005 innovation was defined solely in terms of the product- and process innovation concept, see earlier versions of the Oslo manual. Both are closely related to the broad defined concept *technological innovation*. Consequently the innovation concept that has been used up till now in e.g. The Community innovation Survey I, II an III, see below, includes product and process innovation but not marketing and organizational innovation.

Box 8.3. The definition of innovation.

According to the revised Oslo Manual, see OECD (2005)[17] four types of innovation are distinguished: product innovations, process innovations marketing innovations and organizational innovations. A *product innovation* is the introduction of a good or service that is new or significantly improved with respect to its characteristics or intended uses. A *process innovation* is the implementation of a new or significantly improved production or delivery method. A *marketing innovation* is the implementation of a new marketing method involving significant changes in product design or packaging, product placement, product promotion or pricing. An *organizational innovation* is the implementation of a new organizational method in the firm's business practices, work place organization or external relations. Product and process innovation comprises expenditure on R&D, investments in machinery and equipment including software, costs for market introduction in connection with new products and processes implemented in the firm. Furthermore, acquisition of external technology such as patents, licences, other know-how and consultant services is included in the innovation concept. Courses and training in connection with the implementation of technological new or improved products and processes are also included in the innovation concept. Organizational innovation comprises e.g. changes in the management structure and general internal structure of the firm, changes in relations to other firms such as joint ventures, partnerships, outsourcing. Marketing innovation includes e.g. changes in sales methods such as E-commerce, franchising, direct sales, increased advertising or significant changes in the look, packing or wrapping of the commodities.

There are several statistical indicators for measuring the innovation activity. Patents can be looked at as an indirect indicator of innovation because the number of patents is the result of innovation activity undertaken before applying or obtaining the patent. The Community Innovation Survey (CIS) includes information of the innovative effort the firms. The discussion below gives an introduction to both indicators.

---

17. OECD (2005b) p 47 ff.

8.5.1. The patent activity in Denmark, OECD and EU[18]

The more patents the residents of a country possess or apply for, the more innovative the country is assumed to be. Accordingly, the annual number of patent applications gives an idea of the innovative activity and by studying the geographical coverage of the patent applications give an indication of the value of the invention, because the firm will seek for patents in more countries the more valuable an invention is considered to be.

Box 8.4. The patent system.

> Patent gives exclusive property rights for an invention for a limited period (usually 20 years) for a specific geographical area. In order to obtain a patent, the invention must be new and original as compared with current standards and in addition, it must be clearly inventive compared with prevailing goods or processes. Furthermore, the invention must include potential for significant industrial use. Seeking patents can be done either by submitting an application via national, European or international procedures. Thus, there is no single overall juridical authority for dealing with patents or intellectual property rights. Instead, the patent system is based on a number of international agreements, which have been ratified by the member countries. The international agreements Patent Cooperation Treaty (PCT) and The European Patent Convention (EPK) are administrated by WIPO, The Worlds Intellectual Property Organization, and EPO, the European Property Organisation, respectively. Patents obtained via WIPO or EPO are mutually respected and also respected by national authorities.

Applying for a patent means that the inventor of new and original knowledge tries to gain the property right of the knowledge for a number of years (normally 20), in order to keep other firms from imitating the product or process that the patenting firm has used resources to develop. Consequently, the patenting system protects knowledge created by the inventor and therefore hinders the productive use of diffusion of

---

18. This section relies partly on Madsen et al. (2000), who analyse the patent and R&D activity in Denmark. Their basic conclusion is that Denmark is far from lagging behind technologically. On the contrary, Denmark is on level with the other EU countries with respect to patent activity and there is some evidence that the potential value of the Danish patents ranks relatively higher than in comparable countries. This conclusion is supported by Botazzi (2004) who shows that certain EU countries e.g. Denmark and Finland obtain more innovation from a given level of R&D than other EU member countries.

knowledge to other firms. From a social point of view, barriers for using new knowledge may be considered as sub-optimal. Knowledge is a public good and restricting use of it is not optimal, especially if it further implies that some can exert some market power based on it. However, protection from immediate imitation is necessary in order to stimulate firms to engage in R&D and innovation activities, as these activities are normally considered as risky in an economic sense. Without the opportunity of patenting new ideas, the growth in privately produced knowledge would be to low. The patent system can be seen as a tool for balancing these opposite considerations in order to reach some kind of social optimal level of innovation.

8.5.2. Developments in patent activities of Danish firms

Figure 8.5 illustrates the patents of Danish firms since 1985. The figure clearly illustrates that over the entire period the number of patent applications has increased significantly. Thus, in 2003 the number of resident patent applications was 33 per 100,000 inhabitants, i.e. a more than 100% increase since the mid eighties.

Figure 8.5 also includes the development in triadic patent families per mio. capita held by Danish residents. OECD (2005a)[19] defines triadic patent families, defined as a set of patents filed at the European Patent Office (EPO), The Japanese Patent Office (JPO) and is granted by the US Patent & Trademark Office (USPTO). Triadic patent families gives an indication of the value of the Danish patents. The more valuable the more likely it is that the patent application is extended to more countries. The curve is relatively flat and the number of triadic patents filed in 2003 was around 40 per mio. capita.

Furthermore the figure includes the R&D intensity of the Danish economy as a whole and of the business sector alone. Obviously, there is a positive correlation between the R&D effort, which can be seen as the input in the Danish innovation process and the patent activities.

---

19.   OECD (2005a) pp 69-70

Figure 8.5. *Resident patent applications, number of triadic patent families held by residents (right axis), business and total R&D intensity (left axis), Denmark 1985-2003.*

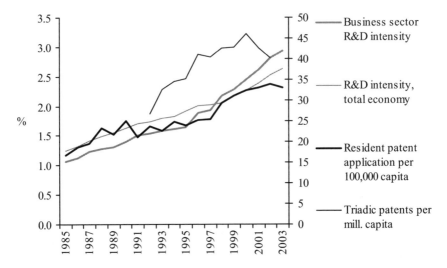

Note: The R&D intensity is defined as the R&D expenditure in per cent of the relevant value added.

Source: MSTI various issues, OECD.

Table 8.4 shows that the patenting activity in Danish firms in international comparison. By using triadic patent families the international comparability of patents is strengthened because the values of the patents are more homogenous across countries. The table shows that the Danish patent activity is significantly below the OECD level. The OECD average is, however, strongly affected by East-Asian countries like Japan and Korea who have traditions for extremely intensive patent seeking. Still, looking at the figures in table it is only countries like Norway and France who are performing worse or like Denmark. Thus the patenting activity is significantly higher in Sweden and Finland.

The superior development in patents and R&D in Sweden and Finland is caused by higher R&D-intensity a the firm level, an industry structure which is beneficial to R&D, i.e. a high fraction of firms in high tech industries and finally specialisation in industries where the particular country has a relative high R&D-intensity. In case of Danish only the latter - the specialisation effect - matters, see Smith (2001).

Table 8.4. R&D and triadic patent families, 2002.

Country	R&D-intensity	Triadic patent families		
		Number 2002	Annual growth 1992-2002 (%)	Number of triadic patent families per mio. capita 2002.
Denmark	2.39	216	4.6	40.2
Finland	3.38	594	10.2	114.2
Norway	1.40	106	3.2	23.4
Sweden	4.29	896	5.1	100.4
Germany	2.46	7,271	6.4	88.1
France	2.30	2,447	4.0	40.0
USA	2.76	18,324	5.1	63.7
Japan	3.07	13,195	4.9	103.5
OECD	2.28	50,494	5.3	48.4

Note: The R&D intensity relates to 2001 and it is measured as Gross Expenditure on R&D (GERD) in per cent of Gross Value Added. The figures on triadic patent families are national results adjusted to meet OECD norms. Some countries report provisional data. Triadic patent families is defined as a set of patents filed at the European Patent Office (EPO), The Japanese Patent Office (JPO) and is granted by the US Patent & Trademark Office (USPTO).

Source: OECD MSTI 2005:2, OECD (2005a).

8.5.3. Innovation expenditure and intensity

Innovation across sectors is shown in Table 8.5 giving the share of firms engaged in innovative activities. Overall Denmark is at the EU average, but somewhat behind the other Nordic countries except Norway. Interestingly the service sector has a relatively low level of innovating firms whereas manufacturing has a high level by international standards.

Table 8.5.   Percentage of innovating firms in the Nordic countries and EU, 1998-2000.

	Denmark	Finland	Iceland	Norway	Sweden	CIS III avg.
Manufacturing	52	49	56	39	47	47
Service	37	40	54	34	46	40
Total industry	44	45	55	36	47	44

Source: Eurostat 61/2004, epp.eurostat.cec.eu.int.

An important question is whether innovating firms account for employment creation According to Christensen (1999), product innovation in manufacturing firms accounted for a positive employment change of 6.7% in CISII. The corresponding figure for process-oriented innovation was significantly lower, i.e. process innovation only accounted for an employment change of 0.3% within the manufacturing firms. Finally, innovation in service industries had a positive influence of 3.9% on employment.[20] An alternative indicator of the growth stimulating effect of innovation is the share of firms' turnover in 2000 that could be referred to technologically new or improved products introduced in 1998-2000, see Table 8.6.

It is easily seen that Finland and Sweden are relatively successful in turning innovation into commercial products. Denmark is lagging a little behind these two countries but do have a medium position among the countries included in the table. Consequently the share of turnover caused by innovation in manufacturing industries is significantly higher in Denmark as compared to Norway, Iceland and Belgium. Looking at service industries the share of turnover caused by innovation is higher in Denmark as compared to Norway, Iceland and The Netherlands.

Table 8.6.   *Share of turnover in 2000 from new/improved products caused by innovation in 1998-2000 as per cent of total turnover in manufacturing and service industries, small North European Countries.*

	Denmark	Finland	Island	Norway	Sweden	Belgium	Netherlands
Manufacturing	24	31	9	18	38	16	24
Service	18	24	3	10	25	23	13

Source: Norges Forskningsråd (2003)

8.6. Education

Human capital is very important for economic growth, cf. also Section 8.3. Much new knowledge is acquired and transmitted via both formal and on the job-training, experience etc. Accordingly knowledge embedded in humans - human capital – is one of the most important channels through which new knowledge is transmitted in society. Growth in human capital

---

20. Note that due to a low overall response rate in CISII these figures should be taken with caution.

is closely related to the educational level of the labour force. A weakness of growth accounting is that the effects of human capital is both appearing in the part which can be attributed to increases in formal educational levels of the work force but also in TFP.[21]

There are various ways of assessing the role of education for both historical growth rates and the potential for future growth. One is to compare the education level across countries and generations. Doing so for Denmark reveals two striking conclusion. First, younger generations tend to be better educated than older generation, see also Chapter 5. This reflects increases in educational investments and efforts over the years. However, improvements for the youngest generations are not as striking as in the past. This is in part caused by late start and late graduation. It is also the case that about 1/5 of a new generation does not obtain any education or formal qualification beyond basic schooling (folkeskolen). Second, in international comparison it may be that Denmark in the past has had a leading position, but in recent comparisons the position is towards the average (see OECD, Velfærdskommissionen). This is partly explained by the facts noted above and partly by the fact that a number of countries have improved their educational levels substantially.

The role of education can also be evaluated by taking a macroeconomic approach in trying to estimate the effects. In an analysis of the role of education for growth the Council of Economic Advisors (2003) finds that between 50% and 90% of TFP growth can be attributed to education and research. This is a significant part, and yet the wide band reflects the measurement problems mentioned above.

An alternative way to analyse the implications of education is to consider both the private and social returns to education based the private and social benefits and costs of education. The former includes effects of education on wages and employment, and the costs comprise direct costs of education and foregone income during education. Considering the private return there are substantial difference across educations. In general the return to education tends to be related to the duration of the education, but there are some deviations since some forms of vocational training (business, financial sector and agriculture) have high returns, cf. Council of Economic Advisors (2003). In general the private return is higher than the opportunity cost, i.e. the market rate of interest. Considering the social return it is also the case that the returns in general are high and above the

---

21. See the Council of Economic Advisors (1997) pp. 242-243 for a fuller discussion of measurement problems of the relation between education and productivity.

opportunity costs. Education clearly has a payoff both to the individual and society.

Comparing the returns to education across countries is difficult but a recent attempt has been made in de la Fuente (2003). Figure 8.6 shows the average private and social returns to education for EU-15 countries (except Luxembourg). This analysis has a number of striking conclusions. First, the return to education is above the opportunity cost (a real rate of turn of 2 -3%). Second, the return – private or social to education in Denmark is not particular high by European Standards. Finally, and surprising the social return to education is lower than the private return, and therefore there is no argument for further public intervention or subsidies in education. Obviously the estimation of such returns are subject to a number of methodological and data problems.

Figure 8.6.   Private and social returns to education – EU-14 countries.

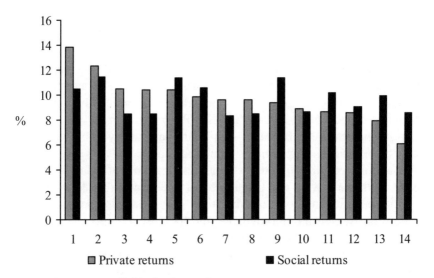

Note: Data not available for Luxembourg
Source: de la Fuente (2003)

A particularly important and difficult question is whether the returns to education can be expected to increase. Associated both with the debate on globalization and new technologies the role of so-called skill-bias play an important role. By skill-bias is understood that labour demand tends to increase for skilled and highly educated groups and to fall for unskilled and low educated groups. Empirical evidence support that this has been the case in the past (see e.g. Fosgerau, Jensen and Sørensen (2000)) and it may therefore be expected also to hold in a forward perspective. Therefore the need to improve the educational level of the work force plays a crucial role in policy debates. This applies both to the requires for new generations to enter the labour market but also for continued learning during work-life (life long learning) (see Trepartsudvalget (2006)).

8.7. Knowledge, New Economy and growth?

Debates on growth and growth policies are often characterized by fads. This may be in the form of pointing to growth miracles in particular countries. Germany was thus a model example in the 1950s and 1960s, Japan in the 1970s and 1980s, and the US in the 1990s. Likewise particular sectors are highlighted as being particularly important for growth. An example of the later includes the revolution in information and communication technologies (ICT) in the 1990s which led to a debate on the "New Economy". The reason was that ICT as associated with outstanding growth rates and substantial improvements in economic well-being. In fact it was even suggested that business cycles would become obsolete. The ICT developments are interesting both because it is an example of a sector highlighted as a "growth engine" and because developments within the ICT area certainly have had wide impacts in recent years.

The economic development in the USA in the 1990ties was highlighted as an example of the "New Economy". Until the new millennium the US economy displayed high growth rates, with an average real growth rate for GDP of more than 3% during the last decade, and as high as 4.5% between 1996 and 2000. Unemployment was reduced to only 4% and inflation had not been soaring. This was taken to reflect that a "New Economy" really had been established in which "Old Economy" phenomena like business cycle fluctuations and tendencies towards increasing inflation when unemployment is low and real growth continues was eliminated. The changes induced by ICT were often singled out as the main explanatory factor for this development. Since the US economy witnessed extraordinary investments in information technologies, and possessed a leading edge on developments of new hardware and software, it was natural to contribute the extraordinary good economic performance to the ICT revolution.

What exactly is ICT? ICT includes activities within computer hardware and software, automation services, telecommunication sectors etc. ICT spending as a percentage of GDP was more than 6% in EU25, hence substantial amounts of resources are going into the sector. Figure 8.7 illustrates see the role of ICT in various EU25 countries.

In principle there are the following three channels: i) it can lead to higher investments and thereby contribute to more growth by increasing the capital stock (this will show up via the entry 'real capital' in growth accounting, ii) there may be further productivity increases in the ICT sector itself, and iii) the use of ICT may lead to productivity increases in general in the economy. According to OECD (2003a) ICT capital has boosted GDP growth. E.g. over the period 1995-1999 ICT capital accounted for nearly 20 percent points of the total output growth in US, 34 percent points in Japan and 18 percent in Western Germany[22] For most countries the contribution to growth coming from ICT capital has increased significantly during 1990s. For some countries the growth contribution from ICT even doubled in the second half of the 1990s as compared to the first part of this decade.

Figure 8.7.   ICT expenditure in percent of GDP in 2004, EU25.

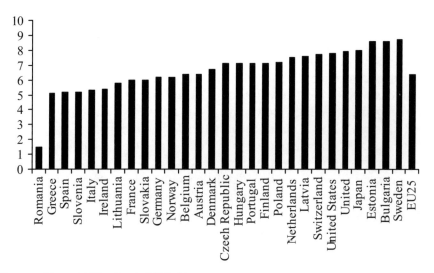

Source: Eurostat Yearbook 2005, Eurostat
Note: ICT includes expenditure on IT equipment, hardware, software and other services plus expenditure on telecommunication equipment, hardware, software and other services.

---

22.   OECD (2003a) figure 1.7.

ICT is lowering transactions and information costs and therefore it has important structural effects. Some of these are associated with the globalization process, cf. Chapter 3. In particular the lowering of these costs has played an important role for some service industries. In the past high information and transactions costs implied that services where confined to national market and therefore "protected" from international competition. This is clearly no longer the case for all services which can be delivered in an electronic form. Through this channel ICT has induced a number of structural changes.

The pervasive role of ICT can be illustrated by considering ICT penetration in various ways. Table 8.7 provides some indicators for EU15 countries. Focussing on Denmark the use of ICT is obviously widespread. Nearly all firms use computers and the internet and 72% of the Danish households have a PC. Finally on average 84% of all Danes has a mobile telephone.

Table 8.7.   Indicators of ICT Penetration in various EU-countries, 2003.

	Share of households with PC, 2002.	Share of households with access to www.	Share of enterprises using computers.	Share of enterprises using internet 2002.	Mobile phone per 100 capita.	Share of enterprises purchasing via www.
Belgium					83	20
Denmark	72	64	98	95	84	21
Germany	65	54	95	84	78	11
Greece	25	16	88	64	84	
Spain	36	28	95	83	90	3
France		31			70	
Ireland		36		83	86	22
Italy	38	42	95	74	96	3
Luxemburg	53	45	97	79	120	14
Netherlands		59	94	85	77	21
Austria	45	37	93	85	88	21
Portugal	31	22	84	69	46	8
Finland	55	47	99	96	91	15
Sweden			99	95	98	23
UK	58	55	88	54		19
EU-15		41	94			12

Source: Eurostat (2003, 2004, 2005).

Today it is clear that ICT has had widespread effects for society at large and economic activities in particular areas. It is equally clear that this has not led to a "New Economy" in which new rules apply and past problems have disappeared. This was underlined by the downturn on world stock markets in 2001 including the huge drop in the NASDAQ-index and in particular for n ICT companies at the New York Stock Exchange. A change which swiftly was spread around the globe. The subsequent the stagnation in the World Economy reminds us that prolonged periods with high growth does not in themselves eliminate business cycles.

References

Andersen P. (2005): *Forskning, globale offentlige goder og velstand* in Andersen, E.A. et al. (ed.): På vej mod nye globale strategier. Jurist og Økonomforbundets Forlag, København 2005.

Andersen, T.M., B. Dalum, H. Linderoth, V. Smith & N. Westergård-Nielsen (2005): *Beskrivende Dansk Økonomi*, 2. edition, Bogforlaget Handelsvidenskab, Aarhus.

Bentzen, J. & V. Smith (2000): The Short-Run Impact of Business Sector R&D Activities on Total Factor Productivity: Empirical Evidence from the Danish Economy. *Journal of Global Business* vol. 12 no. 33, 2001.

Botazzi, L. (2004): R&D and the Financing of Ideas in Europe, CEPS Working Document No. 203, Brussels 2004.

Christensen J.L. (1999): Innovation på dansk - resultater fra den 2. Community Innovation Survey, Notat fra Institut for Erhvervsstudier, Ålborg Universitet, 1999.

Danmarks Statistik (Statistics Denmark) (1995): 50-year review, Copenhagen 1995.

Danmarks Statistik (Statistics Denmark) (2005): Statistisk tiårsoversigt 2005, Copenhagen 2005.

Dansk Center for Forskningsanalyse (2004) *Innovation i Dansk erhvervsliv 2002*, Århus Universitet, Århus 2004.

Durlauf, S., 2002, On the Empirics of Social Capital, Economic Journal, 112, 458-479.

Eurostat (2003): Statistics on the information Society in Europe, European Commision 2003.

Eurostat (2004): Innovation in Europe. Results for the EU, Iceland and Norway, Eurostat, 2004.

Eurostat (2004): Statistics in Focus 16/2004: *Internet usage by individuals and enterprises*, European Commission 2004.

Eurostat (2005): *Eurostat Yearbook 2005*, European Commission 2005.

Eurostat (2005): Statistics in Focus, 8/2005: *Telecommunications in EuropeInternet usage by individuals and enterprises,* European Commission 2005.

Fosgerau, M., S.E.H. Jensen and A. Sørensen, 2000, Relative Demand Shifts for Educated Labour, CEBR Discussion Paper.

Grossman G.M. & E. Helpman (1991): *Innovation and Growth in the Global Economy*, Cambridge MA, MIT Press.

HM Treasury (2004): *Trade and the Global Economy – The role of International Trade in Productivity, Economic Reforms and Growth,*

HM Treasury, UK and The Department of Trade and Industry UK, Crown 2004.

Larsson A. & C.O. Andersen (2001): Chapter 6 in Wille Maus, K. (ed.): Science and Technology Indicators in The Nordic Countries 2000. The Nordic Council of Ministers, TemaNord 2001:539

Madsen, E.S., A.Ø. Nielsen & V. Smith (2000): Patent og Fou-aktivitet i Danmark – en sammenligning med det øvrige Skandinavien, Rapport 2000/5, The Danish Institute for Studies in Research and Research Policy, Aarhus 2000.

Norges Forskningsråd (2003): Det Norske forsknings- og innovasjonssystemet – statistik og indikatorer 2003, Oslo 2003.

OECD (2000a): *Economic growth in the OECD area: Recent trends at the aggregate and sectorial level,* Economic Department working paper no. 248 by Scarpetta, S., A. Bassanini, D. Pilat & P. Schreyer, Paris 2000.

OECD (2003a): *The sources of Economic growth in the OECD Countries,* Paris 2003.

OECD (2004): *The Frascati Manual 2002: Proposed Standard Practise for Surveys.* Paris 2004.

OECD (2005a): *Main Science and Technology Indicators,* No. 2, 2005, Paris.

OECD (2005b): The Oslo Manual, 3rd edition, OECD, Paris 2005.

OECD (2005c): Economic Outlook 2005/2 No. 78, December. Paris 2005.

Putnam,R, 1995, Bolwing Alone: America's decline social capital, Journal of Democracy, 6, 65-78.

Romer, P.M. (1986): Increasing Returns and Long Run Growth, *Journal of Political Economy 94*, pp. 1002-37.

Smith, V. (2001): A comparison of Business Enterprise R&D, Chapter 2 in Wille Maus, K. (ed.): Science and Technology Indicators in The Nordic Countries 2000. The Nordic Council of Ministers, TemaNord 2001:539.

Smith, V., M. Dilling-Hansen, T. Eriksson & E.S. Madsen (2004): *R&D and Productivity in Danish Firms: Some Empirical Evidence, Applied Economics,* 2004, Vol. 36, No. 16.

Solow, R.M. (1957): Technical Change and the Aggregate Production Function, *Review of Economic and Statistics 39,* pp. 313-320.

The Council of Economic Advisors (1997): *The Danish Economy, Spring 1997,* Copenhagen 1997.

The Council of Economic Advisors (2003): *The Danish Economy, Spring 2003,* Copenhagen 2003.

The Danish Ministry of Economic Affairs (1999): *Economic Survey, December 1999*, Copenhagen 1999.

The Danish Ministry of Economics and Business Affairs (2004): *Vækst redegørelse 04 – konkurrencedygtige vækstvilkår*, København 2004.

Trepartsudvalg, 2006 Livslang opkvalificering og uddannelse for alle på arbejdsmarkedet - rapport fra Trepartsudvalget, Finansministeriet.

Tænketanken *Fremtidens Vækst* (2004): Vision 2010 – *Det fleksible og nytænkende samfund*.

Velfærdskommissionen (2006): *Analyserapport II. Fremtidens velfærd – vores valg*. København 2006.

Web addresses

www.afsk.au.dk

www.cfa.au.dk (The Danish Centre for Studies in Research and Research Policy)

www.dst.dk (Statistics Denmark)

www.europa.eu.int/comm/eurostat (EUROSTAT)

www.nifu.no (Studies in innovation, research and Education, Norway)

www.oecd.org (OECD)

www.oem.dk (The Danish Ministry of Economic and Business Affairs)

www.statistikbanken.dk (Statistikbanken, Statistics Denmark)

www.uvm.dk (The Danish Ministry of Education)

www.velfaerd.dk (Velfærdskommissionen)

www.vtu.dk (The Danish Ministry of Science, Technology and Innovation)

www.worldbank.org (The World Bank)

Appendix A

National accounts

The national accounts are different from normal corporate accounts, where the most important result is a profit or a loss. Rather, the aim of national accounts is to give an *overall view of the economy*. National accounts statistics thus provide the data used in most macroeconomic models and therefore include key economic concepts which will be dealt with in this appendix.

The main concept is gross domestic product (*GDP*)

GDP (output based) = Output + taxes less subsidies on products - intermediate consumption

In principle, *output* is the value of goods and services produced by all firms. *Intermediate consumption* is the value of goods and services sold from one firm to another as part of the process of production. By subtracting intermediate consumption GDP becomes a measure of value added (value of goods and services sold to final users) and therefore an important measure of economic performance.[1] By including *taxes less subsidies on products*, GDP is measured at market prices equal to prices which consumer have to pay, cf. section dealing with price concepts.

---

1. Example: Farmer's wheat sold to miller $ 0,30, miller's flour sold to baker $0,55, baker's bread sold to grocer $ 0,90 and grocer's bread sold to consumer $1,00. Then output is $2,75 and contribution to GDP $ 1,00, cf. Baily and Friedman p. 34. In another way, GDP is value added at each stage of production: $0,30 + (0,55-0,30) + (0,90-0,55) + (1,00-0,90)$.

A. Output

Output should include the value of all the goods and services that appear as output in the economic system. This is not possible with the statistical material available, however. There are no fundamental problems involved when goods/services are sold in the market since the value can be computed as an *output volume multiplied by price.* In a number of cases, however, this accounting principle is not used. The most important of these are mentioned below.

a) Banks provide *financial services* which cannot be computed as volume multiplied by price. Here, output is determined as the difference between interest revenues and interest expenditures (net revenues based on the interest differential) plus revenues from charges, etc.

b) Output for *trading industries* is based on gross profits and not on sales.

c) Stocks are, by definition, not on the market, but when similar goods are sold, there is no problem finding a price that can be used to compute output. Stocks are stated in replacement prices.

d) Manufacturers' *consumption of own goods* is included in output. The prices used here are those which corresponding goods are sold for. The consumption of own goods in agriculture, fishing and market gardening is thus computed in this way.

e) *Owner-occupied dwellings* present a pricing problem. These dwellings "produce" a return (gross rent) that is not due to a sale. Actual rentals for housing is therefore used as a price basis when determining the yield from owner-occupied dwellings (imputed rentals for housing).

f) The goods mentioned above are those for which there is a direct market price or where the price can be based on the market price of comparable goods. The price used is thus based on *market activity.* By its very nature, the output for *non-market activity* cannot be based on market prices. The most important non-market activity by far is *public services* (education, hospital treatment, etc.) which are largely free. Output thus cannot be calculated as a volume multiplied by a price. Instead, the *costs* are used, the biggest part of which is employees' wages. This accounting principle is unfortunate (though necessary) since rising costs imply rising output even though it doesn't necessarily mean that there are more services available. Thus, a fall in public-sector employees' performance will not reduce output, and, conversely, an increase in performance will not increase output.

g) One of the main criticisms against the calculation of output is that it ignores several major non-market activities. Households produce major services (child-minding, cooking, cleaning, repairs, gardening, etc.) that are not included as part of output. This naturally makes it difficult to estimate the trend in output, and with it GDP, because the increasing participation rate for women has meant that many services that were previously performed in the home (e.g. child-minding) are now increasingly included in GDP (e.g. child-minding in day-care centres). The growth in GDP thus overstates the real increase in value added.

"normalt"

Household production is proportionately much more prevalent in developing countries than in the industrialised countries; this fact alone thus makes comparisons between developed and developing countries problematical.

B. Price concepts and value added

By subtracting taxes on products (net) from GDP at market prices, we get *gross value added (GVA)* in basic prices. Output is also measured in basic prices. GVA is essential in illustrating activity by industry, cf. Chapter 3.

Taxes on products are duties on cigarettes, beer, petrol, etc., car registration duty, and VAT, while subsidies are EU subsidies to producers, government subsidies to cover public transport losses, interest subsidies to housing, etc.

Basic prices can be said to be the prices that firms receive for their products (Taxes on products (net) belong to the state).

Figure A1.   Prices and value added terms.

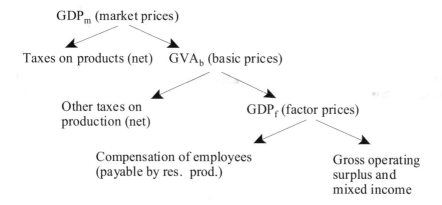

Furthermore, GDP at factor prices or factor costs is GVA less other taxes on production (net). Other taxes on production are, for example, property taxes and weight duty on vehicles used in industry. These taxes can only be levied on industry, not on individual products. All three concepts are dealing with value added but at different prices. Part of GDP at factor costs is received by the employees and dividing this part by GDP we get the wage ratio.

*GDP (income based) = gross operating surplus and mixed income
+ compensation of employees + taxes on production (net).*

Growth in GDP is caused by both price and volume increases but growth in GDP is only a measure of economic growth when growth is based on volume increases. Therefore, to get a measure of economic growth, GDP is worked out in prices prevailing in a base year, e.g. 2000-prices. However, many items being produced in the base year are not produced in the current year and many items have changed in quality since the base year, e.g. computers. Certainly, if quality improvement is undervalued so is economic growth. In 2005, Statistics Denmark as well as EUswitched to chain indices as a measure of economic growth. Each link of a chain Laspeyres' volume index measures year on year growth, see appendix B for further explanation.

C. GDP defined in terms of expenditure

GDP (expenditure based) = final consumption expenditure (C)
+ gross fixed capital formation and changes in inventories (I)
+ export of goods and services (X) - import of goods and services (M)

C is divided into two main groups, *private and government consumption expenditure.* Private consumption consists almost entirely of households' consumption of goods and services. In a national accounting sense, households consume a good at the time of purchase. An important exception is *housing which is not regarded as C but as I.* In consequence, the return from the housing stock (gross rent) is regarded as C. The national accounts thus contain a partially fictitious "industry" called dwellings making up a considerable part of GVA (7.6% in Denmark in 2002 but only a minor part of employment (0.6% in Denmark in 2002).[2] Household consumption in Denmark is obtained by adjusting for purchases in Denmark by non-resident households, etc.

Government consumption expenditure comprises services provided by the general government (education,[3] health services, etc.). In some cases, though, consumers pay part of the cost of these services themselves. Household expenditures on medicine, medical and dental treatment, and childcare centres are thus regarded as private consumption. It should be emphasised that government consumption expenditure does not include income transfers.

Gross fixed capital formation solely concerns industry, excluding housing, and includes goods that are used at least one year in the production process, e.g. machinery, plant, transport equipment and buildings.[4] Capital formation also includes government expenditure on school, hospital and road construction, etc. Expenditure on major repairs to buildings, etc., is also included since this represents an improvement of capital assets while current repairs and maintenance work are regarded as intermediate consumption.

---

2. www.statistikbanken.dk.
3. Some part of expenditure on education increases human capital and should really be looked upon as investment.
4. Expenditure on gasoline appears as C (household) or as intermediate consumption (firm) and a car is regarded as I when bought by a firm, but as C when bought by a household.

D. GDP and other income terms

GDP is the value of all goods and services produced in a year but it also equals the income received by those factors of production which produced the goods and services. Some part of this factor income is received by foreign factors of production (foreign employees, foreign capital, cf. Figure A2) and the remainder, gross national income (GNI), goes to national factors of production. GNI is identical to gross national product (GNP) which is still used in some national accounts statistic. Of course, GNI is bigger than GDP if factor income paid to the rest of the world (ROW) is smaller than factor income received by ROW.

Figure A2.   GDP and other income terms in market prices.

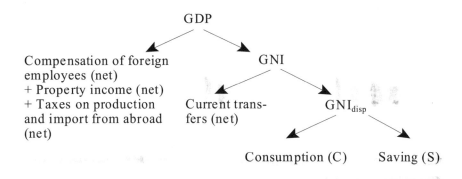

GNI less current transfers to ROW is gross national disposable income which is consumed or saved. Current transfers include development aid, payments to international organizations, e.g. EU, etc.

E. Consumption of fixed capital and net terms

Net domestic product (NDP) is GDP minus the consumption of fixed capital. The general rule in national accounts is that *a net term is the result of a gross term minus the consumption of fixed capital* which represents the technical and physical deterioration of capital assets¹ during the period "to become worse" and which can therefore be regarded as depreciations of capital assets.

Ideally, estimations of the national product should take the deterioration of capital assets into account so, ceteris paribus, net terms are

1: things that can be sold to pay debts.

"becoming worse" [handwritten]
"reduction of value" [handwritten]

preferable to gross terms. Depreciations in the national accounts are very much estimates, however, and therefore extremely uncertain. This is probably why net terms are rarely used in comparisons of economic trends between different countries.

The fact that land (natural resources, the environment) is not depreciated is also seen by many as a problem. There is no doubt that the massive environmental destruction in, for example, the former Soviet Union has significantly reduced future production possibilities. They have, so to speak, run down their "environmental capital". Countries which run down their deposits of non-renewable *ikke-genbrugelige* [handwritten] natural resources also reduce their future earnings possibilities, e.g. oil producing countries are using up their oil capital.

F. Savings (S), capital formation *Creation* [handwritten] (I) and the current external balance

Without any transactions with ROW (closed economy):

GDP = C+I = C+S (cf. Figure A2) or I=S

Including transactions with ROW:

I = S minus surplus on the current external balance or S plus deficit on the current external balance). Since Denmark had deficits before 1990, the relation then was I = S plus deficit on the current account. It seems obvious, however, that domestic capital formation must either be financed by domestic savings or foreign savings where the latter are reflected in deficit on the current external balance.

G. International comparisons

GDP or GNI per capita are often used to compare countries' stage of development or standard of living. Such comparisons only give a rough idea of differences in living conditions. As mentioned previously, there are important problems in using GDP as a measure of overall economic activity, cf. non-market activities by households and government, underground economy, depreciation of natural resources etc.

1: The difference between the amount of something you have and the higher amount that you need. [handwritten]

In addition to this, using exchange rates for international comparisons of economic aggregates the differences between countries correspond not only to differences in volume of goods and services but also to differences in level of prices. In order to obtain a true comparison of volume, differences in level of prices are eliminated by using purchasing power parities (PPP) to convert the values of the countries' economic aggregates expressed in national currency into a common currency (international $). PPP are based on price surveys that estimate what a basket of comparable goods and services cost in different countries.

The difference between PPP and the exchange rate can be considerable. In 2004, GNP (GNI) per capita in China was 17% of GNP per capita in Denmark measured at PPP but only 4% using the exchange rate.[5] Generally, by using PPP instead of exchange rates, the difference in GNP per capita between industrialised and developing countries is substantially reduced.

H. GDP and alternative measures

The criticism of GDP as a measure of prosperity or welfare has resulted in alternative measures. W. Nordhaus and J. Tobin were among the first to calculate an alternative to GNP: Measure of economic welfare (MEW). MEW adjusts GNP in several ways, e.g. MEW includes household production and the value of leisure. Of course, such adjustments are questionable.

Human development index (HDI) is published every year since 1990 in Human Development Report. HDI is a simple average of three indexes based upon: 1) life expectancy at birth, 2) the adult literacy rate and the combined gross, secondary and tertiary enrolment ratio, 3) GDP per capita measured at PPP. In 2003, Denmark was ranked as country number 14 based upon HDI and as number 5 based upon GDP per capita (PPP). The relatively low HDI rank is caused by a relatively low life expectancy at birth index.[6]

For the period 1970 to 1990, a Welfare Indicator (WI) has been constructed for Denmark. WI is private and government consumption minus defensive expenditures, costs of pollution, costs of traffic accidents etc. plus value of household production, value of leisure etc. Defensive

5.   *World Development Indicators* -Database.
6.   United Nations Development Programme: *Human Development Report 2005.*

↓ spending on a particular period of time

expenditures are not directly a source of utility themselves, but are necessary inputs to activities that may yield utility. Examples of government defensive expenditure are spending on police, defence, and health services. WI increased by 23% during the period 1970-1990 while total consumption increased by 40%. Excluding the value of leisure, WI increased by 41%.

The World Bank (World Development Indicators) provides estimates of adjusted net savings (ANS) for a large number of countries. ANS is equal to net savings (gross saving minus the consumption of fixed capita) plus education expenditure and minus energy depletion, mineral depletion, net forest depletion, and carbon dioxide. Expenditure on education is added as a measure of investment in human capital. If ANS is negative capital is reduced which is not sustainable over a long period. You can't reverse the conclusion, however, because the different kind of capital may not be substitutes, cf. Chapter 7. Anyhow, there is a link between ANS and sustainable development.

In recent years, "green national accounts" has been developed. Green GDP is GDP adjusted for the depletion[1] of natural resources and degradation of the environment.

Of course, non-economic values are not measured in GNP, e.g. health, political freedom, crime, leisure, divorce rates etc.

1: to reduce the amount of something.

References

Danmarks Statistik: *Nationalregnskabsstatistik* (text in Danish as well as English).

Maddison, A.: The World Economy. *Historical Statistics*. OECD 2003.

Nordhaus, W.D. and J. Tobin: *Economic Growth*. National Bureau of Economic Research, 50. Colloquium. New York 1972.

Rørmose Jensen, Peter and Elisabeth Møllgaard: *On the Measurement of a Welfare Indicator for Denmark 1970-1990*. The Rockwool Foundation Research Unit, Copenhagen 1995.

United Nations Development Programme: *Human Development Report*.

World Bank: *World Development Report*.

Web addresses

www.europa.eu.int/comm/eurostat

www.imf.org (International Monetary Fund)

www.oecd.org

www.sourceoecd.org (through university libraries)

www.statistikbanken.dk

www.worldbank.org

www.wto.org (World Trade Organization)

Appendix B

Price and quantity indexes

A. Price index formula

The price index represents a total expression of the movement in prices for several goods or services. When all goods and services are included, the price index illustrates the general trend in prices, or the inflation rate. The problem with index calculations is how to determine the weights that appropriately represent price moments for individual goods used in the summary price index. The weight problem is solved in different ways in the following three index formulas.

Laypeyres price index:
$$P_{t:o}^{LA} = \frac{\sum_i p_{i,t} \times q_{i,o}}{\sum_i p_{i,o} \times q_{i,o}} \cdot 100$$

The budget method:
$$= \sum_i \frac{p_{i,t}}{p_{i,o}} \cdot B_{i,o} \cdot 100, \qquad B_{i,o} = \frac{p_{i,o} \times q_{i,o}}{\sum p_{i,o} \times q_{i,o}}$$

$i = 1,....,m,$ $p = $ prices, $q = $ quantity, and $B_{i,o} = $ the budget share for good i in year o.

The numerator indicates the expenditure on the quantities of m goods and services bought in the index base year (year o) valued at the prices in the final year (year t). When this is expressed in relation to the same quantities valued at the prices of the base year of the index (the denominator), the result is the price increase for the m goods and services from year o to year t. The Laspeyres index uses the quantities of the base year of the index as the standard, and this means that this index measures price movements for a fixed combination of goods and services.

The index can also be calculated using the (equivalent) budget method, in which the price increase for the individual good or service is weighted by the share of the expenditure on that good or service in the budget for the base year of the index. The greater the weight, the stronger is the representation of the price increase of this good or service in the price index.

Paasche price index:

$$P_{t:o}^{PA} = \frac{\sum_i p_{i,t} \times q_{i,t}}{\sum_i p_{i,o} \times q_{i,t}} \cdot 100$$

The Paasche price index uses up-to-date weights, which means the weights derive from the current time period.

Normally, consumption of a good will increase relative to the consumption of all other goods when the price of that good decreases relative to the prices of all other goods. The Laspeyres index does not take into consideration this substitution that takes place when relative prices change. This results in a numerator that is too high because prices and quantities relate to different years. Therefore, the index overestimates the real price increase. In contrast, the Paasche index underestimates the real price increase (the dominator is too high).

The calculation of sub-indexes is normally made using the budget formula of the Laspeyres index in that the prices are indexed and the share of the budget is provided. These elements are sufficient for calculating the price index. In the budget formula, you only need to know the relative price (p_t/p_o) and not the individual prices in the two years.

Table B1.   Calculation of a "housing index".

	Weight distribution, jan. 2006, %	Consumer price index	
		Jan. 2000	Jan. 2006
Rentals for housing	19.72	98.1	114.1
Fuel, electricity, gas, heat	2.12	97.2	118.8
Furnishings, household equipment etc.	6.53	99.3	108.7
Maintenance and repair	0.89	100.4	111.0

Total weight in CPI 29.26.
Source: www.statistikbanken.dk.

$$P^{LA}_{jan06:jan00} = \left[\frac{114.1*19.72}{98.1*29.26} + \frac{118.8*2.12}{97.2*29.26} + \frac{108.7*6.53}{99.3*29.26} + \frac{111.0*0.89}{100.4*29.26} \right] 100 = 115$$

In Table B1, the weights are not taken from the base year of the index, the year in which the index equals 100. The weights derive from the values in January 2006. When the year from which the weights are taken for the index lies between the base year and the most current year in the data series, it is not possible to claim that the index overestimates or underestimates the real price rise when substitution takes place.

The weight basis used in calculating the Laspeyres index is often changed. If you use a price index covering a longer period of time, a linkage between the indexes will most likely be necessary. This type of linking is illustrated in Table B2.

If you want the housing price index for 2004, using 1984 as the base year of the index, you must first calculate the index for the year in which the link is being made (1992), with 1992 set equal to 100. Next, the index for 2004 is calculated, with 1992 set equal to 100. Finally, the two indexes are multiplied, yielding the price rise from 1984 to 1992 and from 1992 to 2004.

Table B2.   Linking consumer price "housing indexes".

	1984	1992	
1980=100	139.5	207.6	
1992=100	100.0	148.8	(207.6x100/ 139.5)
	1992	2004	
2000=100	80.4	111.1	
1992=100	100	138.2	(111.1x100/ 80.4)
	1984	2004	
1984=100	100	205.6	(148.8x138.2/ 100)

Source: Statistics Denmark: STO, 1989, 2002, and 2005.

Since the Laspeyres index normally overestimates the real price rise and the Paasche index normally underestimates it, it seems natural to calculate an index that lies between the two indexes. One such intermediate index is the Fisher index, which calculates a geometric average of the two other indexes.

Fisher price index:
$$P_{t:o}^{FI} = \sqrt{P_{t:o}^{LA} \times P_{t:o}^{PA}}$$

B. Quantity indexes

Totally analogous to the price indexes, there are three corresponding quantity indices.

$$Q_{t:o}^{LA} = \frac{\sum_i p_{i,o} \times q_{i,t}}{\sum_i p_{i,o} \times q_{i,o}} \cdot 100, \quad Q_{t:o}^{PA} = \frac{\sum_i p_{i,t} \times q_{i,t}}{\sum_i p_{i,t} \times q_{i,o}} \cdot 100, \quad Q_{t:o}^{Fi} = \sqrt{Q_{t:o}^{LA} \times Q_{t:o}^{PA}}$$

The quantity indices show the real changes in quantities, or the changes given constant prices. Using the various index formulas, it can easily be shown that:

$$V_{t:o} = \frac{\sum_i p_{i,t} \times q_{i,t}}{\sum_i p_{i,o} \times q_{i,o}} \cdot 100 = P_{t:o}^{PA} \times Q_{t:o}^{LA} = P_{t:o}^{LA} \times Q_{t:o}^{PA} = P_{t:o}^{Fi} \times Q_{t:o}^{Fi}$$

V is a value index that relates the value in year t to the value in year o. If you know V as well as a price index, the quantity index can be easily calculated.

In the system of national accounts, the material is reported in both constant as well as current prices. Dividing the value index by the quantity index produces the (implicit) price index. You can calculate this implicit price index for many of the indices presented in the national accounts.

Using base year prices is a problem for periods far apart from the base year. Therefore, one may give preference to chain indices as a measure of real changes in quantities.

Chain Laspeyres' volume index: $Q_{t:0}^{LA} = Q_{1:0}^{LA} \times Q_{2:1}^{LA} \times \ldots\ldots \times Q_{t:t-1}^{LA}$

C. Deflating

If you know the value index and the price index, the quantity index can be calculated by dividing the value index by the price index. Such a calculation is called *deflating*. There is often a need to deflate because it is the real change or movement that is of interest. If you have, for example, an index of hourly earnings (value index) and a Laspeyres price index, an index of movements in real hourly earnings (a quantity index) can be calculated, as in Table B3.

Table B3.   *Index of average hourly earnings in Danish manufacturing – nominal and real changes, 1989-1998.*

	1989	2005
Index of average hourly earnings:		
1980=100	181	323
1989=100	100	178
Consumer price index:		
1900=100	4142	5790
1989=100	100	140
Index of real hourly earnings (quantity index):		
1989=100	100	127[1]

11)   178 x 100 / 140.
Source: www.statistikbanken.dk.

If the weight of goods in the consumption basket of manufacturing sector employees differs substantially from the weights used in the consumer price index, deflating with the consumer price index can be a problem. If the prices for the goods weighted heavily in the consumption basket of a manufacturing employee have increased relatively greatly, deflation with the consumer price index will overestimate the movement in the real hourly wage since this division is with a price index that has risen too little with respect to the consumption choices of manufacturing employees. A corresponding problem applies to retired individuals. If the value of goods consumed by retired individuals is deflated using the consumer price index, the result will most likely be incorrect since retired individuals have another consumption pattern than that of the population in general.

Often, a price index will be used to deflate another price index to illustrate the relative or real price movement. For example, a price index for oil can be deflated with a price index for exported manufacturers. Such an index shows the movement in purchasing power for a barrel of oil measured in manufactured goods.

D. Four general price indexes

1) The *consumer price index (CPI)* is an index of prices for goods and services bought by private households. CPI reflects the price paid by the consumers, i.e. including value added tax (VAT) and duties but minus subsidies. Housing subsidies are not taken into account, however. The index weights are based on total final consumption expenditure according to the national account statistics.
One of the convergence criteria for the Economic and Monetary Union concerns inflation. In order to compare inflation rates in EU countries, an EU-harmonised CPI has been calculated since 1996.

2) Like CPI, the *Index of net retail prices* is an index of prices for goods and services bought by private households, but excluding taxes and subsidies.

3) The *price index for domestic supply* measures price development related to the first commercial transaction of a commodity, i.e. producers' and importers' selling price, excluding VAT and excise duties. The index does not include services. The *raw material price index* is an index for imported unprocessed raw material and is a sub-index of the price index for domestic supply.

4) *Unit value indexes for external trade.*

In foreign trade statistics, products are classified in accordance with so-called product nomenclatures where each product or product group is assigned a classification number. For each item of the nomenclature, a unit value is calculated as:

$$P_i = \frac{V_i}{q_i}$$

where V_i is the recorded value of products under classification number i and q_i is the quantity. The unit value index for imports and exports is then calculated using Fisher's index formula.

The use of classification numbers means that a change in the unit value index can have been caused by both changes in product prices and changes in the nature of the products assigned to the number in question. This is because, as a rule, a classification number comprises several different products of different qualities. Thus, the unit value is not a product price in the usual sense. This also means that a shift within a classification number towards relatively more products of high quality, and thus high price, will be recorded as a price increase, even though there have been no price increases for individual products. There is thus no attempt to solve the quality problem!

The *terms of trade* index for foreign trade is calculated as the unit value index for exports divided by the unit value index for imports. If export prices increase more than import prices, the terms of trade increase accordingly.

References

Statistics Denmark: Statistisk tiårsoversigt (STO)

Web addresses

www.europa.eu.int/comm/eurostat
www.imf.org (International Monetary Fund)
www.oecd.org
www.sourceoecd.org (through university libraries)
www.statistikbanken.dk
www.worldbank.org
www.wto.org (World Trade Organization)

INDEX